T0181331

Progress in IS

"PROGRESS in IS" encompasses the various areas of Information Systems in theory and practice, presenting cutting-edge advances in the field. It is aimed especially at researchers, doctoral students, and advanced practitioners. The series features both research monographs that make substantial contributions to our state of knowledge and handbooks and other edited volumes, in which a team of experts is organized by one or more leading authorities to write individual chapters on various aspects of the topic. "PROGRESS in IS" is edited by a global team of leading IS experts. The editorial board expressly welcomes new members to this group. Individual volumes in this series are supported by a minimum of two members of the editorial board, and a code of conduct mandatory for all members of the board ensures the quality and cutting-edge nature of the titles published under this series.

More information about this series at http://www.springer.com/series/10440

Christoph W. Künne

Online Intermediaries for Co-Creation

An Explorative Study in Healthcare

Springer

Christoph W. Künne
Munich
Germany

Dissertation University of Erlangen-Nuremberg, 2016

ISSN 2196-8705   ISSN 2196-8713   (electronic)
Progress in IS
ISBN 978-3-319-84573-9   ISBN 978-3-319-51124-5   (eBook)
DOI 10.1007/978-3-319-51124-5

© Springer International Publishing AG 2018
Softcover reprint of the hardcover 1st edition 2017
This work is subject to copyright. All rights are reserved by the Publisher, whether the whole or part of the material is concerned, specifically the rights of translation, reprinting, reuse of illustrations, recitation, broadcasting, reproduction on microfilms or in any other physical way, and transmission or information storage and retrieval, electronic adaptation, computer software, or by similar or dissimilar methodology now known or hereafter developed.
The use of general descriptive names, registered names, trademarks, service marks, etc. in this publication does not imply, even in the absence of a specific statement, that such names are exempt from the relevant protective laws and regulations and therefore free for general use.
The publisher, the authors and the editors are safe to assume that the advice and information in this book are believed to be true and accurate at the date of publication. Neither the publisher nor the authors or the editors give a warranty, express or implied, with respect to the material contained herein or for any errors or omissions that may have been made.

Printed on acid-free paper

This Springer imprint is published by Springer Nature
The registered company is Springer International Publishing AG
The registered company address is: Gewerbestrasse 11, 6330 Cham, Switzerland

Foreword

In the digital era, the Internet provides unique possibilities to connect particular groups of stakeholders, like companies with their geographically dispersed customers and partners. Online platforms, in particular, offer distinct features for companies to exchange knowledge and to jointly create ("co-create") innovations with external stakeholders, such as product users, customers, experts, or partners of other organizations.

Given the complicated industry structure and sheer number of stakeholders in the healthcare sector, this sector appears to be particularly promising for crowd-sourced innovation. The Internet can help to facilitate and improve the exchange between pharmaceutical companies, medical technology companies, insurance companies, medical doctors, nursing staff, patients and their family members, and many others. As Christoph Künne convincingly argues, harnessing the creativity of healthcare consumers is a promising means of innovation in healthcare. Healthcare consumers, who are often patients, tend to be intrinsically motivated to improve their current situation, and there are many examples where patients have played a key role in developing solutions to their healthcare challenges, particularly in the context of rare or chronic diseases. Literature suggests that consumers should be systematically supported in doing so.

As such, understanding this bridging role of online intermediaries is a fertile field for research and the central matter of Christoph Künne's thesis. Online intermediaries link two or more parties through online platforms in order to foster co-creation of innovative products and solutions. The author addresses this highly relevant research gap with three consecutive empirical studies using qualitative research designs. The work invites the reader to explore what different types of online intermediaries exist, how they differ regarding their value-creation potential, and what challenges they currently face. The author also clarifies the adoption process to be followed for companies to benefit from co-created innovation outcomes.

Overall, the thesis is comprehensive in its approach and reveals results that are not only of great interest for academia, but also insightful for business practice. It appeals for its readable style, as well as the fresh approach by which the concepts are developed and presented. Also, with specific industry examples, the author helps the reader to follow the research with ease. Christoph Künne's thesis has been accepted as a doctoral dissertation in 2016 by the School of Business and Economics at the University of Erlangen-Nuremberg. I congratulate Christoph Künne on the tangible and convincing results of his research. The book is a must read for all those who have an interest in consumer co-creation for innovation beyond the typical boundaries of the healthcare sector. I wish the book the broad dissemination it deserves and Christoph Künne all the best for his future career.

Nuremberg, Germany   Prof. Dr. Kathrin M. Möslein

Preface

This book concludes my doctoral research activities at the Chair of Information Systems I, especially Innovation and Value Creation in Nuremberg. Looking back, I am glad I pursued this path as it broadened my thinking and sharpened my skills. The printed results you see here are the tip of the iceberg, the end product of a long development process. During this research journey, I relied on the support of several loyal individuals, to whom I owe a debt of gratitude.

First, several senior university professors have influenced my direction. In particular, I am deeply thankful to my doctoral supervisor Prof. Dr. Kathrin Möslein for giving me the opportunity to do academic research and teaching at her chair. I have greatly benefited from all her constructive feedback and the time she spent helping me to develop my hypotheses. Without the trust she put in me, this work would never have been finished. I also want to thank Prof. Dr. Michael Amberg for preparing the second appraisal report on the thesis. During my time in Nuremberg, I felt privileged to have the opportunity to interact with Prof. Dr. Dr. h.c. mult. Peter Mertens, whom I knew long before I started my doctoral research by his esteemed reputation as the godfather of the German Wirtschaftsinformatik. My research was also heavily influenced from overseas, not only through international academic conferences and peer reviews, but also through a research stay at the Robert H. Smith School of Business at the University of Maryland. I feel indebted to Prof. Ritu Agarwal, Ph.D., who gave me a warm welcome to the Washington DC area, who constantly challenged the theoretical robustness of my contributions, and who motivated me through our extremely energizing discussions.

Second, I greatly appreciate the support of a few fellow researchers. Specifically, Dr. Stefan Thallmaier (HHL Leipzig), Dr. Daniel Fürstenau (Free University of Berlin), Prof. Dr. Christoph Ihl (Hamburg University of Technology), Dr. Cécile Cam (Audencia Nantes), and Dr. Shahla Ghobadi (University of New South Wales) have proven to be inspiring sparring partners, helping me to solidify my ideas into outcomes. In addition, I want to extend my thanks to many former and current members of the Wi1 team who took an interest in my research journey. Special thanks go to Dr. in spe Matthias Raß, Dr. Hari Suman Naik, Dr. Constantin Söldner, and Dr. Sabine Brunner for being always approachable, even on non-research topics. Transforming all the constructive inputs into written pages would not have been possible without the very effective work environment at the Bavarian State Library in Munich, which I gratefully acknowledge.

Third, I want to express gratitude to my good friends who shared the highs and the lows. It is like running a marathon; although you are determined about the mission, the finish line often feels far away. Then, unexpectedly, friends show up along the track cheering passionately. Two of them stand out, namely, Dr. Michael Hagenau for his persistent pushing and rigorous reflection, and Christian Siebert for his generous support in many ways and an unparalleled sense of humor.

Finally, I am most indebted to my family, especially my parents Rita Künne and Dr. Wulf-Dieter Künne, and my sister Stefanie. They believed in me during the entire journey. Thank you for listening to my concerns at all times and providing unfaltering encouragement whenever I needed it.

All of those listed above I acknowledge for supporting me through this stage of my life. Now, let us take it from here. Exciting times are ahead.

Munich, Germany   Christoph W. Künne

Contents

Abbreviations

AGOF	Arbeitsgemeinschaft Online Forschung
AJAX	Asynchronous JavaScript and XML; enables modern web applications
B2B	Business to business
B2C	Business to consumer
CEO	Chief executive officer
cf.	Confer (latin); compare with
Chap.	Chapter
e.g.	Exempli gratia (latin); for example
EK	External knowledge
EMA	European Medicines Agency
et al.	Et alia (latin); and others
etc.	Et cetera (latin); and so forth
FDA	Food and Drug Association
Fig.	Figure
GDP	Gross domestic product
HC	Healthcare
HCC	Healthcare consumer
HCO	Healthcare organization
i.e.	Id est (latin); that is to say
ibid.	Ibidem (latin); referring to a previously cited work
IT	Information technology
IVW	Informationsgemeinschaft zur Feststellung der Verbreitung von Werbeträgern
NPD	New product development
OII	Online innovation intermediary
p.	Page
pp.	Pages
PRO	Patient-reported outcome

R&D	Research and development
RQ	Research question
RSS	Rich Site Summary; a standard of web feeds
Sect.	Section
UII	User innovation input
URL	Uniform resource locator
XML	Extensible Markup Language

List of Figures

List of Tables

Chapter 1
Introduction

> *Without radical innovation it seems unlikely that we can sustain the kind of healthcare which we associate with highly developed societies.*
>
> —John Bessant

1.1 Motivation[1]

Healthcare is an exceedingly costly,[2] very complex, and commonly used service that has a pervasive effect on each person's quality of daily life. It is unique in the sense that people consume services that they need but do not necessarily want. Similar to other technical services like repair or appraisal services, consumers are at a significant knowledge disadvantage during service provision which is why healthcare is a credence service in that consumers are hardly able to evaluate the clinical quality even after thFe service is performed (Berry and Bendapudi 2007).

The healthcare sector as a whole is made up of a very diverse set of players representing a wide range of interests (Kennedy and Berk 2011). In fact, five major groups can be distinguished here: regulators, providers, payers, suppliers, and healthcare consumers (see Fig. 1.1). Following these five groups, there are structural characteristics and salient differences compared to other industrial or high technology branches.

---

[1]An earlier version of this chapter is published in the proceedings of the 2012 International Conference on Technology Management as Kuenne et al. (2013) and in a transfer report through the Advanced Institute of Management Research, London as Bessant et al. (2012). For more details concerning the communication of the research, see Annex A.

[2]In 2012, health spending in the EU member states consumed on weighted average 10.1% of their GDP while annual growth in health spending more than doubled GDP growth over the past decade (OECD 2014).

© Springer International Publishing AG 2018
C.W. Künne, *Online Intermediaries for Co-Creation*, Progress in IS,
DOI 10.1007/978-3-319-51124-5_1

Fig. 1.1 Healthcare landscape traditionally dominated by five types of players

First, the regulatory bodies enact healthcare regulations and laws. It aims at ensuring safety, ethical compliance and environmental care, but incurs enormous regulatory-related costs as well, for example the evaluation and approval process of drugs or medical devices (Bohnet-Joschko and Jandeck 2011; Clulow 2013; Fichman et al. 2011). In fact, the healthcare sector entails a *high degree of regulatory requirements* for all participants (Fichman et al. 2011; Field 2008).

Second, at the level of healthcare providers, the adoption of innovation, i.e. new technologies or procedures, poses special challenges partly due to *strongly hierarchical and complex structures* and own professional norms in healthcare (Chreim et al. 2010; Hernandez et al. 2013; Kane and Labianca 2011). That is, doctors are primarily occupied with delivering treatments to patients in their best possible way and consider any other activity as administrative nuisance (Fichman et al. 2011).

Third, at the level of the healthcare payers, one key peculiarity of healthcare as a network of diverse stakeholders becomes obvious. Often, the *payer* of a product or service is *not the same entity* as the *consumer* of the product or service, and the consumer of that product or service is often not the same entity as the *decision-making entity* (Rotnes and Staalesen 2009).

Fourth, at the level of healthcare suppliers, there are, among others, those organizations that develop new products and treatments and heavily invest in research and development (R&D). Due to the enormous complexity of new products, *very long development times*[3] and staggering R&D budgets are typical in this sector (Bohnet-Joschko and Jandeck 2011; Clulow 2013; Hanney et al. 2015).

Fifth, the end consumers of the healthcare sector, who are often patients, are distinctively different from consumers in other areas. Berry and Bendapudi (2007) emphasize that healthcare consumers (HCCs) are *usually sick* and under stress. Hence, they are plagued by illness, pain, uncertainty, sadness, and fear which can cause them to be more emotional, more demanding, more sensitive, or more depending than they would normally be. In the case of chronic or rare disease patients, they are *affected over many years* gathering a tremendous pool of experiential and technical knowledge about their condition and treatments. Common to all is, though, that they are highly *intrinsically motivated* to restore the situation to the better.

To the degree that healthcare systems are struggling with a multitude of challenges, it is not surprising that *innovation* is an activity of central and crucial importance. Indeed, the healthcare sector has continuously been characterized by innovation—in treatments and drugs, in hospital and care systems, in primary and acute care pathways and in chronic disease management. While innovation has traditionally been acknowledged as a collaborative, multi-player activity, in today's knowledge rich environment even large healthcare organizations (HCOs), such as pharmaceutical or medical technology companies, experience a bottleneck of internal knowledge resources, fueling the search to engage a wide range of additional players. Innovation, though, does not necessarily mean the one unique discovery that solves previous challenges. As Chin et al. (2012:26) from the 2012 Forum on Healthcare Innovation at the Harvard Medical School put it:

> There's something undeniably alluring about the breakthrough innovation that suddenly changes everything. [...] However, in a world full of innovations we already struggle to absorb. Perhaps what we need is not simply another 'big idea', but rather better ways of distributing the smaller ideas—the knowledge we have now or anticipate acquiring in the near future.

Related to the increasing need for innovation in healthcare, there is a paradigm shift in managing innovation. Often referred to as *open innovation* (Chesbrough 2003; Huff et al. 2013), this approach is about achieving and sustaining a higher degree of innovation by opening up the traditionally closed innovation process. It suggests that the process of new product and service development should better integrate and leverage external knowledge resources provided by a wide range of external actors, such as customers and users. These external actors enable the innovating organization to learn more easily about their needs, and to benefit straight away from their solution proposals for specific problems they might already have in mind. The integration of such external actors is feasible during earlier stages

---

[3]Especially in biomedical and health research, the time lag between research and its translation into products, policy, or practice has been estimated to be at 17 years (Hanney et al. 2015; Morris et al. 2011).

of the process, such as idea generation and conceptualization, as well as later stages, like development or prototyping. So far, healthcare has not been as advanced as other areas in the use of open innovation approaches which may be attributed to its structural complexity (Clulow 2013; Reinhardt et al. 2014). Considered a subset of open innovation is the concept of *co-creation* (Greer and Lei 2012; Kraemer et al. 2014; Piller et al. 2010). Co-creation denotes a collaborative activity in which consumers and organizations jointly form knowledge that is valuable for the organization's innovation process of new products or services. Hence, this concept distinctively focusses on consumers as a source of innovation.

In the context of healthcare, a promising direction for innovation lies in harnessing the *innovation potential of healthcare consumers* (Boote et al. 2002; Paterson 2004; Rotnes and Staalesen 2009; Wanless 2002). There are many examples where patients have played a key role in developing solutions to their healthcare challenges—and there is evidence that this process is accelerating (Cepiku and Savignon 2015; Habicht et al. 2012; Huener et al. 2011; von Hippel et al. 2011). Clearly, there is considerable potential in approaches which mobilize a wider community, including individual patients and their caregivers as a part of the "innovation front-end" in healthcare.

One powerful set of tools, already widely used in other domains to enable co-creation, are those which leverage the enormous reach of the Internet. The Internet has changed our understanding of collaborative activities in innovation processes. Over the last two decades, various types of tools have emerged that allow a wider community of different people from inside and outside an organization to work together during the shared exploration of healthcare challenges, the generation of new ideas and the design, implementation and evaluation of innovations (Moeslein 2013). The emergence of web 2.0 technology and interactive capabilities in the online space can be an effective source of jointly constructed and shared knowledge through the participation of healthcare consumers, healthcare providers, researchers, and others. In the past decade we observe an increasing number of *health-related online platforms* that, in addition to traditional resources such as health professionals and books, help sick and well people to gather additional information on medical conditions, share their medical experience, and discuss questions and concerns (Cline 2001; Goh et al. 2013; Oh 2012). Based on prior research (Bullinger et al. 2012; Hartmann et al. 2013), some of these online health platforms can support and contribute to innovation activities in modern healthcare systems. Four brief examples are depicted in the following to illustrate how the engagement of healthcare consumers through online platforms may appear. These examples are Edison Nation Medical, PatientsLikeMe, Patient Opinion, and InnovationByYou.

Example one: *Edison Nation Medical* is an innovation marketplace specifically for healthcare products. It aims at individuals such as physicians, nurses, entrepreneurs, patients and caregivers to submit a medical invention idea for detailed feasibility evaluation. If selected, Edison Nation Medical provides the monetary and non-monetary resources to fully develop and potentially commercialize it through a network of implementation partners. At the same time, innovation-seeking

Fig. 1.2 Call for idea search at the innovation marketplace EdisonNationMedical (Screenshot retrieved on August 15, 2015 from www.edisonnationmedical.com)

companies can partner with Edison Nation Medical and publish a call for innovation search on a particular topic that individuals can directly reply to (see Fig. 1.2). Recent innovation searches dealt with topics such as wearable medical devices, first aid products, and remote monitoring for post-surgical patients.

Example two: *PatientsLikeMe*, an online network of patients to better manage their conditions, was working with *Merck*[4] in psoriasis.[5] They launched a community there in 2012 and were doing quarterly surveys on how the different changing seasons affect the disease. Looking at the northern hemisphere, in the winter there is a dry cold, in the summer there is hot humidity, but people also have exposure to other aerosols like sunscreen or mosquito repellent. PatientsLikeMe surveyed the patients in order to get a sense of what is bothering them. For example, around Christmas people drink more alcohol and alcohol can be a trigger for psoriasis. With the returned results from the surveys, PatientsLikeMe was able to complete two patient-reported outcome measures. One is called the Dermatological Life Quality Index, a quality of life measure (see Fig. 1.3), and the other one is called the Body Surface Area percentage that estimates how of much of your body is covered with dermatological psoriasis. After data analysis, the results were shared back with the patients as well as with Merck as one of their commercial clients.

---

[4]Merck Sharp & Dohme is an American pharmaceutical company and one of the largest in the world.

[5]Psoriasis is an immune-mediated disease that affects the skin by red, itchy, scaly patches. It is typically a lifelong condition with currently no cure.

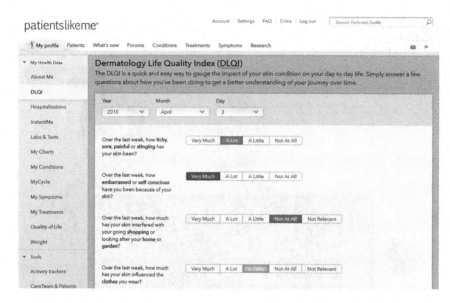

Fig. 1.3 Interface for data collection in the context of psoriasis at PatientsLikeMe (Screenshot retrieved on August 15, 2015 from www.patientslikeme.com)

Example three: *PatientOpinion* aims at improving health services in the UK through giving patients the possibility to publicly, yet anonymously share their experiences (mostly praise and criticism, but often also suggestions for improvement) about the care received at hospitals, surgeries and clinics. However, it is more than a one-way channel. Staff from the respective organizations directly replies to it indicating whether the organization has reacted to the suggestions and implemented change based on the patient's input (see Fig. 1.4). In one report, a patient lady was sent to an overnight stay at hospital for a polysomnography test, a type of diagnostic sleep study. She experienced several dissatisfying circumstances which overall question the effectiveness of such a test. Her experiences include a stuffy, badly ventilated ward in which the window could not be sufficiently opened, loud sound of a plant room from the shared courtyard, incomplete briefing from the unmotivated staff, and lastly an uncomfortable thin mattress. So she suggested revisiting the entire procedure from a patient perspective to ensure the effectiveness of an overnight polysomnography test. Ultimately, through the PatientOpinion platform, the hospital confirmed to having implemented change according to her suggestions.

Example four: At *InnovationByYou*, an online community for continence care and ostomy care patients, the members devise and discuss product ideas that facilitate coping with their condition. One problem area identified by users of ostomy bags is to know the right time when to change the bag. Therefore, they considered a full bag indicator sketching out several ways of how this could be realized (see Fig. 1.5). Along the way, professional support is given by a renowned

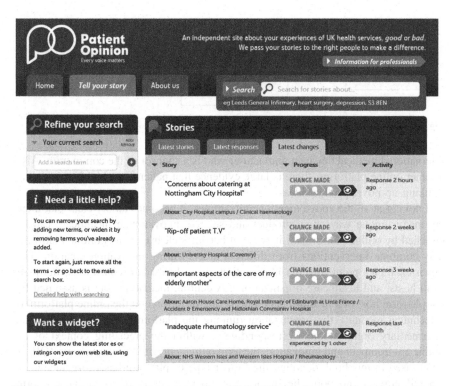

Fig. 1.4 Patients' suggestions put into practice at PatientOpinion (Screenshot retrieved on August 15, 2015 from www.patientopinion.org.uk)

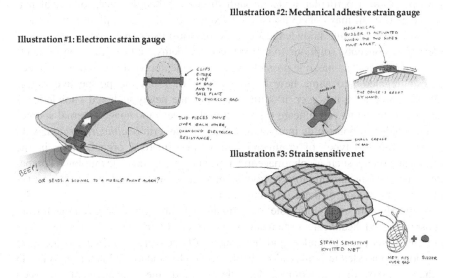

Fig. 1.5 Suggested solutions for a full ostomy bag indicator at InnovationByYou (Illustrations from www.innovationbyyou.com retrieved on February 15, 2013)

Fig. 1.6 Idealized interaction model of different actors

international medical device manufacturer who is a sponsor of the community. Also at other online platforms, there is large evidence that patients are highly creative in thinking up novel product ideas.

Looking at all the above mentioned examples, it becomes amply clear that there are many unique ways how product and service innovation in healthcare can be enriched by online platforms. Likewise, it becomes clear that such online platforms may combine interventions from different actors during innovation creation. The given examples point towards interventions from healthcare consumers, the platform hosts, and healthcare organizations. A central, mediating role is assumed by the platform host of a health-related online platform. Beyond the online platform as a technical medium, the organization running the platform can be considered an intermediary organization. Correspondingly, within the preceding context of an online environment and innovation, the term *online innovation intermediary* (OII) is being used in this book denoting the former type of platform-based organizations. An OII attracts and pools healthcare consumers as users of its online platform according to the platform's leading theme. The healthcare consumers are interested in gathering information on specific medical conditions, or may want to exchange with peers on a particular topic through discussion boards, chats or social networking. The OII may collect users' knowledge over time and exploit it in a variety of ways. The valuable knowledge from the platform users may appear in form of ideas, raw concepts, solutions to experienced problems, and feedback on products or services. For example, one possible way is that the knowledge could be analyzed and aggregated into some new form by the OII. From the perspective of the innovation process, however, it is important that the newly gathered knowledge is being transferred to a healthcare organization that seeks to engage external sources of knowledge to nourish its innovation capacity. The term *healthcare organization* denotes different types of commercial or non-commercial organizations in the healthcare sector such as pharmaceutical companies, medical technology companies, hospitals, or nursing homes. In this line of argumentation, Fig. 1.6 depicts the idealized interaction of these different actors.

Arguably, the mediating role of OIIs in the interaction between healthcare consumers and healthcare organizations is critical to innovation outcomes. The present thesis aims to understand how such OIIs actively contribute to the joint creation of knowledge (co-creation) between the aforementioned actors in order to enhance innovation outcomes. The design and the management of such innovation-enabling online platforms are certainly key influencing factors. Thus, the research question overarching this thesis reads as follows:

> **Research Question**: How do online innovation intermediaries (OIIs) enable effective consumer co-creation for innovation between healthcare consumers (HCCs) and healthcare organizations (HCOs)?

This research question will be further clarified with the help of a thorough literature review on the key concepts involved and the derivation of a theoretical framework. This thesis will explore platform-mediated co-creation for innovation between healthcare consumers and healthcare organizations, and will reveal important findings for researchers and practitioners alike to add new knowledge in this important domain.

The remainder of this chapter is organized as follows. The next section outlines the academic interest that lies in extending knowledge in this topic and why further research is needed. Then, Sect. 1.3 introduces and explains the structure of this thesis with its six chapters.

1.2 Research Gap and Research Questions

The previous section has introduced the thesis' topic from a practical standpoint. Now this section will substantiate its relevance from a scholarly perspective. It mainly draws upon three fields of research that are (i) patient innovation, (ii) co-creation of innovation, and (iii) innovation intermediaries. The following paragraphs outline limitations of current research that together build the scientific motivation of this thesis and justify the research goal formulated by a set of jointly arranged research questions.

The first area that motivates this research is the field of *patient innovation*. The innovative potential of healthcare consumers, who are often patients, to provide inputs to healthcare innovation has been subject of research in recent years (Boote et al. 2002; Cepiku and Savignon 2015; Engström 2012; Habicht and Moeslein 2015; Habicht et al. 2012; Henrike and Schultz 2014; Huener et al. 2011; Oliveira et al. 2015; Paterson 2004; Rotnes and Staalesen 2009). The integration of HCCs is seen as part of the solution to mitigate the current challenges in healthcare. Yet, it has been documented that HCCs are a valuable resource of innovation that is exploited only to a marginal extent so far (Nambisan and Nambisan 2009). Henrike and Schultz (2014) summarize that research on innovation in healthcare mostly focuses on the creation of innovation by healthcare professionals (Fleuren et al. 2004; West and Wallace 1991), on the innovation behavior of healthcare organizations (Hernandez et al. 2013; Salge and Vera 2009; Schultz et al. 2012), and on the innovation adoption and implementation processes by healthcare professionals and hospitals (Berwick 2003; Hoff 2011; Kimberly and Evanisko 1981; Nembhard et al. 2009). A recent survey performed within a group of innovating patients (Cepiku and Savignon 2015) shows that only 10% of patient innovators developed the innovation in collaboration with a business firm and only 1% of patients has communicated their innovation to business firms. That behavior is explained through the same survey in which the profit-making motive ranks low in all cases and never appears as the initial motive. This is in line with what von Hippel (1988) found out: innovating users do not automatically proceed to commercialize their ideas and become entrepreneurs, but they rather develop ideas for their own functional advantage. Academic discourse has highlighted that if knowledge generated by HCCs is not adopted and integrated by professionals, beneficial resources remain unused and patient innovation can hardly unfold its full potential (Argote et al. 2000; Henrike and Schultz 2014). Thus, HCCs, in addition to healthcare professionals, should play a major role in the advancement of healthcare innovation (Henrike and Schultz 2014). In a similar vein, Oliveira et al. (2015) conclude that more research is needed in the area of how HCCs can be supported in their innovation activity, how these patient-driven innovations can be professionally evaluated, and how innovations that are estimated to be of general value can be adopted by a larger audience for broader health advantages. Often though, HCCs are not able to implement ideas alone, they need support from other, mostly professional players to succeed with the implementation (Engström and Snyder 2013). Also Engström and Snyder (2013:316) call for more research in this field by saying:

> While it is often impossible for patients to implement ideas alone, we believe that lead patients can play an important role in innovation. We welcome research that continues to develop blueprints for how users can be involved in the innovation of healthcare.

Therefore, it is necessary to develop a systematic professional approach to make full use of innovative inputs from HCCs. One promising approach is subject of this thesis and will be discussed later.

The second main area that stimulates this research is the field of co-creation, especially *co-creation with consumers.*[6] While co-creation is commonly understood as a collaboration activity between organizations and the consumers of their products for the benefit of new product development (NPD), existing research mostly focused on showing the application of consumer co-creation, often in form of successful examples (Magnusson 2009; Piller et al. 2012). While these examples are helpful for creating anecdotal evidence and generating attention for the underlying phenomenon, they mostly lack a theoretical foundation and a differentiated view on the specific mechanisms enabling consumer co-creation (Greer and Lei 2012; Piller et al. 2012). The vast majority of previous research on co-creation has been conducted in a business-to-business (B2B) context while the business-to-consumer (B2C) context has been neglected (Biemans and Langerak 2015; Hoyer et al. 2010; Magnusson 2009; Spann et al. 2009). This may be due to a

---

[6]The underlying literature equally refers to co-creation with *customers* (e.g., Greer and Lei 2012; Piller et al. 2012) as well as co-creation with *consumers* (e.g., Hoyer et al. 2010; Vernette and Hamdi-Kidar 2013). With regard to the heterogeneity of actors within healthcare (cf. Sect. 1.1), the term *consumer* is considered more suitable in the context of this work.

few differences. In the B2B context, the levels of technical knowledge of consumers and supplier firms are quite symmetrical, as opposed to the B2C context[7] in which knowledge asymmetry is more common (Hoyer et al. 2010). This raises the question whether end consumers bear sufficient technical knowledge to make a meaningful contribution to the innovation process (ibid.). Furthermore, the B2C context is commonly characterized by the heterogeneity of consumers, a large consumer base, a large distance between the firm and its consumers, and quickly changing consumer preferences (Spann et al. 2009). This partially explains why it is more difficult to interact with consumers for the development of new products and why co-creation may impose additional challenges in a B2C setting (Hoyer et al. 2010; Magnusson 2009; Spann et al. 2009). Biemans and Langerak (2015:2) recently confirmed this research gap as they put forward their updated research priorities among which they ask:

> How to manage consumer involvement in NPD? [...] What are the differences in consumer involvement between B2C and B2B? [...] How to leverage the use of digital/social/mobile media in NPD? [...] What is the role of social media in generating new product and service ideas? How can it be used as a complement to traditional idea generation methods?

Especially, methods of virtual consumer integration, i.e. through the Internet, for new product development have become popular in recent years. Yet, Bartl et al. (2012) find that its high potential has been promised by literature, but its practical use is still limited.

Besides the above arguments, previous research tends to emphasize the benefits of consumer co-creation, e.g. the novelty or quality of ideas generated, while the costs and risks related to setting up co-creation processes remain underresearched (Carbonell et al. 2009; Hoyer et al. 2010; Mahr et al. 2014). For example, in order to identify and integrate suitable types of consumers, significant investments in terms of time and money are required by innovating firms (Alam 2002; Luethje and Herstatt 2004). Overall, the arena of co-creation has attracted a lot of attention in recent years. However, it remains a field of research largely unexplored that offers compelling avenues of further investigation (Biemans and Langerak 2015; Hoyer et al. 2010). This research aims to address the gaps described above, notably by shifting the focus towards the B2C context and special challenges imposed. In the end, success or failure of co-creation has to be assessed by its positive outcomes on new product development which requires markets and situations in which co-creation is likely to be a beneficial innovation strategy.

The third main area that ignites this research is the field of *innovation intermediaries*. As illustrated in Sect. 1.1, the number of health-related online platforms has greatly increased over the last years. Some features of these online platforms can support and contribute to innovation activities in modern healthcare systems.

---

[7]The acronym *B2C* needs to be interpreted in the present context of healthcare. While the *B* usually designates private sector businesses, in this work, the *B* stands for healthcare organizations (HCOs) no matter if belonging to the private or public sector. The *C* designates healthcare consumers accordingly.

Correspondingly, the organization behind such a platform can be regarded as an *online innovation intermediary* (OII) that acts in any aspect of the innovation process between two or more parties using the online platform as technical vehicle. At this point, the scholarly perspective of innovation intermediaries becomes important (Howells 2006). If such platform-based organizations are understood as a category of intermediaries, then related literature should be able to provide (partial) explanations for why they do what they do and how they do it. However, as the term intermediary covers a broad class of organizations, explanations for online intermediaries in particular remain scarce. Further research into OIIs follows Howells' (2006) call for research into the range of intermediaries and a more detailed outline of their functions and activities. For any new category of intermediary, key questions need to be answered, such as what the enabling factors of successful intermediation are, or how innovation intermediaries facilitate the creation and integration of knowledge among various parties (Lopez-Vega and Vanhaverbeke 2009). Although a few years have passed since Howells' seminal article, Mele and Russo-Spena (2015:42) recently reconfirmed the need for further research into online (or virtual, as used in the following citation) intermediaries by stating:

> On virtual intermediaries, however, their agency is not fully addressed in the literature. Therefore, there is a need to further understand the agential roles of these virtual intermediaries.

Existing research on online intermediaries has foremost reflected on the ability of online intermediaries to solve specific types of innovation problems (Boudreau et al. 2011; Jeppesen and Lakhani 2010; Terwiesch and Xu 2008). Often, single intermediary cases have been used for analysis which leads Colombo et al. (2013:2) to the following conclusion:

> Hence limited attention has been devoted to analyzing and comparing how different web-based intermediaries organize their service, i.e., how they connect and link seeker firms with solvers.

In addition to that, there is a twofold lack of understanding: understanding the strategies that different intermediaries use when they interact with their knowledge sources and with their innovation-seeking client organizations, and understanding the challenges that client organizations have to overcome when interacting with the intermediary (Colombo et al. 2015). This research aims to address the gaps described above by shifting the focus on the analysis of online innovation intermediaries in healthcare.

Altogether, the above three areas provide the scholarly motivation for this research. In short, the research gap of this thesis arises from (1) healthcare consumers as knowledge source for innovation that is underutilized so far, (2) consumer co-creation in B2C settings that may impose additional challenges for healthcare organizations, and (3) online intermediaries for innovation as a new category that have been insufficiently investigated in terms of their agency. By addressing this gap, this thesis strengthens the understanding of patient innovation

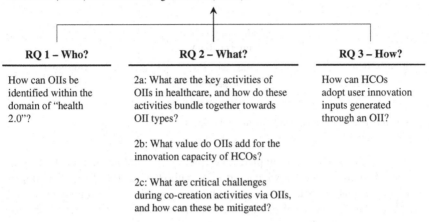

Overarching RQ

How do online innovation intermediaries (OIIs) enable effective co-creation between healthcare consumers (HCCs) and healthcare organizations (HCOs)?

RQ 1 – Who?	RQ 2 – What?	RQ 3 – How?
How can OIIs be identified within the domain of "health 2.0"?	2a: What are the key activities of OIIs in healthcare, and how do these activities bundle together towards OII types? 2b: What value do OIIs add for the innovation capacity of HCOs? 2c: What are critical challenges during co-creation activities via OIIs, and how can these be mitigated?	How can HCOs adopt user innovation inputs generated through an OII?

Fig. 1.7 The research questions of this thesis

as a driver for an organization's competitive advantage and provides conceptual clarity on how this can be achieved using OIIs. If this knowledge is not adopted and integrated by HCOs, critical resources remain unused. Moreover, results may be important for those HCOs that wish to enhance their innovation capacity with external sources, to extract maximum value from collaborating with an innovation intermediary for this purpose, and to design effective mechanisms that integrate contributions from intermediaries into internal innovation.

Based on the above elaboration of the research gap, the overarching research question (RQ) formulated in Sect. 1.1 can be further detailed by additional subordinated research questions. These questions will lead this work and are shown in Fig. 1.7.

The research questions are structured as a group of three and are designed to consecutively build upon each other. Research question 1 aims to identify OIIs on an international scale and thus to provide further empirical evidence. It is a prerequisite to the further analysis. It sets off in the domain of "health 2.0"[8] which incorporates the use of recent, web-based technology in healthcare. Once relevant online platforms are identified, the research questions 2a–2c aim to investigate how the OIIs under analysis work in detail with regard to the key agential activities, the value-add they provide for HCOs, and critical challenges that occurred during co-creation activities. These research questions extract from the formulated research gap on innovation intermediaries and consumer co-creation. Then, research question 3 aims to switch perspective to the HCO side in order to study how inputs that come through an OII are adopted and exploited by organizations. The third research

---

[8]cf. Sect. 3.2.1 for further explanation.

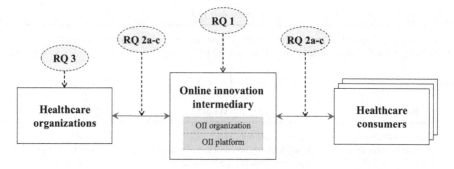

Fig. 1.8 Interrelated research questions in field context

question is important to complete the picture of online intermediaries for co-creation: if co-created knowledge artifacts with HCCs and OIIs are not adopted by HCOs, then its ultimate success might be questionable. The formulated research questions relate to the idealized interaction model given in Sect. 1.1 in the following way (see Fig. 1.8).

With the research questions already foreshadowing a certain structure of this research, the next section will delineate its full structure with its six modular chapters.

1.3   Structure of the Thesis

This work is structured into six overall chapters in order to explore the emerging phenomenon of online innovation intermediaries for consumer co-creation in healthcare. The structure follows the actual stepwise line of research conducted. Thus, each chapter represents one specific research step. All chapters are adjusted to each other and following chapters build on previous ones. Furthermore, the structure is designed in a way that every chapter is divided into sections which, on the lowest hierarchical level, may be subdivided into subsections. The sequence of chapters is explained in the following.

In brief, the current chapter provides the relevance of this topic for practice and academic research and derives clear research questions that serve as work order for the subsequent chapters. Chapter 2 builds the theoretical framework to provide a consistent perspective for the entire work. Building upon the foundation of Chaps. 1 and 2, the subsequent Chaps. 3, 4, and 5 each treat one empirical study. Each empirical study is designed to address a distinct part of the overarching topic. Consequently, each study is motivated by its own subordinated research question that contributes to answering the overall research question in the end. In a similar fashion, each of the three studies builds on its own theoretical underpinnings, different data sources, a distinct research design including data gathering and data analysis methods, and a separate discussion of findings.

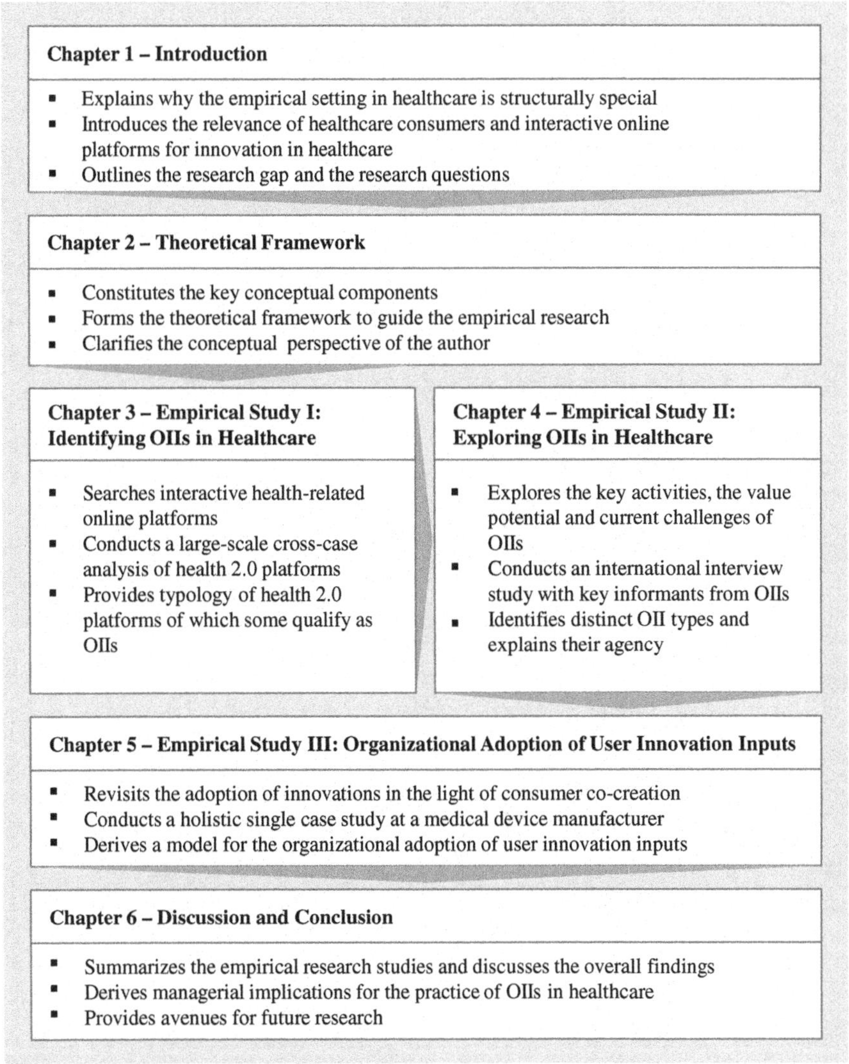

Chapter 1 – Introduction

- Explains why the empirical setting in healthcare is structurally special
- Introduces the relevance of healthcare consumers and interactive online platforms for innovation in healthcare
- Outlines the research gap and the research questions

Chapter 2 – Theoretical Framework

- Constitutes the key conceptual components
- Forms the theoretical framework to guide the empirical research
- Clarifies the conceptual perspective of the author

Chapter 3 – Empirical Study I: Identifying OIIs in Healthcare

- Searches interactive health-related online platforms
- Conducts a large-scale cross-case analysis of health 2.0 platforms
- Provides typology of health 2.0 platforms of which some qualify as OIIs

Chapter 4 – Empirical Study II: Exploring OIIs in Healthcare

- Explores the key activities, the value potential and current challenges of OIIs
- Conducts an international interview study with key informants from OIIs
- Identifies distinct OII types and explains their agency

Chapter 5 – Empirical Study III: Organizational Adoption of User Innovation Inputs

- Revisits the adoption of innovations in the light of consumer co-creation
- Conducts a holistic single case study at a medical device manufacturer
- Derives a model for the organizational adoption of user innovation inputs

Chapter 6 – Discussion and Conclusion

- Summarizes the empirical research studies and discusses the overall findings
- Derives managerial implications for the practice of OIIs in healthcare
- Provides avenues for future research

Fig. 1.9 Structure of the thesis with its six chapters

The perspectives taken of each of the three empirical studies vary though: while Chap. 3 takes an outside perspective on the research subject of online innovation intermediaries, Chap. 4 gives detailed accounts from an inside perspective on the research subject; Chap. 5 then takes the view of a HCO that utilizes the input generated through an OII to enhance its innovation function. Finally, Chap. 6 concludes the entire research results and ends with an outlook for future research. Figure 1.9 depicts the entire structure of this thesis in a compact visualization.

Chapter 2
Theoretical Framework

2.1 Elucidation of Key Components

To guide the empirical studies to be conducted, the present chapter derives the theoretical framework. It aims at clarifying the conceptual components that are used throughout the remainder of this research. Therefore, the first section of this chapter begins with the elucidation of the most necessary conceptual components. First, the concept of *consumer co-creation for innovation* is presented and defined. Second, *healthcare consumers* are introduced as a construct and it is stated that healthcare consumers may serve as promising input factor for consumer co-creation. Third, it is argued that knowledge is an important determinant of innovation and the *knowledge-based theory of the firm* is introduced. Fourth, the concept of *innovation intermediary* is presented which provides the essential foundation to view an organization running a health-related online platform as an innovation intermediary if it is set up in this way. In the second section of this chapter, all components are consolidated to form the theoretical framework.

2.1.1 Consumer Co-Creation for Innovation

Before diving deeper into the concept of co-creation, it is important to define it as there exist numerous interpretations that differ in significant nuances. Solely from a linguistic perspective, the term *co-creation* implies that something is obviously created and it is done in a joint manner between two or more parties as the "co" suggests. These and other essential notions are explained in this section and a suitable definition of co-creation is presented, which will serve as the basis for the entire thesis and its multiple empirical studies in this field.

© Springer International Publishing AG 2018
C.W. Künne, *Online Intermediaries for Co-Creation*, Progress in IS,
DOI 10.1007/978-3-319-51124-5_2

2.1.1.1 Distinguishing Value Creation and Value Co-Creation

During the last years, the traditional view on *value creation* in organizational settings has increasingly been questioned. Earlier literature viewed value creation in a way that value is produced by providers exclusively inside organizations and used up by consumers (Alderson 1957; Bagozzi 1975; Hunt 1976). Value is conceptualized as being exchanged between the producer and the consumer, which often equals the price that consumers pay for the purchased products or services. Newer literature spotlights the importance of consumer engagement in value creation processes and emphasizes the added interactive nature to value creation (Normann and Ramírez 1993; Prahalad and Ramaswamy 2004a; Reichwald and Piller 2009; Vargo and Lusch 2004). Scholars and managers alike have acknowledged consumers as active partners who become involved in firm's value creation processes and are empowered to conceive solutions that better address their needs and expectations (Fuchs and Schreier 2011; Mahr et al. 2014; Nambisan 2009; Prahalad and Ramaswamy 2004a; Sawhney et al. 2005). It is considered to yield major benefits for innovating organizations leading to the development of better products or services while lowering risks and costs of failures at the same time. It is described as a paradigm shift from value creation *for* consumers to value creation *with* consumers (Vargo and Lusch 2004). This newer view specifies that value is jointly created, or co-created, during the interaction between the provider and the consumer. Therefore, the latter view is often denoted under the term *value co-creation.*[1]

2.1.1.2 Defining Consumer Co-Creation for Innovation

There are certainly many areas in organizational settings where consumers can be involved in co-creation (Romero and Molina 2011; Wind and Mahajan 1997). However, one area in particular where co-creation is increasingly crucial is the area of product and service innovation (Hoyer et al. 2010). In many organizations, the innovation capacity for new products and services is structurally accommodated in the new product development (NPD) or research and development (R&D) function. Co-creation for innovation is supported by a stream of scholarly literature that understands co-creation as the active involvement of consumers in the innovation process (Foss et al. 2011; Greer and Lei 2012; Hoyer et al. 2010; Kraemer et al. 2014; Lee et al. 2012; Lorenzo-Romero et al. 2014; Mahr et al. 2014; O'Hern and Rindfleisch 2010; Piller et al. 2010; Russo-Spena and Mele 2012; Weber 2011). They argue that the firm's innovation performance can be improved through the

---

[1]Depending on the applied linguistic vocabulary, the prefix 'co' has been adopted from different, yet closely related word families beginning with 'co', such as collaborative, cooperative, or collective. Originally, this prefix has roots in the Latin. It signifies a relation between two subjects or objects that interact in a notion of together, mutually, or jointly (Stoller-Schai 2009:34).

Table 2.1 Selected definitions of consumer co-creation for innovation

Authors	Definition
O'Hern and Rindfleisch (2010), Hoyer et al. (2010), Lorenzo-Romero et al. (2014)	• A collaborative new product development activity in which consumers actively contribute and select various elements of a new product offering
Piller et al. (2010)	• An active, creative, and social process, based on collaboration between producers (retailers) and customers (users) in the context of new product development
Kraemer et al. (2014)	• Active, creative, and social collaboration activities of firms and users within new product and service development
Mahr et al. (2014)	• Customer co-production of knowledge that is valuable for the firm's innovation process
Greer and Lei (2012)	• The process of engaging in the creation of new products or services in collaboration with customers or users
Russo-Spena and Mele (2012)	• Innovation can be understood as a co-creation process within social and technological networks in which actors integrate their resources to create mutual value
Weber (2011)	• A process where product manufacturers and/or service providers engage with their end users in (parts or phases of) innovation projects to jointly perform innovation activities and co-create value, with the aim of increasing effectiveness and efficiency of the innovation process

involvement of consumers by tapping into their knowledge, skills, experiences, and interests. Ultimately, it will contribute to achieve sustainable competitive advantage over the competition (Prahalad and Ramaswamy 2004a). Yet, successful innovation requires a profound understanding of consumer needs and product developments efforts that meet those needs.

Reviewing available definitions from the last five years (see Table 2.1) reveals that they greatly overlap, but also show slight differences. It is commonly recognized that consumer co-creation for innovation (i) is stipulated as a process or activity, not a static event, (ii) is based on collaboration, (iii) between firms and consumers, (iv) highlights and also depends on the active and central role of the consumer, (v) is valuable for the development of new products or services. Beyond the sometimes abstract concept of value inherent to co-creation, Mahr et al. (2014) add the concept of knowledge to it. It helps to describe value through knowledge that is created, gathered and exploited during co-creation activities. Therefore, taking all these aspects into account, the following definition is concluded and proposed as conceptual basis for this research. If at some points in this document it should be referred to as 'co-creation' only, then the reader should interpret it according the definition beneath.

> **Definition**: Consumer co-creation for innovation describes a collaborative activity in which consumers and organizations jointly form knowledge that is valuable for the organization's innovation process of new products or services.

The above definition integrates four central elements. First, it acknowledges the pivotal role of knowledge to develop innovations (Madhavan and Grover 1998; Mahr et al. 2014). Second, the definition relates to the distinct consumers' involvement in the formation of valuable knowledge. Third, while still being a universal definition, the definition avoids the terms "customers" and "firms" and uses "consumers" and "organizations" instead to better accommodate the healthcare context. Fourth, the definition relates to the value-in-use-view by Vargo and Lusch (2008) who argue that value is always determined by the beneficiary. In co-creation, there are at least two types of beneficiaries, the organization and the consumer. This research focuses on the benefits for organizations similar to preceding studies (Blazevic and Lievens 2008; Hoyer et al. 2010; Lau et al. 2010; Magnusson 2009; Mahr et al. 2014; Sawhney et al. 2005). From an organization's perspective as the beneficiary, the value of knowledge formed through co-creation highly depends on how the beneficiary organization can make effective use of it in a certain situation at a specific moment in time.

2.1.1.3 Clarifying "Innovation"

Regarding the outcome of co-creation for innovation, an important distinction has to be made at this point. Co-creation in whichever form is at its core linked to the joint creation of value between an organization and consumers. The notion of value may be translated in an operational notion of knowledge among other. When co-creation is bounded to the area of innovation, sustainable innovation shall ultimately be the outcome of this endeavor. However, innovation as a definite outcome cannot be planned with certainty. Therefore, innovation can still be the result of co-creation, but co-creation does not necessarily have to lead to innovation (Ophof 2013).

Innovation, though, is a very broad concept. A plethora of definitions of innovation has resulted in ambiguity of how the term 'innovation' is operationalized in the scholarly literature on innovation and new product development (Garcia and Calantone 2002; West and Bogers 2013). Some papers even reference 'innovation' and 'idea' interchangeably (e.g., Di Gangi and Wasko 2009), thus amplifying the ambiguity of terms. Hence, I find it important to clarify the understanding that I adhere to in this research. Generally speaking, innovation can mean scientific inventions, patents, technological breakthroughs, or even a simple new way to do things (Lee et al. 2012). For example Rogers (2003:12) defines it rather broadly by focusing on the perceived newness as a distinguishing notion for innovation:

> An innovation is an idea, practice, or object that is perceived as new by an individual or other unit of adoption. It matters little [...] whether or not an idea is objectively new as measured by the lapse of time since its first use or discovery. The perceived newness of the idea for the individual determines his or her reaction to it. If an idea seems new to the individual, it is an innovation.

Mueller-Prothmann and Doerr (2009) add the notion of diffusion to it by stating that an invention is only an innovation if it reaches a certain level of diffusion in a user group, i.e. a market. Hauschildt and Salomo (2011) go further and link an innovation to its commercialization. This is in line with Freeman (1982:7) who argues:

> Inventions do not necessarily lead to technical innovations. In fact the majority do not. An innovation in the economic sense is accomplished only with the first commercial transaction.

However, because innovations can have economic or societal impact even if diffused through a non-commercial process, a more generalized definition is given by Roberts (1988:12):

> Innovation is composed of two parts: (1) the generation of an idea or invention, and (2) the conversion of that invention into a business or other useful application.

The same author continues by putting it in a formula-like statement by saying that "Innovation = Invention + Exploitation", while the latter is usually the commercial diffusion (Roberts 1988). From an organizational perspective, innovation is directly tied to value creation when a new idea or approach is applied and new value is created, either economically, socially, or technically (Lee et al. 2012).

West and Bogers (2013:13) add an elucidating remark noting that not all of the research on co-creation for innovation and other co-creation related concepts involves the creation of innovations. In particular, most user-generated content would not qualify as an innovation in the sense of Roberts' definition above (Bogers and West 2012). In the context of this research, I follow Roberts' definition, i.e. an initial new idea generated by consumers on an OII platform becomes an innovation only if it is professionally matured into a product or service and successfully diffused into a user group.

2.1.1.4 Key Reasons for the Emergence of Co-Creation

There are two main reasons that have favored and furthered the emergence of co-creation. First, new technological opportunities, foremost the Internet as a valuable communication medium, have provided consumers with access to unlimited amounts of information and an ability to communicate with other consumers and companies anywhere in the world (Hoyer et al. 2010; Prahalad and Ramaswamy 2004a). Especially through the developments towards Web 2.0 as well as the emergence of numerous social media platforms, consumers are easily enabled to interconnect worldwide exchanging personal, social and scientific knowledge with like-minded individuals (Lee et al. 2012). Thereby, consumers are better informed, have easier access to product information and product alternatives, and become more conscious about their needs. This has contributed to a new level of consumer empowerment in a way that consumers desire to take a more active and influential role in the process of value creation with companies (Hoyer et al. 2010; Lorenzo-Romero et al. 2014).

The same technological opportunities have opened up new opportunities for firms to integrate consumers more widely, more effectively, more interactively in their innovation processes (Nambisan and Nambisan 2008). The Internet acts as a means of coordination, a means of aggregation as well as a means of distribution (Zwass 2010). At the same time, it is available to a large majority of people. For these reasons, the Internet has been and still is a major driver in the development of the co-creation concept but also in its realization.

Second, even large firms realize a bottleneck of internal knowledge resources for innovation despite a knowledge rich environment. Industry-specific challenges even increase the need for an uninterrupted flow of innovation (Mahr et al. 2014). Both inevitably involve a higher demand for need and solution related information. Using co-creation to harness consumers' knowledge about their experiences und usage appears as a logical step. The involvement of consumers in this process transforms them into a valuable knowledge resource through which firms can address the challenges and improve their innovation performance (Vargo and Lusch 2004).

2.1.1.5 Related Concepts and Their Differentiation

The concept of co-creation has occurred in the guise of many similar and partly overlapping concepts. For example, a systematic literature review by Greer et al. (2012) in this field has used the following terms for their search: co-development, co-innovation, co-production, collaborative innovation, customer new product development, joint development, open innovation with customers, participatory innovation and user-centric innovation. However, two closely associated concepts to co-creation are 'open innovation' and 'user innovation' that are briefly illuminated next to show how they differ.

The *open innovation* paradigm has been used to describe a system where innovation is not only performed within an internal research and development department of a firm, but in a cooperative manner with other external actors (Chesbrough 2003; Reichwald and Piller 2009). Chesbrough et al. (2006:1) define it as:

> Open innovation is the use of purposive inflows and outflows of knowledge to accelerate internal innovation, and expand the markets for external use of innovation, respectively. [This paradigm] assumes that firms can and should use external ideas as well as internal ideas, and internal and external paths to market, as they look to advance their technology.

It is opposed to closed innovation that has been the dominant model in the past; the latter is characterized by closely managed networks of vertically integrated partners (Chesbrough 2003; Lee et al. 2012). Open innovation in contrast requires the organization's boundaries to be permeable to knowledge flows.

Co-creation can be considered a subset of open innovation (Greer and Lei 2012). Common to both is the integration of external sources of knowledge in a firm's innovation process. While open innovation includes many different forms of external sources and actors set up in formal or informal relationships serving a firm's innovation process, consumer co-creation constrains to firm-driven approaches of open innovation with consumers only (Piller et al. 2012). Thus, co-creation is less comprehensive than open innovation as, for example, open innovation can also occur without interaction with consumers.

The second strongly related concept to co-creation is *user innovation*. User innovation is about the role of users in innovation and links to the seminal works of von Hippel (1976, 1978, 1986, 1988, 2005). It postulates that not only are firms' R&D functions sources of valuable innovations but that also users have the abilities to develop innovations themselves (von Hippel 1988). The 'users' are typically consumer users such as individual end-users or user communities, or intermediate users such as user firms (Bogers et al. 2010). The 'innovation' that they generate is typically (i) the innovation of novel products, services, or technologies, (ii) the innovation in configuration of existing products, services and technologies, and (iii) the innovation of use, while the majority of user innovations concentrates on the latter two (Weber 2011). Clearly, the motivations are very different: firms usually aim at selling the innovation and making profit from it, while users innovate to better attend to their needs and requirements (von Hippel 2005).

Integral part of von Hippel's studies on user innovation is the idea of *lead users* (von Hippel 1986). Lead users face specific needs for a product or service much ahead of the general market participants and create a workable solution for it by themselves. In this case, users are taking over the role of the innovator entirely. They are characterized as being highly intrinsically motivated while performing the innovation process independently and without an interaction with a manufacturing firm. Many firms show high interest in the resulting discoveries of lead users, and firms "just" need to identify and capture their solutions (Piller et al. 2010).

Common to user innovation and co-creation is that both consider users/consumers as valuable sources of innovation. However, co-creation takes the perspective of a firm-driven approach that facilitates the interaction with the consumers by providing tools and methods to jointly create a solution. Figure 2.1 briefly summarizes commonalities and differences of the related concepts.

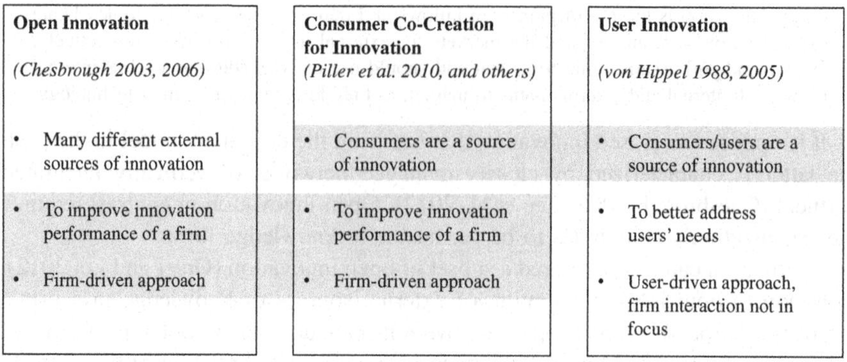

Open Innovation *(Chesbrough 2003, 2006)*	Consumer Co-Creation for Innovation *(Piller et al. 2010, and others)*	User Innovation *(von Hippel 1988, 2005)*

• Many different external
  sources of innovation
	• Consumers are a source
	  of innovation
		• Consumers/users are a
		  source of innovation

• To improve innovation
  performance of a firm
	• To improve innovation
	  performance of a firm
		• To better address
		  users' needs

• Firm-driven approach	• Firm-driven approach	• User-driven approach,
		  firm interaction not in
		  focus

Fig. 2.1 Related concepts in overview

2.1.2   Healthcare Consumers as Source for Co-Creation

The previous section has explained the changing perspective of the consumer in creating value over recent years. In a similar vein, the perceived role of healthcare consumers has also changed which is elucidated in this subsection.

2.1.2.1   HCC Involvement in Healthcare

The HCC stands at the end of a complex industry whose leading rationale is to improve his own well-being and health status. More strikingly, the HCC is the source where health issues originate—or at least where they come into appearance. His health status and diseases are the subject matter of the players involved in healthcare. While the HCC has traditionally been regarded as a receiver of care only, who is described as weak, exposed and dependent on the immediate environment, the role has transformed towards one of a consumer who actively manages his health status, seeks information online, makes distinct choices and thus creates value (Nordgren 2009).

At this point, it is recommendable to clarify the term "healthcare consumer" (HCC). In its broadest sense, a healthcare consumer can be simply defined as both actuator and receiver of all health-related efforts. However, there are various terms used in literature to describe healthcare receivers, such as *patient, service user, lay person, sufferer* and *client* (Bastian 1994; Boote et al. 2002). There is no overall agreement about the terminology applied and it highly depends on the context and, in particular, on the role and mission of the person or organization using the term. On the one hand, words as *client, customer* and *consumer* could overstress a notion of market-orientation and a commercial relationship which is problematic in health. On the other hand, *patient* and *sufferer* are less popular because it may emphasize sickness and disempowerment. Although it may not be perfect, the term *healthcare consumer* bridges best the gap between sickness and health. This term refers to people who receive or who have the potential to receive healthcare. A healthcare consumer does not have to be a patient who is sick while he may undergo preventive treatments yet. For the purpose of this research, I prefer to adhere to the widely accepted term *healthcare consumer* which will be used throughout the document under the given considerations.

The new active role of the HCC, which is often noted as one path to address the current challenges in healthcare system, is gaining acceptance in the scholarly healthcare discourse (Berry and Bendapudi 2007; Bessant and Maher 2009; Engström 2012; McColl-Kennedy et al. 2012; Nambisan and Nambisan 2009). Beyond that, an increasing stream of literature argues for a more prominent role of healthcare consumers in the provision of healthcare (Bartl 2009; Echeverri 2013; Elg et al. 2012; Ferguson 2007; Hardyman et al. 2015; Henrike and Schultz 2014; Longtin et al. 2010; Rozenblum and Bates 2013; Voorberg et al. 2014).

The involvement of HCCs in healthcare delivery spans a continuum from HCC's preferences being used as input to treatments to HCC taking over tasks within their own care (Engström 2012). Different versions of it are also found under terms such as patient centeredness (Robinson et al. 2008; Rozenblum and Bates 2013), patient empowerment (Anderson and Funnell 2000; Bodenheimer et al. 2002; Salmon and Hall 2004), patient partnership (Brennan 1999; Cahill 1996), and shared decision making (Smith 2003; Wills and Holmes-Rovner 2003). Benefits that come along HCC involvement are often denoted with decreased costs for the provider, increased freedom for the HCC, and better adherence to treatments and thus improved health outcomes (Elg et al. 2012; Robinson et al. 2008). It is contestable if this shift towards a more active role of HCCs is always in the best interest of the HCCs (Nordgren 2009) as not every HCC wants to necessarily adopt this active role.

2.1.2.2 HCC as Source of Innovation

However, the stream of literature on HCC involvement in healthcare provision does not yet consider the innovation capacity of healthcare consumers (Cepiku and Savignon 2015; Habicht et al. 2012; Henrike and Schultz 2014). Even recent research on 'patient-centered innovation' neglects the direct role that HCCs can play in the innovation process (Hernandez et al. 2013). Only few scholarly publications have commenced to explore it so far (e.g., Cepiku and Giordano 2014; Engström and Snyder 2013; Henrike and Schultz 2014; Nambisan and Nambisan 2009). Henrike and Schultz (2014) observe that research on innovation in healthcare has mainly focused on either the generation of innovation by healthcare professionals themselves (e.g., Fleuren et al. 2004; West and Wallace 1991), on the innovation behavior of HCOs (e.g., Hernandez et al. 2013; Salge and Vera 2009; Schultz et al. 2012), or on the innovation adoption by healthcare professionals and hospitals (e.g., Berwick 2003; Hoff 2011; Kimberly and Evanisko 1981; Nembhard et al. 2009).

Recent research has found that HCCs conceive a multitude of valuable solutions to improve their own personal medical situations (Cepiku and Savignon 2015; Engström 2012; Frost et al. 2011; Habicht et al. 2012; Oliveira et al. 2015). These solutions range from simple tools for everyday use, through discovery of previously unknown therapies, to highly sophisticated solutions. The HCCs with their devised solutions and their generated expert knowledge through course of their ailments may thus induce stimuli for innovation by professional stakeholders. Henrike and Schultz (2014:330) defines the innovative behavior of HCCs as emerging incremental adaptations or the creation of completely new solutions for products, services, or processes to significantly benefit the care situation of HCCs. The source of their knowledge comes from two sources. First, the frequent use and consumption of products or services gives the consumers broad usage experiences. Such learning by doing leads to lively, practicable and plausible knowledge (Schreier and Prügl 2008). Second, consumer knowledge comes from knowledge related to the product or service environment, i.e. structural knowledge about the design of products, technical knowledge about technologies applied in existing products, or general knowledge about market trends (Lüthje 2004). Prior research shows that more informed consumers relate positively to the likelihood of innovation and decreased development costs in comparison with innovation that is influenced by less informed consumers (Lüthje 2004; Ozer 2009). From other domains such as telecommunication services, it can be concluded that ideas provided by consumers tend to be more original and of higher creative value than those from R&D departments (Kristensson et al. 2004). This is in line with Wiley (1998) who found that consumers' ideas differ in content as well as quality because consumers are often unaware of technical or organizational restrictions.

For example, in a survey-based analysis Oliveira et al. (2015) study disease-related innovation by HCCs. In a sample population of 500 rare disease patients, they find that 36% (182) of surveyed patients had developed (product as well as service related) improvements to the management of their disease. Further evaluation by expert medical evaluators showed that 22% (40) of these claimed improvements are assessed as new-to-the world, while the rest was new to the person who conceived it, but not new to medicine. Considering self-selection bias of the rare disease patients in the sample, the reported innovation levels might be lower in broader populations, but still it gives clear evidence of HCCs developing innovative solutions. However, from a qualitative enquiry, Engström (2012) adds that the inventiveness and ability to generate ideas varies substantially among HCCs. Therefore, he proposes the idea of *lead patients* that extends von Hippel's idea of lead users to the healthcare domain, arguing that some of the HCCs inquired make substantially more contributions than the average (Engström and Snyder 2013; Engström 2012). Not only do those lead patients show unique innovative capabilities, but also strong relational capabilities. In addition to exploring new solutions to address their unmet needs, they express openness and empathy toward peers and they seem to extract intrinsic rewards from making the efforts to innovate without necessarily being able to benefit from their ideas themselves (Engström and Snyder 2013).

2.1.2.3 Status Quo of Consumer Co-Creation in Healthcare

Identifying HCCs as a valuable source of innovation is just one necessary part for co-creation. Exploiting HCCs' potential for the benefit of a firm's innovation process of new products or services is a second part necessary for co-creation as defined above (cf. Sect. 2.1.1.2). Yet, scholarly literature that explores HCOs engaging with HCCs in the context of consumer co-creation for innovation remains scarce. For example, Davey et al. (2010) show that innovating with HCCs can exceed the dyad of physician and HCC through systematically integrating HCOs from different medical areas.

There is, indeed, a number of research on co-creation for innovation between HCOs (such as manufacturing medical firms) and the users of their products (Biemans 1991; Bill et al. 2011; Bohnet-Joschko and Kientzler 2010; Chatterji and Fabrizio 2008; Demonaco et al. 2006; Huener et al. 2011; Lettl et al. 2006, 2008; Luethje 2003; Richter 2008; Shaw 1985; von Hippel and Demonaco 2013; von Hippel 1976). These studies, which cover a broad range of application domains, from advancing drug therapies to improving medical equipment technology, show a high share of user involvement in product innovation and have documented the abilities of product users to develop substantial innovations that are commercially successful in the market. Beyond that, they investigate facets and outcomes of the collaboration between manufacturing firms and participating users. For example, Luethje (2003) explores that, in a study among surgeons in Germany, deep product-related knowledge of users is positively associated with a higher innovation propensity. Chatterji and Fabrizio (2008) find that, in the field of medical device inventions by US physicians, inventions by users have a greater importance relative to manufacturer inventions. Bill et al. (2011) identifies types and roles of participating users in the innovation process of a Swedish medical technology company offering sterilization equipment of surgical instruments, with hospitals as its main customer segment. Von Hippel and Demonaco (2013) observe that, in the setting of new off-label uses of approved drugs, there is an under-diffusion of this type of innovation because the incentives for physicians to do so are too little.

A common understanding of all these studies is that the product users involved in these cases generated their contributions from their direct work environment in the role as clinicians or surgeons. They can be considered as professional user innovators, i.e. opposing lay user innovators such as healthcare consumers. In other terms, it is consumer co-creation conducted in the B2B context (Hoyer et al. 2010). In this research, however, I question the role of healthcare consumers within co-creation shifting the focus to the B2C context. The integration of lay consumers into the innovation process of firms is a different and sometimes more challenging task than in a B2B environment (Adams-Bigelow 2004; Stevens and Burley 2003). Usually, the B2C context is described by a greater relational distance between firms and consumers, the presence of many middlemen such as retailers, lower degree of consumer loyalty, and fast changing consumer preferences (Spann et al. 2009).

Nevertheless, expected and realized benefits of HCC involvement in co-creation are well reported and are measured by the value created for HCOs and HCCs. For

HCOs, the benefits relate to enhanced innovativeness and reduced time to market that may translate into savings of financial and other resources (Nambisan and Nambisan 2009). For HCCs, the benefits relate to higher consumer loyalty, consumer satisfaction, and consumer quality perceptions (Bendapudi and Leone 2003) which in return also yields benefits for the HCO's customer relationship management. Especially in the context of rare or chronic conditions, HCCs have gathered extensive lay knowledge that may exceed the knowledge of professionals such as physicians or nurses, and hence the involvement of HCCs into the creation or improvement of a product or service can make it more effective. However, there are barriers as well that need to be balanced. Professionals may also doubt if the HCCs' lay knowledge is representative and legitimate which may be fueled through negative past experience with HCC interactions (Hudson 2015). Apart from that, collaborating with HCCs may incorporate high risks and may slow down the innovation process (Henrike and Schultz 2014).

In sum, current literature does acknowledge the large potential of HCCs for innovation. However, specific applications of consumer co-creation in healthcare remain scarce in the B2C context. Existing studies have mainly explored either co-creation with professional users (e.g. physicians), or the HCC involvement in the delivery of care while the latter rarely utilizes the creative input from HCCs for the advancement of innovation at HCOs.

With regard to HCCs and co-creation, the body of literature is developing though. Available studies point to motivations, competencies, roles of HCCs, and the potential adaptations required to exploit the HCC contributions (Engström 2012). In practice, there are certainly several commercially successful examples of consumer co-creation for innovation in healthcare, but at least in the academic literature I have not located any reports about it. Overall, research on methods, practices, and outcomes with regard to the collaborative interaction between HCOs and HCCs is lacking.

2.1.3 Knowledge as Determinant of Innovation

Following my line of argument, there are in many cases in which HCCs either have conceived an innovation that eventually is commercialized by an established HCO or hold knowledge crucial to an established HCO for the development of a novel product or service innovation. While certainly both sides, the HCCs as well as the HCOs, gain benefits from such knowledge exchange, I focus in this research on the HCOs as main beneficiaries. This section deepens the conceptualization from the perspective of the HCO. As knowledge is the key construct that influences innovation performance of an HCO, this section serves to clarify the knowledge-based theory of the firm, the importance of external knowledge for innovation, and the value of consumer co-created knowledge.

2.1.3.1 Knowledge-Based Theory of the Firm

The importance of knowledge and knowledge management is widely discussed in academic discourse (e.g., Alavi and Leidner 2001; Lehner 2014; Probst et al. 2013). According to the *knowledge-based theory of the firm*, knowledge is considered as the most strategically important resource of an organization (Grant 1996; Spender 1994). This view builds on and extends the resource-based theory of the firm that was first conceived by Penrose (1959) and later extended by others (Barney 2001; Conner 1991; Wernerfelt 1984). While knowledge-based resources are usually difficult to imitate and socially complex, the knowledge-based view suggests that an organization's distinct entirety of knowledge artifacts is the major driver for corporate performance and hence sustained long-term competitive advantage (Alavi and Leidner 2001). The knowledge is hold and conveyed through various entities such as organizational culture, regulations, processes, documents, systems, and individual employees (Grant 1996; Nelson and Winter 1982; Spender 1996).

Following the knowledge-based view, an organization's ability to integrate disparate sources of knowledge is concurrent to increased levels of competitive advantage. As such integration of knowledge has to pass significant hurdles, organizations that succeed in doing so are more likely better at generating innovative products and services (Dyer and Singh 1998; Grant 1996; Kogut and Zander 1992; Nahapiet and Ghoshal 1998; Tsoukas 1996). Therefore, knowledge work involves crossing various functional, occupational, hierarchical, and inter-organizational boundaries (Levina and Vaast 2005).

2.1.3.2 Externality of Knowledge

From the product ideation phase to the product testing phase, the creation of new knowledge is the central theme during the development of new products and services (Leonard-Barton 1995; Madhavan and Grover 1998; Nambisan 2002). Traditionally, the largest share of knowledge-based resources was developed within the boundaries of the organization. Nowadays, only few organizations can retain their innovativeness and competiveness by relying purely on internal resources (Powell et al. 1996). Increasingly, they are leaning on externally created knowledge requiring to transfer and apply it internally. Hence, organizations align their processes to acquire, disseminate and interpret new knowledge from external sources. A recent empirical review by Kruse (2012) demonstrates the wide range of potential sources of external knowledge in the context of open innovation. He suggests six main categories: (1) customers, in terms of users, consumers, or clients; (2) competitors; (3) business partners, such as suppliers, intermediaries, consultancies, service providers; (4) institutional sources, such as academic and private research institutes and governmental institutions; (5) media, such as documentations of patents or regulations, mass media like the Internet, and events like tradeshows or conferences; and (6) alliances and other forms of networks.

On a conceptual level, Antons and Piller (2015) model the perceived externality of a knowledge source as determined by three types of boundaries. First, externality regarding the disciplinary context of the knowledge—it relates to knowledge perceived as external when it originates from another technical domain of expertise. Second, externality regarding the spatial distance between the knowledge source and its recipient—a growing geographical or spatial distance is assumed to increase the resistance toward the external knowledge. Third, externality regarding the organizational affiliation of the source unit holding the knowledge—if knowledge is transferred between different organizations or institutions, it is commonly classified as external knowledge. Overall, these three types of boundaries might coincide which causes a self-reinforcing impediment to the transfer of knowledge.

While the promised benefits of exploiting external knowledge are numerous, it has to be tempered with the additional challenges that it induces. Therefore, Kruse (2012) has investigated the positive and negative influences that external knowledge (EK) may have on the innovation process. Table 2.2 summarizes these influences along the five-stage innovation process by Desouza et al. (2009) and additional cross-process influences.

Table 2.2 Influences of external knowledge on the innovation process (Kruse 2012)

Stage	Positive influence	Negative influence
(1) Generation and Mobilization	• Compensates low R&D resources • Skimming spillover from EK bearers • Increases innovativeness • Increases number of ideas and degree of novelty • Generates new knowledge	• Increases dependency on EK bearers • Cannot guarantee uniqueness of EK • Cannot automatically increase innovativeness
(2) Advocacy and Screening	• Facilitates radical innovation • Supports technological innovation • Allows selection of complex innovation	• Causes non-observance of opportunities • Leads to miss of chances
(3) Experimentation	• Shortens time to develop • Increases innovation quality • Enables new knowledge combinations	
(4) Commercialization	• Decreases risk and insecurity • Increases mutual benefit in collaborative agreements • Increases probability of successful realization • Increases return on R&D investment • Shortens time to market	• Increases risk and insecurity • Increases costs for search, acquisition, integration of EK • Causes problems with intellectual property rights • Cannot automatically increase business value • Cannot exclusively belong to organization

(continued)

Table 2.2 (continued)

Stage	Positive influence	Negative influence
(5) Diffusion and Implementation	• Deregulate loss/outlet of knowledge • Increases number of new products, new processes, and patents • Avoids redundancies • Enhances organization knowledge base • Incorporates new capabilities Enhances existing skills	• Causes conflict between sharing and protection • Impedes exchange by over–protection • Pollutes internal body of knowledge
(1–5) Cross-process	• Knowledge integration develops into core competency • Facilitates acquisition/transfer of EK • Increases competitiveness • Increases flexibility and visibility • Complements internal knowledge/R&D • Depends on previous knowledge/R&D • Shortens innovation process • Decentralizes innovation processes • Reduces complexity of internal R&D • Improves internal R&D	• Causes not-invented-here syndrome • Causes leakage of internal knowledge • Causes "over-search" through exorbitant number of sources • Causes lock-in effect • Cannot replace internal R&D • Cannot complement internal R&D • Cannot secure correctness of EK • Requires cultural changes • Requires organizational changes • Leads to immoderate openness • Reduces internal R&D activities • Increases complexity of relationships • Increases complexity if sources are widespread • Slows down process if number of sources is low

2.1.3.3   Consumer Co-Created Knowledge

While the knowledge-based theory of the firm reveals the ubiquity of knowledge and its impact on organizational performance, consumer co-creation enriches it by integrating consumers as a knowledge resource that is beyond the firm's boundaries (Mahr et al. 2014). Following the preceding conceptualizations on knowledge externality, consumers are one viable source of external knowledge for organizations. These organizations can learn about their consumers' needs, preferences, suggestions for improvement, and new product- or service-related ideas. During consumer co-creation, consumers are involved in creating different types of knowledge, both individually as well as in groups (Nambisan 2002). For example, new knowledge can be generated through converting tacit knowledge into explicit knowledge, e.g., a consumer conceives an accessory product to better manage his disease in the daily life and shares it with others, or through combining explicit knowledge, e.g., a consumer summarizes other consumers' experiences with a specific medical device in an online community.

These differences in the nature of knowledge creation imply the need to incorporate a range of knowledge management mechanism during consumer co-creation. Conversely, the created knowledge has to deliver value that aligns well with the goals of the respective innovation project.[2] Previous studies attempted to capture the value dimensions of consumer co-created knowledge by referring to aspects such as novel insights (von Hippel 2005), usefulness (Alam 2002), or the need for minimal physical effort (Sawhney et al. 2005). More recently, Mahr et al. (2014), by following the classic economic theory, argues that the value of consumer co-created knowledge is the relative balance between the benefits and the costs attached to its development and use. The benefits can be achieved by exploration and exploitation of knowledge (March 1991). Explorative activities cover experimentation and discovery among others and thus locate knowledge holding a wide range of new insights, new ideas, and new inspiration (Im and Workman 2004; Kristensson and 2002). Therefore, knowledge *novelty* is a key dimension that provides benefits from explorative activities. Exploitative activities, however, include implementation and refinement among others. They thus unveil knowledge that is directly applicable to a particular project and certain tasks and is easily implementable without further transformation (Im and Workman 2004; Kristensson et al. 2002). Hence, the knowledge *relevance* is another critical dimension that provides benefits from exploitative activities. Both dimensions increase the value of consumer co-created knowledge and subsequently the innovation performance.

Nevertheless, the positive value has to be moderated with the costs incurred. Knowledge *costs* not only signify monetary but also temporal expenditures to create, access, transfer, and use external knowledge from consumers. For example, R&D staff spends a significant amount of time to identify and select appropriate sources of external knowledge as well as to manage and perform the communication with them (Piller and Ihl 2009). The knowledge costs are also contingent on the nature and complexity of knowledge, the readily availability of consumers holding such relevant knowledge, the chosen knowledge transfer channel (Gupta and Govindarajan 2000; Winter 1987). Other scholars (Dahlander and Gann 2010; Grant 1996) highlight the costs of coordination and costs of competition when collaborating with external knowledge sources. Costs of coordination emerge from organizational boundaries that need to be crossed or from maintaining too many relationships with external sources. Costs of competition occur when intellectual property needs to be protected against others having access who could potentially exploit it in bad faith. As a result, knowledge costs can vary considerably across innovation projects. It may explain why organizations engage (or not) in co-creation

---

[2]Innovation, i.e. the development of new products or services, in organizational settings is usually carried out in projects (Joshi and Sharma 2004).

activities with consumers leading to fruitful inputs from external sources being adopted (or rejected) for organizational innovation projects (Alam 2002; Hoyer et al. 2010; von Hippel 2005).

To summarize, the value of consumer co-created knowledge that organizational innovation project members can draw from increases with greater novelty and greater relevance and decreases with greater costs. So the relative balance between these value dimensions is important. It has to be evaluated against the backdrop that consumers enable access to knowledge which organizations are barely able to produce in-house and which may prove crucial to greater innovation performance (Gardiner and Rothwell 1985; Neale and Corkindale 1998; Pavitt 1984) and subsequently to the organization's competitive advantage (Desouza et al. 2008; Lilien et al. 2002).

2.1.4 Innovation Intermediaries

Against the backdrop of a myriad of health-related online platforms that has evolved during the last years, this research argues that some of the organizations behind these health-related online platforms can act as an OII when bridging the gap between the online crowd of healthcare consumers and healthcare organizations seeking to innovate. This section, therefore, will describe and apply concepts from the scholarly discourse on innovation intermediation.

2.1.4.1 Traditional Innovation Intermediaries

Different strands of research elaborate on the importance of external sources of knowledge for enhancing firms' capability to innovate, e.g. research on technological change (Rosenberg 1982), collective invention (Allen 1983), user innovation (von Hippel 1988), and open innovation (Chesbrough 2003). Across this large body of research, it is well acknowledged that firms with large and heterogeneous networks outperform firms with less access to external sources (Baum et al. 2000; Gulati et al. 2000). However, sharing knowledge between partners is not straightforward as knowledge can be tacit in nature and can be embedded in people (Nonaka 1994). The challenges that come along with codifying and transferring knowledge have been investigated by Kogut and Zander (1993).

To facilitate these knowledge flows, a large number of organizations emerged in the last decade that serve as intermediaries in the innovation process, i.e. that bring into the innovation process of established firms a wider range of external players including their expertise. Innovation intermediaries perform functions[3] beyond simple information retrieval and dissemination to extend their offering towards

---

[3]Refer to Sect. 4.2.1 for a more detailed elaboration.

knowledge creation, knowledge brokering and knowledge diagnosis (Lopez-Vega and Vanhaverbeke 2009) while they get involved in the innovation process of their stakeholders. A rich literature describes and analyses the role of intermediaries as third parties mediating between manufacturing firms and their customers (see review by Howells 2006). The key function of the intermediaries is to connect, transform, translate, and consequently support the fragility of knowledge (Nonaka and Takeuchi 1996). From a network perspective, intermediaries connect an actor, e.g. a manufacturing firm, with different sources of knowledge and ideas, e.g. the users of their products (Diener and Piller 2010). It is their structural position between sources of knowledge and potential adoptions that is the key to the value they generate (Winch and Courtney 2007). Because innovation is often the outcome of novel connections among pieces of previously unrelated knowledge (Kodama 1993; Schumpeter 1934), innovation intermediaries stimulate innovation by coupling knowledge domains that are otherwise disconnected (Hargadon and Sutton 1997; Hargadon 1998).

Innovation intermediaries rather describe an overarching class of organizations that Howells (2006:720) broadly defines as follows:

> An organization or body that acts as an agent or broker in any aspect of the innovation process between two or more parties. Such intermediary activities include: helping to provide information about potential collaborators; brokering a transaction between two or more parties; acting as a mediator, or go-between, bodies or organizations that are already collaborating; and helping find advice, funding and support for the innovation outcomes of such collaborations.

This general definition is valid to all such organization whose organizational purpose is to enable innovation. In this regard, it also includes organizations such as industry and trade associations, economic development agencies, chambers of commerce, science, technology or business parks, business incubators, research consortia and networks, research institutes, or standards organizations (Dalziel 2010). Also scholars within the innovation literature have studied the variety of such intermediaries on a conceptual level and found different forms such as *intermediaries* (Watkins and Horley 1986), third parties (Mantel and Rosegger 1987), *bridge builders* (Bessant and Rush 1995; McEvily and Zaheer 1999), *superstructure organizations* (Lynn et al. 1996), *knowledge brokers* (Hargadon 1998), *innovation brokers* (Klerkx et al. 2009; Winch and Courtney 2007), *innomediaries* (Mele and Russo-Spena 2015; Sawhney et al. 2003), *virtual knowledge brokers* (Verona et al. 2006), and *open innovation accelerators* (Diener and Piller 2010). Many innovation intermediaries involve a role of brokering knowledge across the intermediary's network. Hargadon (1998:2) defines knowledge brokers as:

> Organizations that span multiple markets and technology domains and innovate by brokering knowledge from where it is known to where it is not.

They gain their unique network position by obtaining knowledge from different sources and domains, recombining it and providing it in the form of a solution to their clients' innovation problems (Colombo et al. 2015; Hargadon 1998). Conceptually, brokering knowledge as a third party is deeply rooted in the theory of structural holes (Burt 1992) that explains how certain organizations can bridge knowledge gaps. Knowledge gaps, i.e. structural holes, occur due to missing relationships between parties in an industry. A key property of an intermediary in such a network is the structural autonomy. It implies that the intermediary has no structural holes in all the relationships at his own end, while the other parties involved are rich in structural holes at their end (Burt 1992:45). It helps the knowledge broker to be the only owner of the innovation outcome to be transferred to the innovating client of the intermediary (Verona et al. 2006).

According to the above definitions, innovation intermediaries can help in two ways: either by helping innovating organizations to find and assimilate external knowledge or ideas more rapidly, or by helping the same to find more markets where their own ideas can be used by others for mutual benefit (Chesbrough 2006). Hence, the knowledge exchange can be beneficial in two directions (Dahlander and Gann 2010): outward and inward. Outward indicates the external commercialization of internally developed knowledge that does not readily find implementation in the organization's own portfolio. Inward relates to the sourcing and adoption of external knowledge that benefits the organization, the organization's product portfolio, or the organization's innovation capacity. In this research, I mainly focus on innovation intermediaries that manage the inward flow of knowledge. This is in line with the definition I gave earlier on consumer co-creation for innovation which sets a distinct interest to form knowledge that is valuable for the firm's innovation process of new products or services.

2.1.4.2   Online Innovation Intermediaries

In the last years, a new category of innovation intermediaries has appeared that take advantage of the increased ubiquity of the Internet and the penetration of web 2.0 technologies (Colombo et al. 2013, 2015; Mele and Russo-Spena 2015; Verona et al. 2006). These are called *online innovation intermediaries* (OIIs) whereas 'online' may interchangeably be understood as 'virtual' or 'web-based' or 'digital'. Related literature alternatively describes them as *innomediaries* (Sawhney et al. 2003) or *virtual knowledge brokers* (Verona et al. 2006). Their goal is to facilitate knowledge exchange in virtual environments and to offer their clients the opportunity to access large communities of individuals with experiential, educational, or professional knowledge in diverse geographical and disciplinary fields (Boudreau et al. 2011; Colombo et al. 2015; Jeppesen and Lakhani 2010). Leaning on Verona et al. (2006), the key roles of OIIs are described as to collect dispersed sources of knowledge, to recombine the collected knowledge to empower innovation, and to transfer it to new contexts (e.g. healthcare organizations).

In contrast to innovation intermediaries in the physical world, those who operate in virtual environments are able to offer significantly richer capabilities[4] with regard

---

[4]Refer to Sect. 4.2.2 for a more detailed elaboration.

to *network access, knowledge absorption, knowledge integration,* and *knowledge implementation* (Verona et al. 2006). Organizations that employ OIIs can greatly benefit from it for two reasons (Verona et al. 2006): first, OIIs help to augment the network access by enhancing the reach in engaging with consumers; and second, organizations can gain richness through bidirectional interactions and higher quality content.

However, there are also restrictions just because of the virtual character of the environment. The processes of knowledge transfer between consumers and OII and organizations, are all determined by the nature of knowledge (Nonaka 1994) and, in particular, by the level of knowledge codification. OIIs allow those types of knowledge to be exchanged that are codified. Knowledge artifacts that are codified can be replicated and hence exchanged (Szulanski 1996). Generally, tacit knowledge is more difficult to be exchanged over the Internet than explicit knowledge (Afuah 2003), yet, this does not mean that tacit cannot be codified, but it is just more difficult to do so. The degree of possible codification depends on the tools and methods implemented on the OII platform.

In order to best exploit the advantages of the virtual environment, Verona et al. (2006) suggest that OIIs should develop strong web-specific competencies in tracking and profiling consumers, creating incentive systems to reward participation, and managing and moderating two-way communication channels to create emerging social and individual knowledge. Further, they need to have the ability to evaluate and analyze the generated knowledge in order to recombine and transfer it to their clients.

Beyond the differentiation of engaging with innovation intermediaries in the virtual or in the physical world, there is another noticeable differentiation in the scholarly discourse: the differentiation between innovation intermediaries in a B2B or in a B2C context. The vast majority of scholarly research on innovation intermediaries has been conducted in the context of B2B,[5] in which it is argued that the technical knowledge of the parties being mediated is fairly symmetrical (Magnusson 2009). On the other hand, neither offline nor online-based intermediation between businesses and consumers (B2C) has been hardly studied.[6] This is in line with similar observations in the literature on co-creation (cf. Sect. 2.1.1) that has also studied B2C interactions to a far lesser extent.

To summarize, Table 2.3 outlines the major differences between different access types to external knowledge, i.e. access via an OII, access via a traditional

---

[5]For further reference, the following studies deal with innovation intermediaries in the B2B context, distinguished by virtual as opposed to physical environments: physical B2B (Bessant and Rush 1995; Dalziel and Parjanen 2012; Howells 2006; Huizingh 2011; Perkmann 2009; Winch and Courtney 2007), virtual B2B (Billington and Davidson 2012; Frey et al. 2011; Hossain 2012; Katzy et al. 2013; Lichtenthaler and Ernst 2008; Lichtenthaler 2013; Sieg et al. 2010; Verona et al. 2006).

[6]The following studies relate to innovation intermediaries in the B2C context and give some anecdotal evidence: physical B2C (Siguaw et al. 2014), virtual B2C (Bugshan 2015; Di Gangi and Wasko 2009; Nambisan 2002; Prandelli et al. 2006; Sawhney et al. 2005).

Table 2.3 Comparison of access types to external knowledge (building on Hallerstede 2013; Verona et al. 2006)

Dimension	Online innovation intermediary	Traditional innovation intermediary	Direct access without intermediary
Environment	Virtual	Physical	Physical
Type of contact	Mediated	Mediated	Direct
Type of orientation	Network orientation	Client orientation	Firm orientation
Source of knowledge	Broad, from consumers and industries	Limited, mainly from industries	Limited to own reach
Amount of processable knowledge	High	Medium	Low
Core competence	Network access	Knowledge absorption	Knowledge implementation
Main limitation	Knowledge implementation	Network access	Network access

innovation intermediary, and direct access of a company without using an intermediary. Hence, OIIs offer different kind of strengths than traditional innovation intermediaries. Primarily, OIIs have a greater reach in sourcing knowledge from a broad user base, whereas the transfer of knowledge is restricted to knowledge that can be codified. Hence, the implementation of knowledge is harder for OIIs than for traditional innovation intermediaries.

2.1.4.3 Existing Research on OIIs in Healthcare

Reviewing the literature yields little evidence for the scholarly analysis of OIIs in the healthcare domain and the related positive contribution on innovation outcomes. Prior scholarly analysis on OIIs in healthcare is summarized in the next paragraphs.

For example, patient-reported outcomes have been used to evaluate off-label uses of drugs on *PatientsLikeMe*,[7] an online patient network and research platform (Frost et al. 2011; Nakamura et al. 2012). It thus helps to understand efficacy and safety of some treatments and gives evidence for secondary drug uses. Also, it allows evaluation over a longer time period than feasible through traditional clinical trials. In a similar vein, Armstrong et al. (2012) evaluate the efficacy of acne treatments in real-world patient population via *CureTogether*,[8] a crowdsourcing platform for high-volume patient data and experience. They note that, in traditional trials of acne treatments, predefined inclusion and exclusion criteria select for a

---

[7]www.patientslikeme.com

[8]www.curetogether.com

homogenous population of study subjects that may not be representative of the real-world patient population. Eventually, these approaches render a contribution on innovation through identifying potential targets for treatments to be studied systematically in traditional research settings.

On other types of platforms, so-called "share-your-experience" websites, patients can review their personal health experiences, e.g., from the last hospital or doctor's visit, and read reviews posted by others. Adams (2011) acknowledges the role of such sites as mediators between patients and other stakeholders and sees the potential of repackaging solicited feedbacks by the platform operator in order to link it back to hospitals, insurance companies, policy makers, or others. Nevertheless at the point of research, the analyzed websites simply did not have enough information to address further institutional or policy consequences. Three of the four websites under study by Adams (2011) are shut down by today, the remaining one is UK-based *PatientOpinion*.[9]

Evidence for the suitability of open innovation practices to integrate healthcare consumers is given by studies about two publicly funded online platforms in Germany. Bullinger et al. (2012) study the adoption of *GemeinsamSelten*,[10] an open health platform for rare diseases, through analyzing attraction of platform users and intensity of peer communication. Hartmann et al. (2013) developed *Ideenschmiede*,[11] an online platform for systematic ideation, which is part of a virtual community for patients with amyotrophic lateral sclerosis. Both platforms enable a collaborative and systematic process of idea development between platform users and expect a higher idea quality than in uncontrolled settings.

In other domains than healthcare, however, there is evidence in academic literature that manufacturing firms work together with OIIs [e.g., chemical industry (Sieg et al. 2010), machinery industry (Piller and Wielens 2011), science problems (Jeppesen and Lakhani 2010)]. For instance *InnoCentive*,[12] an OII running innovation contests in various industries, is often described as a prominent example and has received significant attention in academic literature (Chesbrough 2006; Huston and Sakkab 2006; Lakhani et al. 2007; Nambisan and Sawhney 2007; Sawhney et al. 2003; Terwiesch and Xu 2008; Verona et al. 2006).

The far majority of the literature on health-related online platforms emphasizes the impact on easier information retrieval, sharing, and creation supported by anecdotal evidence. A dedicated link towards innovation, i.e. developing ideas with HCCs and exploiting those ideas through HCOs, is mostly neglected. Beyond the rather infrastructural level of an online platform, there is no further consideration of this class of platform-based organizations as possible intermediaries for the innovation process of HCOs.

---

[9]www.patientopinion.org

[10]www.gemeinsamselten.de

[11]www.dgmideenschmiede.de

[12]www.innocentive.com

2.2   Derivation of Theoretical Framework

Based on the research questions proposed in Chap. 1 and the elucidation of the four key concepts on the previous pages in this chapter, the present section will derive, explain and graphically depict a theoretical framework that will guide the empirical research.

The theoretical framework explicates the author's view on the interrelation of the identified key concepts. It is a necessary step in exploratory research to clarify the underlying assumptions for the empirical studies to be conducted (Herek 2010). As Herek (2010) notes, there are at least four reasons why a theoretical framework strengthens the research piece. First, theoretical assumptions that are explicitly stated can be critically evaluated. Second, the theoretical framework permits to pair and substantiate own research studies with existing theoretical discussion in academic literature. Third, it enables the researcher to go beyond simple description of a specific phenomenon by constructing generalizations to other situations or domains. Fourth, having a theoretical framework sets a focus and thereby establishes limitations to those generalizations. The development of the theoretical framework for this research follows the approach suggested by Herek (2010) who states that

> the task of developing a theoretical framework starts with asking a research question, proceeds through the task of identifying key variables and the relationships among them, and results in a plan for empirically observing those variables and relationships.

The overarching research question as outlined in Chap. 1 reads as:

Research Question: How do online innovation intermediaries (OIIs) enable effective consumer co-creation for innovation between healthcare consumers (HCCs) and healthcare organizations (HCOs)?

This research question is situated in the context of healthcare. As outlined in the previous chapter, healthcare is a domain with many peculiarities compared to other industries (cf. Sect. 1.1). This fact justifies the distinct angle of the above research question. Generalizations beyond the domain of healthcare may be applicable, but are not covered by the scope of the present research. Furthermore, this research question is based upon the following assumptions. Assumption #1: Some healthcare-related OIIs can be effective mediators for co-creation. Especially in healthcare, where trust and privacy is important, a third-party can better embody independence in the process of co-creation. Assumption #2: From their medical history and their experiences gained often over years, HCCs possess specific knowledge that is valuable for the HCO's innovation process of new products or services. Assumption #3: If effectively implemented, consumer co-creation through OII platforms can increase innovation performance for HCOs. To frame the assumptions in the theoretical framework, four key concepts are used. The concepts have been substantiated with literature through the literature review conducted in Sect. 2.1.

First, there is the concept of *consumer co-creation for innovation*. The present thesis deals with a subset of value co-creation by focusing on a type of value co-creation that serves the innovation capacity of organizations and that is fueled by input from consumers. As per the definition used here, co-creation exhibits as collaborative activity in which consumers and firms jointly form knowledge that is valuable for the firm's innovation process of new products or services. It specifies that consumers are considered as a source for co-creation.

This leads to the second key concept, the *healthcare consumers as source of innovation* (by the term it encompasses more than patients only). While tradition-ally regarded as a receiver of care only, HCCs in many places have proven to adopt a very active role in managing their medical situation. By that means, they possess a significant pool of knowledge that they are also willing to share with others, i.e. peers or organizations. Many examples have shown that HCCs qualify as a source of innovation because they have developed solutions to their problems before commercial organizations did.

Third, the definition of co-creation indicates that *knowledge* is a central element. Similarly, from an organizational perspective, knowledge is considered the most strategically important resource of an organization according to the knowledge-based theory of the firm (Grant 1996). Knowledge assets are a major driver for greater innovation performance and sustained competitive advantage (Desouza et al. 2008; Dyer and Singh 1998; Grant 1996; Kogut and Zander 1992; Lilien et al. 2002; Nahapiet and Ghoshal 1998; Neale and Corkindale 1998; Tsoukas 1996). Hence integrating the HCCs' knowledge has been acknowledged a logical step for HCOs.

Fourth, the type of a platform-based organization that enables and orchestrates co-creation activities is conceptualized as an *online innovation intermediary*. This approach allows connecting the actors involved through interactive online platforms and the social as well as technological features of the Internet. An OII helps to mediate between the actors and engages in brokering relevant knowledge. Dependent upon the service model and the interventions of the intermediary, the value (in terms of innovation performance) that HCOs draw from co-creation activities may be increased or decreased. However, the question that remains is how this occurs and why.

Finally, the research question as well as the four key concepts help to assemble the theoretical framework for this thesis. The main intention of the research question is that co-creation shall be enabled in a specific way. According to the given definition of co-creation (cf. Sect. 2.1.1.2), co-creation serves the purpose of providing valuable inputs to an organization's innovation process which ultimately contributes to the organization's innovation performance. In the context of this work, that is the *HCO innovation performance*. To provide such valuable inputs to HCO innovation, this work argues for the approach of *co-creation with healthcare consumers* whose innovation potential is considered underutilized (cf. Sect. 2.1.2).

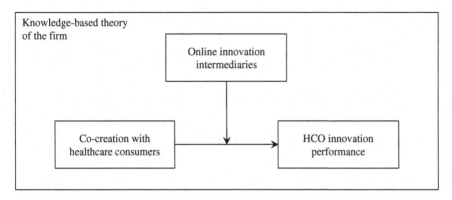

Fig. 2.2 Theoretical framework for thesis

Due to recent technological opportunities, *online innovation intermediaries* can act as an effective mediator for co-creation (cf. Sect. 2.1.4). Therefore, OIIs are modeled as a moderator in the relationship between the process of co-creation with healthcare consumers and the goal to increase the HCO innovation performance. Eventually, the exchange between the actors involved is based on the exchange of knowledge assets, which can be valuable resources for the HCO innovation performance. Hence, the *knowledge-based theory of the firm* provides a distinct lens for this research (cf. Sect. 2.1.3). Following this line of argumentation, the theoretical framework can be derived as shown in Fig. 2.2.

The above framework will guide the answering of the overarching research question. The framework predominantly provokes the development of theory of explanatory nature (Gregor 2006) as it aims at explaining how the phenomenon of OIIs influences consumer co-creation between HCCs and HCOs. In order to answer the overarching research question in a systematic way, it will be split up into multiple empirical studies that are directed by the subordinated research questions given earlier (cf. Fig. 1.7). This approach helps to reduce the complexity of the phenomenon under study and helps to structure the research process in a meaningful manner. The following chapter will present the first of three empirical studies.

Chapter 3
Empirical Study I: Identifying Online Innovation Intermediaries in Healthcare

3.1 Needs and Goals[1]

The previous chapter has set the conceptual foundations to deal with online intermediaries for co-creation in healthcare. This chapter presents the first of three empirical studies. Integral part of each OII is an online platform through which co-creation activities with HCCs are enabled. From a user perspective, it seems difficult to distinguish the broad range of health-related online platforms available. In addition to traditional resources, such platforms help sick and well people to gather additional information on medical conditions, share their medical experience, and discuss questions and solutions (Cline 2001; Fox and Duggan 2013; Oh 2012). A survey by the Pew Research Center reports that 59% of US adults, or 72% of US Internet users, have looked online for health information (Fox and Duggan 2013; Miller and Washington 2012). This makes it the third most popular activity on the Internet.

Surprisingly, given recent trends and challenges in healthcare, several scholars state that there is insufficient research about the impact of recent technological developments of the Internet, often subsumed under the term *web 2.0*, on healthcare (Boulos and Wheeler 2007; Leimeister et al. 2008; Randeree 2009). Leimeister et al. (2008) add that online healthcare communities are receiving increased research attention as new special interest groups, but much is still unknown about the design and impact of these groups. A few studies attempt to classify the landscape of web 2.0 platforms in healthcare (Birnsteel et al. 2008; Goerlitz et al. 2010; Kordzadeh and Warren 2012; Kuehne et al. 2011; Weber-Jahnke et al. 2011). However, the potential of web 2.0 in healthcare towards innovation and consumer co-creation remains under-researched.

---

[1]An earlier version of this chapter is published in the proceedings of the 21st European Conference on Information Systems (ECIS) as Kuenne et al. (2013). For more details concerning the communication of the research, see Annex A.

© Springer International Publishing AG 2018
C.W. Künne, *Online Intermediaries for Co-Creation*, Progress in IS,
DOI 10.1007/978-3-319-51124-5_3

The interactive character of so-called "health 2.0" platforms offers a unique possibility to access a wide and yet profound knowledge pool of healthcare consumers and other online users that my otherwise be more difficult or even impossible to address. As stated by recent scholarly analysis, the potential of patients knowledge pool is of high value for innovation (Cepiku and Savignon 2015; Habicht et al. 2012; Henrike and Schultz 2014; Oliveira et al. 2015). Hence, if there is a systematic approach to address and exploit these knowledge pools via mediating online platforms, then this may be an effective way to stimulate innovation. A special interest lies in identifying platform operators who, on the one hand, make use of the innovation potential of healthcare consumers and professional stakeholders (e.g., in form of knowledge, experiences and ideas) and, on the other hand, hold a bridging role between seekers and providers of innovation-related knowledge.

For example, this may become true through either consumers exchanging their ideas and solutions, or healthcare organizations searching to better meet consumers' needs and requirements by adopting their contributions. For participating users, it may be an appealing approach as healthcare organizations may integrate their creative inputs and provide the resources to professionally develop and produce a novel product. According to a recent study, approximately 90% of patients with innovative ideas have not started working together with companies in this regard, which may lead to a lack of diffusion (Cepiku and Savignon 2015). For healthcare organizations, this may positively influence the innovation performance and, ultimately, lead to competitive advantage.

For the above reasoning, this chapter looks at recent developments in the domain of health 2.0 which enable user integration in the innovation process. Based upon a myriad of online platforms available in the health domain, it is the goal of this empirical study (i) to provide a classification for health 2.0 platforms from an innovation perspective and (ii) to distinguish those platforms that may act as intermediaries in the above sense. For that goal, an extended review of relevant online platforms is performed and it is examined if they fulfill qualifying attributes. In absence of relevant databases or repositories that identify relevant intermediary platforms, data has to be collected from scratch via an extensive collection procedure. Therefore, the research question of this chapter formulates as:

> **RQ 1**: How can online innovation intermediaries be identified in the domain of "health 2.0"?

To answer the research question, the remainder of this chapter is organized the following way. Section 3.2 introduces further theoretical underpinnings from literature on web 2.0 and health 2.0 arguing that health 2.0 platforms are an adequate entry point to access the profound knowledge pools of HCCs. After reviewing existing typologies, a new typology is proposed and elucidated. The subsequent Sect. 3.3 presents the qualitative, case study based method to perform the large-scale cross-case analysis. Section 3.4 focuses on the findings of the analysis, evaluates the data sample and provides an in-depth analysis of different types of cases. Then, Sect. 3.5 discusses the findings by specifying propositions, and presents limitations and avenues for further research. Finally, Sect. 3.6 summarizes and concludes this chapter.

3.2 Theoretical Underpinning

Besides the theoretical foundations given in Chap. 2, there are a few additional conceptual notions that are of importance for this chapter. The present study aims to identify OIIs through the phenomenon of health 2.0 platforms. It argues that health 2.0 platforms are places that accumulate HCCs as platform users, and hence such platforms may be an adequate vehicle to access the consumers' distinct knowledge pool. The availability of and the access to HCC knowledge is a prerequisite for effective co-creation, as argued earlier in Chap. 2. Therefore, this section introduces the characteristics of health 2.0, reviews existing typologies, and proposes a new typology that caters for the innovation-related context of this research.

3.2.1 Web 2.0 in Healthcare

The term *web 2.0* was initially introduced following the O'Reilly Media Web 2.0 conference in 2004. It summarizes the economic, social, and technological changes that had happened on the Internet and the way in which its users deal with it. It commonly refers to online platforms that enable increased information exchange between lay users, social networking, and collective knowledge production (Adams 2010; O'Reilly 2005). Compared to the *web 1.0*, the so-called first generation of the Internet, the difference of web 2.0 is foremost about user interaction. While web 1.0 was mainly about unidirectional information retrieval, users can create and add information and content to the web. For that reason, the amount of user-generated content has increased enormously.

Berge and Buesching (2008) identified key factors that support the proliferation of web 2.0 services. First, web 2.0 is about improved availability of essential technologies. Namely, web service interfaces, AJAX, and RSS have been developed and advanced in recent years. These technologies enable the simplified interactive use of online services by consumers and providers. Second, the technical infrastructure has highly improved in the past. Particularly the diffusion of broadband Internet enabled the distribution of data-intensive content. Third, the increasing number of so-called digital natives[2] and their different use behavior has highly influenced the development of the Web.

---

[2]Digital natives are users, who belong to a generation growing up with personal computers, the Internet, and communication via electronic media.

As available definitions of web 2.0 are not congruent, Adams (2010) pinpoints the following common points: (1) in web 2.0, lay users are important producers of content; (2) users interact with themselves or the online platform; and (3) social opportunities are facilitated through, e.g., community building and online collaboration.

As a discipline-related adaptation of web 2.0 in healthcare, the term *health 2.0* was coined (Eysenbach 2008; Fischer and Soyez 2014; Hughes et al. 2008). Van de Belt et al. (2010) have done a review on available definitions of health 2.0 concluding by the following characteristic themes: (1) Web 2.0 is the underlying means for communication and information sharing; (2) increased participation of healthcare consumers; (3) increased participation of health professionals or other stakeholders such as payers, providers, researchers; (4) emergence of online communities and social networking; (5) improving collaboration between healthcare consumers and professionals; (6) health information that is patient-driven and user-generated; and (7) positive impact on the healthcare system in terms of higher quality and efficiency. A multitude of online platforms that attempt to incorporate (parts of) the above aspects have emerged in recent years. In the remainder of this work, such platforms will be referred to as *health 2.0 platforms*.

Virtual and online communities are one of the more popular forms of user interaction in the Web 2.0 (Ba and Wang 2013; Correia et al. 2010; Eysenbach et al. 2004; Kuehne et al. 2011; Leimeister et al. 2008; Romm et al. 1997). Users obtain easier access to health-related information and thereby are able to gain better understanding of their health status. In online health communities, users not only provide each other with experiences and (sometimes emotional) support, they also enable one another to comprehend the necessary medical information and science in the context of the respective disorder (Frost and Massagli 2008; Hoch and Ferguson 2005). Such communities are characterized by a high degree of interaction between users, and reciprocal exchange of information. The emergence of these interactive capabilities enable online health communities to be an effective source of jointly constructed and shared knowledge through participation of healthcare consumers, professionals and other stakeholders. Within the academic world, community research has a longstanding tradition. Existing literature addresses a variety of facets, terms and definitions, such as communities of practice (Brown and Duguid 1991; Wenger 1998), virtual communities (Bieber et al. 2002; Leimeister et al. 2008), knowledge communities (Ardichvili et al. 2003), and innovation communities (Bansemir 2013). To different degrees, they focus on aspects of organizational learning, collaborative work, and knowledge sharing.

3.2.2 Typology of Health 2.0 Platforms

A small number of prior studies has already reviewed and classified the landscape of health 2.0 platforms (Birnsteel et al. 2008; Goerlitz et al. 2010; Kordzadeh and Warren 2012; Kuehne et al. 2011; Weber-Jahnke et al. 2011). One extensive approach comes from Weber-Jahnke et al. (2011) who suggest a functional taxonomy from a dedicated consumer perspective. They categorize online healthcare services as information aids, decision aids, education aids, management aids, health sales services, and meta/ratings services. Furthermore, Goerlitz et al. (2010) provide a review of German-speaking web portals in healthcare and classify their results along utilization of web 2.0 components and specialization in healthcare. Another review examines health insurance online platforms and counts their use of web 2.0 technologies and social networks (Kuehne et al. 2011). A more practitioner-oriented industry review of web 2.0 in the health sector from Birnsteel et al. (2008) takes a UK perspective. It profiles selected providers from around the world and discusses potential for scalability within the UK. A recent approach comes from Kordzadeh and Warren (2012). They develop a typology using a stakeholder approach, namely healthcare professionals and healthcare consumers who both can serve as either support provider or support recipient, resulting in a two-by-two matrix. To summarize, it can be stated that all of the above classification approaches do not overlap regarding the classification dimensions employed, i.e. each approach is set in a distinct view. It becomes clear that the potential of health 2.0 platforms towards open, collaborative innovation remains under-researched in these works.

In order to sort the multitude of available health platforms from an innovation-related perspective, a new conceptual classification for health 2.0 platforms may be expedient. For this purpose, I propose the following dimensions: (i) *the qualification as an OII platform* and (ii) *the degree of collaboration* with users. These two dimensions are the basis for a two by two typology (see Fig. 3.1). Further explanation for both dimensions is given next.

Regarding the first dimension, it is assumed that some health 2.0 platforms can qualify as an OII platform under certain circumstances. With regard to the conceptual foundations on OIIs (cf. Sect. 2.1.4.2), the key roles of OIIs were described as to collect dispersed sources of knowledge, to recombine it to empower innovation, and to transfer it to new contexts (e.g. healthcare organizations). Thus, for the purpose of this investigation, two essential attributes are derived from this. Each of the attributes is defined as Boolean value (yes or no). When both of the attributes are fulfilled, a health 2.0 platform is regarded suitable as an OII platform.

Fig. 3.1 Typology of health 2.0 platforms from an innovation perspective

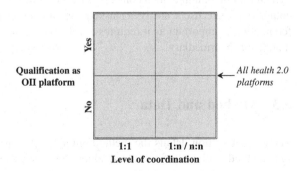

The first attribute is the *explicit enquiry towards the platform users*. The health 2.0 platform has a determined interest in gathering data, information or knowledge from its users. Hence, the users are explicitly asked to share their health data, treatment experiences, unmet needs, preferences, opinions, ideas, or solutions to their problems. From the intermediary's view, the user is regarded as a valuable source of knowledge. The second attribute is the *exploitation of the received user knowledge*. Once user knowledge is collected, the platform operator should exploit it in some way to extract value from it. One possible option is that the knowledge could be analyzed and aggregated into some new form by the intermediary himself. Another option is that the newly gathered knowledge is being transferred to an innovation-seeking organization for the research and development of new products or services.

The second dimension stresses the *level of coordination*. According to the literature on co-creation (Piller et al. 2010) as well as on intermediaries (Lopez-Vega and Vanhaverbeke 2009; Simmel 1902), it is an important dimension for differentiation. It refers to the structure of the underlying relationships in a co-creation setting (Piller et al. 2010). As per the definition of intermediaries (cf. Sect. 2.1.4.1), intermediaries operate as middle link in triadic relationships between HCCs and HCOs (see Fig. 1.6). In its simplest form, it could be a one-to-one-to-one relationship. However, in a system that aims to access knowledge from across boundaries, intermediaries are increasingly involved in more complex relationships, such as 'many-to-one-to-one' or 'many-to-one-to-many' (Howells 2006).

For the purpose of the present study, it is crucial to understand the relationship between the platform and its users first. Thus, the level of coordination applied here relates to linkage between the platform and the users only. Either the platform communicates one-to-one (1:1) at a time, one-to-many (1:n) at a time, or many-to-many (n:n) at a time. One-to-many and many-to-many coordination is prevailing at platforms of which the concepts are based on group dynamics. Many-to-many refers to networks of users who communicate among themselves more or less independent from the platform (Piller et al. 2010). For example, online communities with its social and behavioral effects can have a significant impact in innovation outcomes (Franke and Shah 2003; Fueller et al. 2004). One-to-one coordination is found at platforms of which the concepts are not based on group dynamics. For example, idea contests, where users submit a solution, or survey-like enquiries, where users are being asked for their opinion or experience. This differentiation is important as it requires a different set of methods and skills from the innovation intermediary.

3.3 Method and Data

The present section details the method employed to answer research question one. The method will be differentiated along the distinction of the overall research approach and the research design, which details the phases and research steps undertaken. Thus, this section is divided into two subsections. Section 3.3.1 introduces the overall research approach und justifies the application of an explorative and qualitative case study method. Then Sect. 3.3.2 introduces the research design along the three major phases undertaken and details the operational research steps in separate subsections.

3.3.1 Research Approach

In order to explore the phenomenon of OIIs in healthcare, a qualitative and explorative research approach is selected. The rationale for this selection is twofold. First of all, a qualitative approach makes it possible to answer research questions that intend to find out what new phenomenon are, how they occur or why they occur (Creswell 2009). In this way, the approach adds new facets and aspects to the understanding of hitherto unknown or relatively new phenomenon (Eisenhardt 1989). Secondly, a qualitative research approach is an appropriate means to identify types of occurrences and to derive systematic typologies, which are of relevance to the phenomenon under investigation (ibid.). Hence, the qualitative research approach fits the needs of the present study, which aims to identify dominant approaches of OIIs and their systematic differentiation in the health 2.0 context.

Various forms of qualitative research approaches exist. One frequently applied approach is case study research, in which researchers conduct an *in-depth analysis* to explore a certain *phenomenon* within its *real-life context* (Yin 2014). Hence case study research fits the needs of the present study: it enables OIIs (*phenomenon*) to be explored within healthcare settings (*real-life context*), with the aim of identifying dominant approaches and an appropriate classification by way of an (*in-depth*) analysis. The following aspects need to be considered when choosing a case study approach: (1) the number of cases and (2) the units of analysis. A very useful differentiation in this regard is provided by Yin (2014). In order to distinguish various case study methods, he proposes the following four abstract approaches: (1) single-holistic, (2) multiple-holistic, (3) single-embedded and (4) multiple-embedded (ibid.). The approach selected depends on the objective of the study in question.

For the present study, a multiple-holistic case study approach is selected. A *case* is generally a bounded entity, such as a person, an organization, an event, and it serves as the main unit of analysis in a case study (Yin 2014). With regard to the current study, this means that one case equals one health 2.0 platform. In this way, the case study research makes it possible to iteratively analyze within a case as well as cross-case to identify approaches of OIIs and derive an appropriate systematization. The following section will deliver a detailed explanation of each research phase and its respective steps.

3.3.2 Research Design

As mentioned in the previous section, the present study approaches the empirical field with a multiple-holistic case study design. To accomplish this, the research design is further divided into three phases as depicted in Fig. 3.2. This gradual research design follows the framework for case research proposed by Maimbo and Pervan (2005:1283) who build upon the step-by-step process developed by Eisenhardt (1989:533).

Hence phase 1 comprises the starting point including the identification of an appropriate data source as well as the case selection according to strategy of theoretical sampling by Glaser and Strauss (1967). Phase 1 concludes with the preparation of the instruments for data gathering and analysis as well as the coordination of multiple investigators. In phase 2, the empirical field is entered to collect qualitative data on each single case. Furthermore, the analysis is conducted through constant comparison within as well as across cases. Phase 2 yields preliminary results concerning dominant approaches and characteristics of health 2.0 platforms. Based on that, phase 3 begins to enfold literature by relating those preliminary results to the theoretical underpinnings introduced in Sect. 3.2. This alignment resulted in the sharpening of the explored insights, which are presented in the findings section. Finally, phase 3 reached closure as marginal improvements became negligible. In the following, each of the three stages is explained in greater detail to increase the reliability of the research conducted.

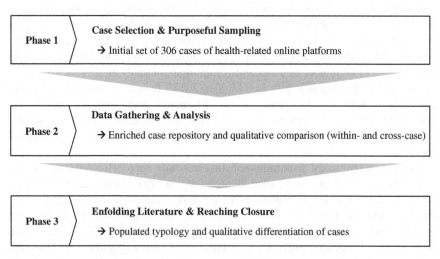

Fig. 3.2 Research design of Chap. 3

3.3.2.1 Case Selection and Purposeful Sampling

The first research phase started with the identification of an appropriate data source to provide a comprehensive overview of OIIs. However, existing resources like databases or third party case repositories were not available. In a study by Diener and Piller (2010), 43 intermediaries for open innovation are profiled, but they are lacking a connection to healthcare. Consequently, a sample of health or medicine-related online platforms had to be created. To do so, a desk research approach using a broad online search was employed. Unlike similar studies (Goerlitz et al. 2010; Weber-Jahnke et al. 2011), I did not solely apply a keyword-based web search to find relevant platforms, but built on the following three key sources.

First, an initial sample was populated by health-related online platforms show-cased at three leading conference series in the field. It is assumed that operators of especially successful, innovative, or recently launched platforms would speak up there. For the period 2007 until 2013, agendas and speaker affiliations were screened from 19 "*Health 2.0*",[3] 5 "*Medicine 2.0*"[4] and 2 "*Doctors 2.0 and You*"[5] conferences.

Second, the *Arbeitsgemeinschaft Online Forschung* (AGOF[6]) and the *Informationsgemeinschaft zur Feststellung der Verbreitung von Werbeträgern (IVW[7])* are working groups for online media research. They bring together the leading online marketers in Germany. They publish market media studies on a regular basis and also special reports on certain industries such as healthcare. These reports help to identify those health-related websites in Germany with highest commercial reach (measured by page visits). For the analysis, the AGOF internet facts 03/2012, the AGOF special report on healthcare Q2/2012, and the IVW online usage report 05/2012 were screened.

Third, the sample was enlarged by screening scientific and practitioner-oriented articles (Allison 2009; Birnsteel et al. 2008; Boulos and Wheeler 2007; Bullinger et al. 2012; Dannecker and Lechner 2007; Frost and Massagli 2008; Goerlitz et al. 2010; Hartmann et al. 2011; Leimeister and Krcmar 2005; Miller and Washington 2012; Pharma Relations 2010; Randeree 2009; Seeman 2008; Swan 2009; Weber-Jahnke et al. 2011). The identified references originate from a search using "health 2.0" and "web 2.0 +healthcare" as search terms in *Google Scholar*.

The case selection was carried out along the strategy of theoretical sampling as proposed by Glaser and Strauss (1967). The predefined criteria for this sampling mechanism focused on platforms that offer knowledge or instruments to advance the user's desire for better health. The user should directly benefit from using the

---

[3]www.health2con.com

[4]www.medicine20congress.com

[5]www.doctors20.com

[6]www.agof.de

[7]www.ivw.de

platform, e.g. through gaining new health knowledge, exchanging with peers or as a
source of support, or should have the opportunity to contribute his knowledge and
experience. Therefore, some exclusions were applied: (i) pure corporate represen-
tations of companies or associations, and (ii) platforms that already stopped operations at the point of study. The goal of the selection process was to create a not
necessarily complete, but broad repository of health platforms available. Achieving
a large variability in the data set supported the objective of mapping the landscape
of health-related online platforms. This first research phase yielded 306 cases for
the subsequent phase of data gathering and analysis.

3.3.2.2 Data Gathering and Analysis

The phase 'data gathering and analysis' follows four major research steps. Each of
these research steps is further detailed in the next paragraphs and graphically
exhibited in Fig. 3.3.

In step 1, structured case vignettes were developed for all cases in the sample.
This was done through intensive investigation of each of the websites. The procedure followed the method of *third-party web assessment* (Irani and Love 2008).
The case vignettes are stored in a structured table in Microsoft Excel. The data
collected describes the purpose and nature of each health platform in general and, in
particular, its suitability as innovation intermediary, and the level of coordination.
Initial dimensions of description were derived from the conceptual dimensions of
the suggested typology (cf. Sect. 3.2.2). Furthermore, an opportunistic data collection in the form of qualitative field notes and screenshots was performed. As
Eisenhardt (1989:533) explains,

> Opportunistic data collection allows investigators to take advantage of emergent themes
> and unique case features.

Gathering data followed the same procedure for each platform: reading the
"about us"-page, the imprint, and the FAQs; skimming through the main categories
of the platform; registering a user account if possible; testing the members area
including its communication features; and searching via Google for third party
articles about the respective platform (e.g., Wikipedia).

As per step 2, in order to ensure the "2.0" character of the health platforms, the
vignettes were screened for cases that offer a minimum level of user involvement,
i.e. allow users to create, add or share content. Only those cases were retained and
remaining cases without any kind of user involvement were removed from the
sample. Users can be healthcare consumers, healthcare professionals or other
stakeholders—depending on the context of the online platform. For instance, pure
health information portals were removed through this step. At the end, a reduced
sample of designated health 2.0 platforms was generated. With the data gathered up
to this point, it is possible to populate the typology from Sect. 3.2 with real cases.

In step 3, the repository of health 2.0 case vignettes underwent a second in-depth
investigation that followed typical procedures of qualitative content analysis

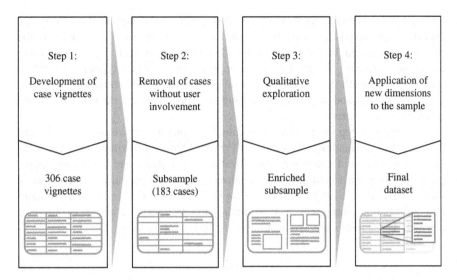

Fig. 3.3 Process of data gathering and analysis in Chap. 3

(Mayring 2000). The elicitation of new dimensions oriented along the characteristic themes of health 2.0 (cf. Sect. 3.2.1). Beyond the earlier defined, comparatively unstructured dimensions, additional dimensions related to the types of users involved, the methods of participation, and the degree of interaction were elicited in multiple iterative rounds until saturation was reached. The definition of these new dimensions aimed at increasing the degree of a structured interpretation of data, i.e. qualitative information was separated and structured into columns as far as possible.

Finally, step 4 covered a coding process based on the new dimensions identified in step three. Two researchers independently assessed each of the health 2.0 platforms according to the new dimensions (Mayring 2000). To ensure consistent coding, several measures applied: In case of different assessments between the researchers, the characteristics were determined together until consensus was reached; and anchor examples were chosen. At the same time, the process of analysis was initiated through constant comparison within a case and across cases (Glaser and Strauss 1967). Based on the comparison of cases, this research step produced the results of this study. Finally, descriptive statistics on the distribution of characteristics within the sample were traced. Having finalized the step of data gathering and analysis, phase three began to relate those findings to existing literature.

3.3.2.3 Enfolding Literature and Reaching Closure

The third and last phase within the given research design focuses on enfolding the relevant literature and eventually on reaching closure for the study. Based upon the prior analysis in phase two, the findings with respect to the populated typology and prevailing characteristics of health 2.0 platforms were compared and related to the literature presented in the theoretical underpinning (see Sect. 3.2) and to other emerging literature. The final results comprise the populated typology including four types of health 2.0 platforms, a detailed qualitative differentiation along five key dimensions, and a statistical account of the empirical distribution of the qualitative characteristics.

This research step sharpens the conceptual idea and directly relates to an existing theoretical understanding (Maimbo and Pervan 2005). Furthermore, it strengthens external validity and analytical generalizability of findings and creates an appropriate anchor point for further investigations to expand, contradict or verify those findings (Eisenhardt 1989). This last phase in the research design ended as no more new information emerged from these final considerations and, hence, closure was reached. The findings are synthesized in the following section.

3.4 Findings

3.4.1 Populated Typology

The sample collection yielded 306 health or medicine-related online platforms (research phase 1) of which 183 are health 2.0 platforms with user involvement (research phase 2). This sub-sample will be the basis for the following analyses. Figure 3.4 shows the distribution of cases, i.e. online platforms, according to the above-defined typology. Please refer to Annex B for a complete repository of all cases included. The distribution of cases into the four fields of the typology reveals that the far majority of 84% does not fulfill the two criteria to qualify as an OII platform. It is not surprising though as OIIs are still a recent phenomenon, which is one reason why more academic research is needed in this field. However, the sample includes 30 online platforms that do qualify as innovation intermediaries. For illustration, detailed case profiles of these 30 OII cases are presented in Annex C.

Fig. 3.4 Empirically populated typology of health 2.0 platforms

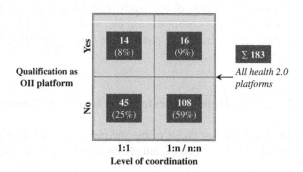

Each of the four fields of the typology accumulates cases of a certain kind. Dominant approaches of each type are described in the following.

The upper left field represents cases that qualify as an OII platform and are characterized by a one-to-one coordination (see Table 3.1). The majority of cases of this group (8 cases) essentially work as an online idea contest. At an idea contest, users of the platform submit contributions within a limited period on a given topic, mostly in form of suggestions, ideas, or solutions (Bullinger and Moeslein 2010; Piller and Walcher 2006). Idea contests often create its attraction from prize money, a board of judges and a competitive atmosphere. Here, one-to-one coordination means that individual users interact with the platform at a given while the users do not connect with each other. For example, within the set of the identified cases, user contributions deal with software applications for healthy children (*Apps for Healthy Kids*), process optimization in the field of radiology (*Medical Valley Innovation*), experiences of nurses in their clinical practice (*Connecting Nurses Care Challenge*), tools that improve life with diabetes (*Diabetes Mine Design Challenge*), and others. Another type of cases relates to "share-your-experience" platforms that collect feedback from users on rendered healthcare services and actively work with the providing entity on resolving issues and improving service (*iWantGreatCare* and *Patient Opinion*).

The upper right field of the typology represents cases that qualify as an OII platform and are characterized by a one-to-many coordination (see Table 3.2). Typical for all cases in this group is the existence of an online user community that entails the one-to-many coordination. In such a setting, users do not only interact with the platform but also with other users which creates a more dynamic environment. It means that the OII not only relies on individual users but also on the entire community of users when enquiring external knowledge. For example, *My Handicap* had invited interested members of their online community to a live chat together with representatives from a leading manufacturer of arm and leg

Table 3.1 List of OII cases with one-to-one coordination level

• AED4.eu	• CrowdMed	• iWantGreatCare
• Apps for Healthy Kids	• Data Design Diabetes	• Medical Valley Innovation
• Army of Women	• Diabetes Mine Design	• NHS Innovation Challenge
• Ashoka Changemakers	Challenge	Prizes
• Connecting Nurses Care	• Edison Nation Medical	• Patient Opinion
Challenge	• Health Tech Hatch	

Table 3.2 List of OII cases with one-to-many coordination level

• Cancer Commons	• Gemeinsam für die	• Inspire
• Coliquio	Seltenen	• My Handicap
• Cure Together	• Ginger.io	• Patient Innovation
• DGM	• Hamburg Living Labs	• PatientsCreate
Ideenschmiede	• Health Unlocked	• PatientsLikeMe
• Doctors.net.uk	• Innovation By You	• Sermo

prostheses. The goal of the live chat was to establish a direct link between firm engineers and prosthesis users and to discuss requirements and product improvements suggested by the users. Other examples in this group are the introducing examples of *PatientsLikeMe* and *InnovationByYou* (cf. Sect. 3.1).

The lower left field of the typology represents cases that do not qualify as an OII and are characterized by a one-to-many coordination. Typical for cases in this group is also the existence of an online user community. However, a key differentiation is that the OII operates the community functionality mainly as a service for the users, i.e. there is no primary intent to exploit the user-created content from the community discussions for any sort of innovation-related insights. This group of cases, which is the largest within the typology, mainly contains health or medicine-related information portals with attached community features (e.g., *WebMD*, *NetDoktor*, *Onmeda*), platforms for the exchange of often condition-related support groups (e.g., *Daily Strength*, *Cancer Connect*, *Fertility Planit*, *Rehacafé*), and medical wikis (e.g., *Wiki Surgery*, *AskDrWiki*).

The lower right field of the typology represents cases that do not qualify as an OII and are characterized by a one-to-one coordination. The dominant approaches found in this group are platforms relating to personal health records or patient data management (e.g., *Hello Health*, *Health Vault*, *Practice Fusion*), simple appraisal platforms (e.g., *Jameda*, *RateMyHospital*, *RateMDs*), and platforms to obtain a second medical diagnosis (e.g., *iDoc24*, *Was hab' ich*, *2ndMD*).

3.4.2   Key Differentiations

A qualitative content analysis of the case vignettes (research phase 2, step 3) provided further dimensions which describe crucial aspects of health 2.0 platforms in general and OIIs in particular. Table 3.3 lists the dimensions, related key questions and their possible answer values. Explanations on these dimensions and their empirical occurrence are presented in the remainder of this section, while Table 3.4 shows all findings in figures.

3.4.2.1   Involvement of Healthcare Consumers

To gain a deeper understanding of who the users of such platforms actually are, the sample was screened by user types. On the top level, it is suggested to distinguish between healthcare consumers and healthcare professionals. *Healthcare consumers* can be distinguished by the level of their affectedness into three general categories: (1) consumers who are *well*, (2) those who are *newly diagnosed* with an illness, and (3) those who are *chronically ill* including their medical caregivers (Cain et al. 2000). According to Cain et al. (2000), HCCs who are *well* make up approximately 60% of the consumers searching for health-related content online. Because these consumers are well, they do not often think about disease-related issues. So they

Table 3.3 Elicited dimensions

Dimension	Question	Answer choice* and answer values					
Healthcare consumer involvement	Is the platform designed to involve consumers? If yes, which type of consumer?	mv	No	The well	Newly diagnosed	Chronically ill and their caregivers	
Healthcare professional involvement	Is the platform designed to involve professionals? If yes, which type of consumer?	mv	No	Providers	Suppliers		
Level of interaction	Which level of interaction can be attained by the users?	sv	Information	Communication	Consultation	Cooperation	Collaboration
Stage of innovation process	At which stage of the innovation process the users' input can be utilized?	mv	None	Fuzzy Front End	New product development	Commercialization	
Online community (availability and access)	Does the platform offer an online community to its users? If yes, are there access restrictions?	sv	No	Non-restricted	Restricted		

*sv—single value only; mv—multiple values possible

Table 3.4 Descriptive statistics on the sample of health 2.0 platforms

		Absolute figures							Relative figures						
		OII Platform				OII Platform			OII Platform				OII Platform		
		No		Yes		Subtotal			No		Yes		Subtotal		
		Coordination		Coordination					Coordination		Coordination				
Dimension	Attribute	1:1	1:n	1:1	1:n	No	Yes	Total	1:1	1:n	1:1	1:n	No	Yes	Total
	Subtotal	45	108	14	16	153	30	183	100%	100%	100%	100%	100%	100%	100%
Consumer Involvement	None	2	22	3	4	24	7	31	4%	20%	21%	25%	16%	23%	17%
	W*	5	10	0	0	15	0	15	11%	9%	0%	0%	10%	0%	8%
	W+ND*	10	21	0	0	31	0	31	22%	19%	0%	0%	20%	0%	17%
	W+ND+CI*	17	4	8	2	21	10	31	38%	4%	57%	13%	14%	33%	17%
	ND+CI	9	31	2	6	40	8	48	20%	29%	14%	38%	26%	27%	26%
	CI	2	20	1	4	22	5	27	4%	19%	7%	25%	14%	17%	15%
Professional Involvement	None	29	64	5	3	93	8	101	64%	59%	36%	19%	61%	27%	55%
	Provider	15	35	1	0	50	1	51	33%	32%	7%	0%	33%	3%	28%
	Provider+Supplier	1	9	7	11	10	18	28	2%	8%	50%	69%	7%	60%	15%
	Supplier	0	0	1	2	0	3	3	0%	0%	7%	13%	0%	10%	2%
Level of Interaction	Information	23	0	0	0	23	0	23	51%	0%	0%	0%	15%	0%	13%
	Communication	2	101	0	2	103	2	105	4%	94%	0%	13%	67%	7%	57%
	Consultation	13	1	13	2	14	15	29	29%	1%	93%	13%	9%	50%	16%
	Cooperation	7	6	1	4	13	5	18	16%	6%	7%	25%	8%	17%	10%
	Collaboration	0	0	0	8	0	8	8	0%	0%	0%	50%	0%	27%	4%
Stage of Innovation Process	None	45	108	3	2	153	5	158	100%	100%	21%	13%	100%	17%	86%
	FFE**	0	0	10	9	0	19	19	0%	0%	71%	56%	0%	63%	10%
	FFE+NPD**	0	0	0	5	0	5	5	0%	0%	0%	31%	0%	17%	3%
	NPD**	0	0	1	0	0	1	1	0%	0%	7%	0%	0%	3%	1%
Community Access	None	45	0	14	0	45	14	59	100%	0%	100%	0%	29%	47%	32%
	Non-restricted	0	92	0	10	92	10	102	0%	85%	0%	63%	60%	33%	56%
	Restricted	0	16	0	6	16	6	22	0%	15%	0%	38%	10%	20%	12%

* W - Well consumers; ND - Newly diagnosed consumers; CI - Chronically ill consumers incl. their caregivers

** FFE - Fuzzy Front End; NPD - New Product Development

Highlighted cells are referred to in the text.

often use the Internet for preventive medicine and wellness information in the same way they look for news and products. Individuals who are *newly diagnosed* are a smaller group of online HCCs, about 5% of the total (ibid.). Many of these HCCs look for online platforms that help them with their illness and cover a lot of knowledge in the first few weeks after their diagnosis. They often reach out to get help from a diffuse network of sources. The third group, the *chronically ill and their caregivers*, make up about 35% of HCCs who go online (ibid.). Cain et al. (2000) state that this group has the biggest potential to affect and be affected by new forms of healthcare-related interactions through the Internet. Many individuals living with a chronic illness gather expert knowledge because they manage that illness on a daily basis.

Analyzing the data sample reveals that the big majority (83%, 152#) of health 2.0 platforms address HCCs as user group while almost half of the platforms (45%, 82#) enable professional stakeholders to get involved.[8] Looking specifically at the consumer segmentation of the designated OII platforms, the data shows that each OII platform with HCC involvement does address the chronically ill as part of their target user group. In combination with newly diagnosed consumers, these two subgroups bring along a certain level of experience and knowledge about particular disorders. In contrast to this, the service and content offerings of non-OII platforms are more often designed to meet the demands of the well consumers.

3.4.2.2 Involvement of Healthcare Professionals

Concerning the involvement of *professional stakeholders in healthcare*, empirical evidence for the following two subgroups was found: (1) *Providers*, e.g., doctors, nurses, other health professionals and medical experts who provide care in hospitals, doctor's surgeries, nursing homes, and others; (2) *Suppliers*, e.g., scientific institutions and research groups, pharmaceutical and medical technology companies who develop new products and treatments and heavily invest in research and development; pharmacies and wholesalers who mostly do resale (cf. Fig. 1.1).

Regarding the professional involvement, OII platforms are more open to integrate healthcare professionals than non-OII platforms. The relative shares of professional involvement are 73% for the OII platforms versus 39% for the non-OII platforms. Additionally, the OII platforms target a wider professional audience, notably providers and suppliers, while the non-OII platforms mostly focus on providers. In summary, OII platforms in health 2.0 are seemingly interested in a broad user group (i.e., consumers and professionals) that provides a rich base of knowledge and experience.

---

[8]For easier verification of the numbers cited in the text, the same numbers (or the numbers used for its calculation) are graphically highlighted in Table 3.4.

3.4.2.3   Level of Interaction

The *level of interaction* refers to the structure of the underlying relationships between the initiating platform and its users. For further differentiation, five levels of inter-action are proposed here, in order of increasing intensity of interaction. (1) *Information*: The first level of interaction serves the purpose of an informational exchange. It can be characterized by a unilateral relationship between the platform and one user at a time. (2) *Communication*: The next level of interaction refers to a two-way exchange within a virtual community. The members are motivated by personal benefits and each individual's interest in an overarching topic which is also shared by the rest of the community. On behalf of the platform and community operator, the members' exchange is not tied to a common, innovation-related goal and requires little coordination efforts only, i.e. the community is highly self-governing. Online discussion boards, support groups and forums are examples in this category. (3) *Consultation*: It describes a deliberate enquiry regarding a specific question towards the healthcare consumers or other users. Hence, the interaction is based on a dyadic relationship. Consumers are asked about their perspectives, needs, or priorities. Among others, appraisal platforms and innovation contests are usually settled in this category. (4) *Cooperation*: When online communities start to develop a momentum on its own, one can find a community-based relationship between the platform and a network of users. Basically there are n:n relationships between the members in the community and 1:n relationships between the platform operator and the members. Cooperation in this context is characterized by partnerships between users themselves and the platform operator. They work together for a common goal on an irregular and little formalized basis in order to bring a joint topic or project forward. (5) *Collaboration*: Collaboration can be considered as a more intense form of cooperation. On a regular basis, users work closely together in well-defined team structures. They share a common goal for the advancement of a joint project. Typically, the degree of coordination by the platform operator increases.

   Looking into the empirical data, it becomes apparent that the levels of interac-tions differ greatly between the four types of the typology. For example, when looking at non-OII platforms with one-to-one coordination level, the levels 'in-formation' and 'consultation' show the highest counts. Compared to this, OII platforms with one-to-many coordination level have their highest count on 'col-laboration'. Thus, it seems that the levels of interaction become more intense when the OII attribute is true and the coordination level is more complex. This partly reflects the constituting attributes of an OII as it requires an 'explicit enquiry towards the users' (cf. Sect. 3.2.2)—reversely, the latter attribute can only be true when the level of interaction is at least consultation, cooperation, or collaboration.

3.4.2.4   Stage of Innovation Process

The dimension *stage of innovation process* describes the time at which the users' input and knowledge can be utilized and integrated into the innovation process. To

Fuzzy Front-end	New Product Dev	Commercialization
Idea Generation I Idea Assessment	Concept Dev I Prototyping	Product Test I Market Launch

Fig. 3.5 Linear phase model of the innovation process (Diener and Piller 2010)

operationalize it, a linear phase model of the innovation process employed by Diener and Piller (2010) is used here (see Fig. 3.5). It suggests three major stages: (1) *Fuzzy front end*, comprising idea generation and evaluation; (2) *New product development*, comprising concept development and prototyping; and (3) *Commercialization*, compromising product test and market launch. After assessing the empirical data, it suggests that the identified OII platforms have the potential to support the innovation process—notably at two stages, the fuzzy front end (80%) and new product development (20%).

3.4.2.5 Community Access

Some OIIs provide free access to their community, some others restrict the access. Online communities without access restriction trust the mechanism of self-selection of members. For reasons of simplicity, it is distinguished between restricted and non-restricted access to online communities. Interestingly, OII platforms restrict user access to specialist communities to a greater extent than non-OII platforms do. It can be observed in the relative share of restricted access communities of OII platforms compared to that of non-OII platforms (38% vs. 15%). On the one hand, this is due to the fact that some physician-only platforms in this subset require professional certifications during registration process. On the other hand, some other platforms also ask consumers to apply for membership through explicating their qualification or motivation levels.

3.5 Discussion

The previous section has provided the evidence for five key observations that will be discussed in the following. First, OII platforms in health 2.0 are looking for profound experience from the healthcare consumer. In particular, they focus on the chronically ill, i.e. patients with a high degree of affectedness. Hence, this can be understood as a shift away from the generalist consumer experience towards a detailed knowledge base on specific disorders. While the focus of many online health communities is on emotional support among peers, the OII cases discussed here put emphasis on a pragmatic exchange of knowledge and potential solutions.

Second, apart from healthcare consumers only, such intermediary platforms are interested in a broad and professional knowledge base. In general, they are more open to professional involvement and professional contributions respectively. In particular, they look beyond medical providers by also targeting suppliers. Nevertheless, this still means that other key players of the healthcare sector are not involved yet (i.e. not involved within the sample investigated). Notably *payers* (e.g. statutory health insurance, private health insurance, and government agencies) and *regulators* (e.g. ministry of health, national or regional committees who set regulatory guidelines) could act as users and contributors as well. On this point, I hypothesize that the perceived benefits of engaging with healthcare consumers through the Internet are still too low for payers and regulators, but might be part of an on-going paradigm shift.

Third, the OII platforms engage for more intense interactions with or between their users. Thus, knowledge exchange is made easier. And eventually, it can foster the emergence of new ideas and the support of innovative activities. The five levels of interaction that are discovered within the analyzed sample are close to existing taxonomies which classify the degree of integration of the public (Arnstein 1969; Boote et al. 2002; Piller et al. 2010). These models confirm the benefits generated by a higher degree of integration of and interaction among consumers. In each of the most intense forms of integration, the authors proclaim that participants/consumers can enter into partnerships with powerholders or even obtain the majority of decision-making (see Table 3.5).

Fourth, early stages of the innovation process (i.e. idea generation to concept development) are more supported than later stages (i.e. commercialization). However, it remains difficult to systematically involve users at the early stages as evidence for such activities is little. Furthermore, users of health 2.0 platforms do not seem to be actively employed during the commercialization stage of novel products—at least, the data sample did not provide clear evidence for this.

Fifth, access to specialist communities is more restricted at OII platforms. Evidence remains low on this point, but it may be interpreted as a tendency. This observation supports the previous hypothesis that OIIs search for particularly suitable and qualified users. By restricting access to their communities, the operator gains more control over the user recruitment process.

This study has three main limitations, which in turn have implications for future research. Firstly, the identified number of innovation intermediaries in health 2.0

Table 3.5 Classifications of consumer interaction levels in comparison

Level	Kuenne	Arnstein (1969)	Boote et al. (2002)	Piller et al. (2010)
1	Information	Non-participation	–	–
2	Communication	Tokenism	–	Listen
3	Consultation		Consultation	Ask
4	Cooperation	Citizen power	Collaboration	Build
5	Collaboration		Consumer-controlled research	

cannot be considered large despite the comprehensive search. The sample revealed 30 of such OII platforms only. Hence, it may be delicate to draw generalizations from the findings. Nonetheless, the findings can function as well-grounded directions for further studies. Within the sample of the identified OIIs, it became apparent that none of the OII runs their current service model solely on intermediation-related services. Their core activity usually lies in something else. This supports the fact that using specific online platforms as an instrument for innovation intermediation currently remains a developing topic. To cater for the scope of this study, the search aimed at platforms with a distinct healthcare focus only, i.e. platforms with a multi-industry approach were neglected. On the one hand, this search approach should uncover potential healthcare-specific implementations. On the other hand, it possibly excluded successful implementations from other domains.

Secondly, the scope on innovation intermediaries is somewhat limited to a bridging role between the healthcare consumers/professionals and third party healthcare organizations. For this purpose, two rather simple criteria were applied which qualify an online platform as an OII platform. This pragmatic approach could be reconsidered and enhanced by other functions (see Howell 2006 for more).

Thirdly, the present analysis is based on a desk research approach. Therefore, the assessment of the dimensions was accomplished with a blend of publicly available information, i.e. the websites including their self-descriptions, and third-party reports from the web, online encyclopedia and academic articles. Consequently, more field research on and with OIIs in healthcare may produce a higher level of understanding regarding their motivation, function, processes and relationships. In particular, it would be useful to explore the types of knowledge created by users on the platform (also claimed by Verona et al. 2006) and, subsequently, how the platform operators add value to the intermediation process by e.g. recombining or refining the knowledge artifacts. Expert interviews with OIIs could confirm or revoke the current assessment. Particular insight could come from OIIs that failed (also raised by Hossain 2012).

Furthermore, studies on the perceived strengths, weaknesses, requirements, and needs by users of OII platforms and by R&D departments of HCOs (as potential clients and beneficiaries of such innovation intermediaries) can be a fruitful approach to further knowledge in this field. The just conducted analysis focused on the user-intermediary interface instead of the intermediary-HCO interface. It is due to the user-oriented definition of health 2.0 that was applied straight from the beginning. Hence, for the subset of health 2.0 platforms that qualify as OII platforms, it is advisable to deepen the understanding of the interface between such intermediaries and third party HCOs. Another area for future research could be the search for successful business models between HCOs and OIIs.

3.6   Conclusion

This chapter focused on one of the new avenues along which the engagement of healthcare consumers and healthcare professionals might take place—the growing use of interactive online platforms in the healthcare sector. Hence, the research question aimed at identifying health 2.0 platforms that can serve as intermediary platforms in the innovation process. This study contributes to an answer in a threefold way.

First, it enhances the academic discussion by creating a novel link between the domains of health 2.0 platforms and co-creation for innovation. It thus puts emphasis on the role of such platforms as advocates of innovation and supporters of the innovation process.

Second, it suggests an essential classification and description of the variety of health 2.0 platforms. Instead of structuring along technical features of online platforms (which are usually easy to observe and to count), the proposed classification scheme scrutinizes the purpose for which each platform is run. I started out by proposing an initial typology to differentiate health 2.0 platforms. The suggested classification scheme distinguishes along two axes: (i) health 2.0 platforms that mediate between innovating companies and external stakeholders, and those who do not; as well as (ii) health 2.0 platforms with a simple or complex coordination level towards the platform users. Based on case vignettes and a cross-case analysis, further dimensions for classification were elicited: involvement of healthcare consumers, involvement of professional stakeholders, level of interaction attained by users, the supported stage of innovation process, and the access to online community (cf. Table 3.3).

Third, it provides a state-of the-art review of health 2.0 platforms with an international scope that does not restrict to consumer services only, but also includes services for doctors and other professional stakeholders. With the examples given in this chapter, the case repository and the case profiles available in Annexes B and C, it is possible to sketch a preliminary picture of the market for OIIs in healthcare. Based on this, it gives practitioners from corporate environments the necessary orientation when it comes to the decision whether to start their own online innovation platform or to engage with already existing actors in the field.

Chapter 4
Empirical Study II: Exploring Online Innovation Intermediaries in Healthcare

4.1 Needs and Goals[1]

The previous chapter has provided the necessary findings to locate and differentiate online innovation intermediaries. Now this chapter goes one step further by investigating their inner workings. It follows the initial theoretical framing of this research that OIIs are an effective instrument to promote and execute consumer co-creation in healthcare. OIIs are understood as a new category of intermediaries that fits into the current explications of the overarching intermediary literature. However, for any new category of intermediaries, key questions need to be answered, such as what the enabling factors of successful intermediation are, or how innovation intermediaries facilitate the creation and integration of knowledge among various parties (Lopez-Vega and Vanhaverbeke 2009).

In particular, the agency of OIIs and their agential roles are still not sufficiently understood in the literature, as recently noted by Mele and Russo-Spena (2015). Further research into OIIs also follows Howells' (2006) call for research into the range of intermediaries and a more detailed outline of their functions and activities. The sparsely available literature on OIIs mostly produces findings from single intermediary cases, which complicate the search for conceptual generalizations. Therefore, Colombo et al. (2013) have called for a comprehensive cross-case analysis about how several online intermediaries organize their service.

This research argues that OIIs, through their agency, have the ability to advance consumer co-creation for innovation. Mahr et al. (2014) traced that most literature tends to emphasize the benefits of consumer co-creation while the risks and costs involved remain underresearched. It seems that not much scholarly insight was added since Hoyer et al. (2010) found that too little was known about the challenges to consumer co-creation and more research was needed in this area.

---

[1]An earlier version of Chapter 4 is published in the proceedings of the 12th International Conference on Wirtschaftsinformatik as Kuenne and Agarwal (2015). For more details concerning the communication of the research, see Annex A.

© Springer International Publishing AG 2018   65
C.W. Künne, *Online Intermediaries for Co-Creation*, Progress in IS,
DOI 10.1007/978-3-319-51124-5_4

In addition to the research needs derived above, further research should also take into consideration the structural differences of the healthcare sector. For example, organizations have to deal with a much higher degree of regulatory requirements and patients are involuntarily forced to be end consumers of healthcare products and services once an illness occurs. This could have implications for the design and management of OIIs in this field.

It can be concluded that extant knowledge about the nature, functioning, and effects of OIIs and how they accommodate the distinctive healthcare set-up is limited. To the degree that OIIs will become increasingly significant in a sector where knowledge resources within organizational boundaries are limited, it is the goal of this chapter to address the research needs formulated above. It particularly aims at investigating the OII agency in terms of the key activities performed and typical configurations of these activities. This is the basis for a further analysis of the value potential provided through OIIs and possible challenges inhibiting current developments in consumer co-creation mediated through OIIs. To increase the contribution of this chapter, specific mitigations for the challenges shall be proposed to the extent of the analyzed data possible. Therefore, the following research questions are addressed in this chapter:

> **RQ 2a**: What are the key activities of OIIs in healthcare, and how do these activities bundle together towards OII types?
>
> **RQ 2b**: What value do OIIs add for the innovation capacity of healthcare organizations?
>
> **RQ 2c**: What are critical challenges during co-creation activities via OIIs, and how can these be mitigated?

The remainder of this chapter is organized as follows. In the next section, the conceptual underpinnings in relation to the three research questions are presented, notably elaborating on functions of OIIs, the value potential of OIIs and reported challenges in adjacent areas. Section 4.3 describes the qualitative research design based on numerous expert interviews as well as how the interview data analysis was performed. Section 4.4 depicts the findings and is structured around the topics of the research questions. The findings including rich empirical evidence are based on interviews with key informants from OII organizations across several countries. Section 4.5 provides a discussion of findings by reflecting to existing knowledge and proposing directions for future research. The final Sect. 4.6 concludes this study.

4.2 Theoretical Underpinning

This section builds on and extends the conceptualizations given in Chap. 2 as part of the theoretical framework. In particular, based on current literature, it adds conceptual considerations on online innovation intermediaries and explains how OIIs influence co-creation activities between consumers and organizations. This helps to frame the

Table 4.1 Activities of innovation intermediaries (Lopez-Vega and Vanhaverbeke 2009)

Group	Function	Activities
Connection	• Gatekeeping and brokering	Link innovation providers and seekers; facilitating knowledge flows; integrating knowledge from different domains
	• Middle men between science policy and industry	Facilitate communication on a system level; connecting on a system level
	• Demand articulation	Provide interfaces between users and firms
Collaboration and support	• Knowledge processing and combination	Combine knowledge from stakeholders; mobilizing research
	• Commercialization	Support marketing, sales and funding
	• Foresight and diagnosis	Align research toward client needs
	• Scanning and information processing	Scan, scope and filter external markets
Technological services	• Intellectual Property	Manage and control intellectual property
	• Testing and training	Test, prototype, diagnose, analyze, validate technology
	• Assessment and evaluation	Assess and evaluate technology
	• Accreditation and standards	Provide advice on standards and standard-setting
	• Regulation and arbitration	Support regulation, self-regulation and arbitration

three research questions of this empirical study and, thus, provides a baseline to which the findings can be related. Section 4.2.1 explains what innovation intermediaries actually do when they mediate between parties. The identified functions enable a distinct value potential (Sect. 4.2.2) but current practices also demand to deal with a set of challenges that impede co-creation initiatives via OIIs (Sect. 4.2.3).

4.2.1 Functions of OIIs

Innovation intermediaries in their traditional notion,[2] and thus OIIs as particular type of innovation intermediaries, can realize various functions for their clients (Howells 2006; Lopez-Vega and Vanhaverbeke 2009; Verona et al. 2006). Table 4.1 gives an overview and outlines typical activities performed to fulfill these functions. Lopez-Vega and Vanhaverbeke (2009) suggest that innovation intermediary functions fall into three groups: (i) *connection*, (ii) *collaboration and support*, and (iii) *technological services*.

---

[2]cf. Sect. 2.1.4.1 for the definition.

In the first group, OIIs connect innovation seekers and innovation providers and, hence, they integrate detached domains of knowledge. Generally, this can include linking organizations to consumers, non-consumers, peers, initiatives, policy and science. The intermediary acts as a trusted and neutral third party in the relationship between the remote parties. Thus, OIIs help to overcome the reluctance of innovation providers towards contributing to an organization's innovation problem.

In the second group, OIIs render collaboration and support services. They utilize their knowledge-gathering and processing competence to help organizations "*compensate for the lack of relevant innovative capabilities*" (Bessant and Rush 1995:100). Moreover, OIIs advise organizations on technological and managerial issues, foster in-house research, technology intelligence and trend analysis, and provide marketing and sales support (Lopez-Vega and Vanhaverbeke 2009). In the third group, OIIs render technological services through testing and prototyping, controlling intellectual property, and supporting regulation and standard-setting.

As Hallerstede (2013) notes, there are some OII functions that seem to be dominant over others due to the environment in which OIIs operate. First, *gatekeeping and brokering* is more dominant as OIIs can draw on a broad spectrum of knowledge and possess the competence to process high amounts of knowledge. Second, consumer *demand articulation* is more dominant as OIIs can act as an unbiased and trustworthy third party with access to a broad array of potential innovation providers. Third, both *knowledge processing and combination* and *scanning and information processing* are more dominant as user interactions are facilitated through the OII online platform. This enables the OII to codify knowledge in a structured manner and to keep up with current markets. And fourth, the function *assessment and evaluation* is more dominant as it can be performed on a large and distributed scale.

The following two sections outline the value potential and possible challenges that result from these functions based on prior literature.

4.2.2 Value Potential of OIIs

In contrast to traditional innovation intermediaries, OIIs work in a virtual environment, i.e. they use online platforms to integrate consumers into co-creation activities with organizations. Hence, working with OIIs yields a distinctive value potential for HCOs. Some value derives from working with innovation intermediaries in general, some other value originates from the specific virtual environment that OIIs exploit. Both are introduced in the following.

In general, OIIs help their client organizations to *reduce the lack of managerial skills and innovative capabilities* that are needed to absorb and assimilate external inputs, as stated by Bessant and Rush (1995). The authors find that key capabilities are lacking with regard to the recognition of requirements, the exploration, comparison and selection of option, along with the acquisition, implementation and operation of the innovation inputs (ibid.). The value potential of OIIs for innovation-seeking organizations lies in several areas. OIIs help them to develop key management capabilities in order to manage innovation projects and processes more effectively. This also allows reducing costs and chance of failure. Through institution building, OIIs accumulate a critical mass of knowledge that stimulates the generation of innovations. Moreover, OIIs are able to reach out more directly to relevant target groups, i.e. a more efficient targeting of support creates value for the client organization. The involvement of OIIs leads to a more decentralized mode of operation, which means less monitoring and control for the client organization.

With regard to the virtual environment of OIIs, there is an additional value potential resulting from it. Four areas have been identified in existing research (Verona et al. 2006): the virtual environment offers new opportunities in *network access, knowledge absorption, knowledge integration*, and *knowledge implementation*.

Concerning *network access*, virtual environments amplify the ability to create direct ties between the actors, i.e. direct relationships with a large number of potential innovators. This becomes possible for a number of reasons. Virtual environments break the usual trade-off between media richness and physical reach that is inherent to traditional channels (Evans and Wurster 1999). Additionally, virtual environments enable participants to communicate almost cost-free without temporal or geographical limitations (Craincross 1997). Furthermore, positive network effects exist that can attract even more direct ties (Downes and Mui 1998; Katz and Shapiro 1985). On the one hand, one additional new user can be reached at progressively decreasing costs due to the prevalence of fixed cost (Shapiro and Varian 1998). On the other hand, new users increase the value of the network for existing users (Gladwell 2000). Apart from direct ties, the virtual environment also helps generating indirect ties, i.e. ties to "friends of friends", that give access to an even broader knowledge base (Ahuja 2000). The high number of ties brings the OII in a position of strong structural autonomy (cf. Sect. 2.1.4.1) which allows the OII to exploit (or sell) the same information towards different client organizations (Werbach 2000).

Concerning *knowledge absorption*, the virtual environment offers a number of IT-based methods for OIIs to absorb knowledge from individuals. Existing research distinguishes five classes: innovation contests, innovation communities, innovation marketplaces, innovation toolkits, and innovation technologies (Moeslein 2013). In addition to that, OIIs can employ traditional methods like observation of online behavior, surveys, and conjoint analyses to obtain knowledge (Verona et al. 2006). Regardless of the method chosen, the virtual environment increases the speed of interaction between the actors and thus accelerates knowledge absorption.

Concerning *knowledge integration*, electronic interfaces are inherent to virtual environments. This facilitates knowledge integration since knowledge can be stored, transmitted and shared more easily. The formal mechanisms of knowledge sharing through an OII platform enable systematic information access and raise the awareness of available knowledge. This facilitates the recombination of assimilated knowledge. Apart from that, virtual environments also empower informal social integration between the participants, especially in online communities (cf. Sect. 3.2.1).

Concerning *knowledge implementation*, the ultimate value of knowledge as a driver for innovativeness does not stem from just owning it but implementing it to a particular technical context, according to the knowledge-based theory of the firm (cf. Sect. 2.1.3.1). In virtual environments, any kind of knowledge shared must be made accessible in an explicit, codified form. This makes it easier for OIIs to internalize, implement and recombine knowledge. In contrast, any knowledge, which is tacit, is difficult to implement for the OII. Yet, there are new ways to assimilate tacit knowledge through virtual environments, such as innovation toolkits (Piller and Walcher 2006), co-design platforms (Thallmaier 2014), or artificial intelligence agents (Avery 2016).

To summarize, OIIs provide a unique value potential for HCOs most of which derives from the virtual context. Turning to the theoretical framework given in Chap. 2, it means that (i) OIIs are able to supply HCOs with critical knowledge artifacts, which are regarded as the most strategic assets according to the knowledge-based theory of the firm, (ii) OIIs draw their strategic advantage from the virtual environment, and (iii) OIIs possess richer capabilities with regard to accessing, absorbing and integrating external knowledge. However, the value potential explained above has to be tempered with potential challenges that are outlined next.

4.2.3   Challenges in the Intermediary Ecosystem

The positive value potential that organizations may extract from co-creation via OIIs does not come without new challenges. Prior literature has often emphasized net positive benefits, although the several challenges[3] with co-creation via OIIs are receiving more attention (Greer and Lei 2012; Hallerstede 2013; Hoyer et al. 2010; Nambisan 2002; Ojanen and Hallikas 2009; Ophof 2013; Schultze et al. 2007; Sieg et al. 2010). As OIIs are yet a recent phenomenon, most of the discourse centers on organization-level challenges and their organization-consumer interface that is crucial for consumer co-creation. Only a small share of the discourse deals with OII-level challenges and the related organization-OII interface. These referenced challenges are introduced in the following, organized around six thematic blocks.

First, co-creation initiatives can produce large amounts of consumer inputs which may possibly lead to *information overload* (Hoyer et al. 2010). Especially at the ideation stage of the innovation process, the wide end of the innovation funnel becomes even wider if co-creation with consumers is involved, making it a key challenge for organizations to screen the large number of inputs. One approach to alleviate this effect is to integrate the consumers in evaluating the contributions of others (Haller 2012).

Second, besides the sheer quantity of input, firms may run into challenges related to the *quality of the input*. Thus, mechanisms are required to monitor and control for the development of quality and efficiency (Ophof 2013). For example, in spite of

---

[3]Literature refers to it as challenges, problems, difficulties, risks, or impediments.

the high number of contributions, many of the novel ideas provided by consumer co-creators may be infeasible from a manufacturing view (Magnusson et al. 2003). Hence, from a firm perspective, the management of misperformance due a lack of skills may occur as a critical challenge during co-creation activities (Hoyer et al. 2010). However, firm efforts to manage consumer co-creators may be limited as consumers are not employees and thus not under direct control. For example, consumers could choose to unexpectedly interrupt participating in co-creation activities which had a negative effect on the NPD process (Nambisan 2002). Yet, misperformance in its various facets depends on the standpoint: preferred outcomes for consumers may be divergent from firm-preferred outcomes (Hoyer et al. 2010). So a key challenge is how consumers can be incentivized to participate on a continuous basis (Hoyer et al. 2010) and, equally, how firms are able to ensure the sustainability of collaborative efforts if participants fluctuate (Greer and Lei 2012).

Third, innovation-seeking firms report *concerns about secrecy* when they engage in intense co-creation activities (Hoyer et al. 2010). Often, co-creation may involve the disclosure of proprietary information to consumers about internal development trajectories that would otherwise remain secret much longer (Prahalad and Ramaswamy 2004b). Maintaining confidentiality and avoiding knowledge leakage (potentially through the involved consumers to competitors) in co-creation settings is hence a key challenge for firms (Greer and Lei 2012). Closely related to the latter are questions around the ownership of intellectual property that is created in co-creation settings (Greer and Lei 2012). While some consumers could freely hand over their contributions to the collaborating firm, others could expect to keep full ownership of intellectual property. For firms, this might entail legal entanglements that are not favorable (Hoyer et al. 2010). In situations where secrecy and confidentiality are crucial, the presence or absence of trust in a relationship becomes crucial. Trust has been highlighted in the literature as being a critical factor for innovation with consumers and successful collaboration (Brockhoff 2003; Lichtenthaler 2013; Littler et al. 1995; Ritter and Walter 2003).

Fourth, working with external sources of knowledge challenges the existing routines present at most organizations. Studies have noted that *prevailing organizational structures and processes* need to be reconsidered or new mechanisms need to be set up to support the assimilation of consumer knowledge and insights (Greer and Lei 2012; Lei and Slocum 2002; Ophof 2013). In a similar vein, the coupling of external consumers with internal employees, e.g. from NPD teams, may turn out to be a challenge that should not be underestimated as different mindsets and languages prevail (Nambisan 2002). Furthermore, literature reveals that an initial reluctance by employees is common (Sieg et al. 2010). This reluctance is twofold: on the one hand, reluctance towards using external sources of knowledge and related technical instruments (e.g. posting a call on an online platform) and, on the other hand, reluctance towards integrating the externally generated knowledge.[4]

---

[4]Sometimes also referred to as the 'not-invented-here syndrome' (e.g., Antons and Piller 2015; Katz and Allen 1982).

Fifth, there are challenges with regard to organizational strategy, notably the *decreased control* over an organization's strategic management and planning (Hoyer et al. 2010). Relying (partly) on the inputs of consumers during the innovation process and thus giving the consumers some degree of control over the outcomes exacerbates an organization's strategic planning efforts (Moorman and Miner 1998). Besides diminishing control, the complexity of managing organization's objectives increases due to the empowerment of consumers as co-creators and the interests of diverse stakeholders (Bendapudi and Leone 2003; Hoyer et al. 2010).

Sixth, particular challenges arise when working together with innovation intermediaries. The above-mentioned challenges have been extracted from literature on direct organization-consumer co-creation. A limited stream of literature to date addresses emerging problems on co-creation mediated through third parties such as OIIs. Sieg et al. (2010) analyzed a set of case companies and found that selecting the *right scope of topics* to be addressed through OII platforms seems hard. Not every topic per se is suited to be dealt with by consumers through an online environment. A topic or problem statement needs to be understandable, formulated appropriately, may not be too complex, and should be adjusted to the skills of the audience. Rightly scoping topics becomes important here, an area in which some intermediaries may provide advice due to their experience. Additionally, a study from Lichtenthaler (2013) indicates intermediary's difficulties in matching providers and seekers of innovation-related knowledge.

In sum, this review of challenges yields areas for critical development, but is eclectic in nature. Consumer co-creation in general but also consumer co-creation via OIIs in particular has been insufficiently investigated and requires further research, as stated by Hoyer et al. (2010) and Greer et al. (2012). It can be assumed that some of the cited organizational challenges may apply to OIIs in a similar or modified way if the OII becomes the first point of contact in the co-creation process for the participating consumers.

Based on the theoretical framework of Chap. 2, this entire section has given additional nuance on OIIs which will lead the interpretation of findings. The next section dives into the execution of the second empirical study.

4.3 Method and Data

This section details the method and the data of the empirical study. Section 4.3.1 introduces the general research approach, which argues for a qualitative design. Then Sect. 4.3.2 describes the steps of data gathering and details the applied techniques. Finally, Sect. 4.3.3 outlines the process of data analysis.

4.3.1   Research Approach

OIIs in healthcare are a fairly new phenomenon in research. As a consequence, the current understanding of how such intermediaries impact the process of co-creation between HCCs and HCOs is still very limited. Against this backdrop, the identification and description of already existing OIIs in healthcare requires an exploratory research approach for which qualitative research designs are seen as most appropriate (Creswell 2009; Eisenhardt 1989; Robson 2011). In particular, qualitative research is conducted inductively which means that generalizations are drawn from and are grounded in the observations of the respective field.

In this chapter, the interviewing method is chosen, which is the most commonly used method of data collection in qualitative research (King and Horrocks 2010). The research question for a qualitative interview study should not focus on establishing causal relationships or generalized patterns of behavior. It should rather focus on meaning and experience, with reference to a particular group of participants. According to King and Horrocks (2010:9), the defining characteristics of the generic qualitative interview are: (i) it is flexible and open-ended in style, (ii) it tends to focus on people's actual experiences more than general beliefs and opinions, and (iii) the relationship between interviewer and interviewee is crucial to the method. In the following, the process of data gathering will be detailed.

4.3.2   Data Gathering

4.3.2.1   Sampling

The process of data collection started with the selection of appropriate cases, i.e. OIIs in healthcare. The main input to the selection procedure are the results of the previous Chap. 3 that provided a list of 30 OIIs. With this list at hand, the platforms were contacted through email or social networks expressing the request for an expert interview. It yielded a surprisingly positive response rate: 22 contacts agreed to support this research endeavor and to be available for an expert interview. It should be noted that among the 22 there are 19 B2C platforms and 3 B2B platforms (namely *Sermo*, *Colliquio*, *Doctors.net.uk*). Although this work focuses on healthcare consumers as sources for co-creation, the other 3 platforms that rather target medical doctors were kept in the sample for two reasons. First, if there were co-creation practices in place that work in the B2B context, then this could potentially guide the development of co-creation in the B2C context. Second, as the interface between HCO and OII is crucial for co-creation, these cases could provide additional insight. Moreover, to gain a comprehensive view on this topic, 2 more cases were added to the interview sample (namely *Netdoktor.de* and *Onmeda*). These 2 cases do not actually qualify as OII at the moment, but they run large online communities of healthcare consumers. Thus, they might be able to speak

Table 4.2 Overview of interviewed key informants showing international reach

Interview with platform (URL)/Role of interviewee	Headquarted in City/Country	
Sermo (www.sermo.com) *SVP Global Community & Marketing*	Boston	United States
PatientsLikeMe (www.patientslikeme.com) *Director of R&D*	Boston	United States
Army of Women (www.armyofwomen.org) *Founder & CEO*	Los Angeles	United States
Cancer Commons (www.cancercommons.org) *Founder & CEO*	Palo Alto	United States
Inspire (www.inspire.com) *Founder & CEO*	Princeton	United States
CrowdMed (www.crowdmed.com) *Founder & CEO*	San Francisco	United States
Diabetes Mine (www.diabetesmine.com/designcontest) *Founder & Editor-in-Chief*	San Francisco	United States
Ginger.io (www.ginger.io) *Founder & CEO*	San Francisco	United States
Health Tech Hatch (www.healthtechhatch.com) *Founder & CEO*	San Francisco	United States
PatientsCreate (www.patientscreate.com) *Founder & CEO*	London	United Kingdom
Health Unlocked (www.healthunlocked.com) *Founder & Chief Medical Officer*	London	United Kingdom
Doctors.net.uk (www.doctors.net.uk) *CEO*	Oxford	United Kingdom
PatientOpinion (www.patientopinion.co.uk) *Director of Research and Informatics*	Sheffield	United Kingdom
AED4.eu (www.aed4.eu) *Founder & CEO*	Nijmegen	The Netherlands
MyHandicap (www.myhandicap.ch) *Managing Director*	St. Gallen	Switzerland
Patient Innovation (www.patient-innovation.com) *Chief Operating Officer*	Lisbon	Portugal
OnMeda (www.onmeda.de) *Editor-in-Chief*	Cologne	Germany
Hamburg Living Labs (www.hamburglivinglab.de) *Project Leader*	Hamburg	Germany
DGM Ideenschmiede (www.dgmideenschmiede.de) *Research Associate*	Kassel	Germany
Coliquio (www.coliquio.de) *Founder & CEO*	Konstanz	Germany
Netdoktor.de (www.netdoktor.de) *Senior Community Manager*	Munich	Germany
Gemeinsam für die Seltenen (www.gemeinsamselten.de) *Research Associate*	Nuremberg	Germany
InnovationByYou (www.innovationbyyou.com) *Senior Market Manager*	Humlebæk	Denmark
Connecting Nurses (www.connecting-nurses.com) *Steering Committee Member*	Toronto	Canada
Total number of interviews		24

about the innovation potential of large user communities and how it could be systematically addressed. The following table (see Table 4.2) shows the total of 24 interviewees who agreed to participate while testifying the international reach of this study.

4.3.2.2 Developing the Interview Guide

Flexibility is a key requirement of qualitative interviewing. The interviewer must be able to respond to issues that emerge in the course of the interview in order to explore the perspective of the participant on the topics under investigation. Therefore, qualitative interviews use an "interview guide" that outlines the main topics the researcher would like to cover, but is flexible regarding the phrasing of questions and the order in which they are asked (King and Horrocks 2010). It allows the participants to lead the interaction in unanticipated directions.

Topics to include in the guide are fueled by three main sources: (1) own personal experience of the research area, e.g. first-hand experience, and stories and anecdotes told by people, (2) research literature on the subject to see what previous research suggests, and (3) informal preliminary work to focus the thinking about the area. Eventually, developing the interview guide for this study followed the three main criteria proposed by Stigler and Felbinger (2005).

The final interview guide is formulated in proper sentence form and consists of five main questions that have also been shared with each interviewee upfront (see Table 4.3). Each main question is enhanced by five to ten further, more detailed sub-questions which allow the interviewer to stimulate the discussion if needed. The entire interview guide is included in Annex D. Regarding the structure of the guide, the first question intends to give the interviewee an easy start while making sure that both, the interviewee and the interviewer, continue the interview on the basis of a joint understanding of the platform. Then, the following interview questions aim at addressing the context and the core of the scientific research questions formulated earlier. At the same time, the interview questions ensure the open-ended nature of the interview by allowing unexpected responses from the

Table 4.3 Main questions contained in the interview guide

#	Main question
1.	Please provide a short overview of the goals of your organization! Please also describe your personal responsibility in this setting
2.	Who is involved in using or benefiting from the platform?
3.	What is your organization's role between these stakeholders?
4.	What are your positive/negative experiences while working together with the platform users?
5.	What are your positive/negative experiences while working together with healthcare organizations?

interviewee. At the end of each interview, interviewees were given the opportunity to add or highlight aspects that have been considered insufficiently according to their individual judgement. Before going live, this interview guide has been validated and re-adjusted with researchers from other universities in an iterative, multistage process.

4.3.2.3 Conducting the Expert Interviews

As shown above, 24 experts agreed to participate, from OIIs across eight nations, including the United States, the United Kingdom, Germany and other countries. Respondents were predominantly CEOs and/or founders of the respective online platforms. Due to the geographical spread, the interviews were conducted by telephone during August until November 2013 and lasted 63 min on average. 17 interviews were conducted in English, 7 interviews in German. The interviews were guided conversations rather than structured queries. This has ensured (i) a consistent line of inquiry and (ii) the open-ended nature of interview at the same time (King and Horrocks 2010). With the consent of the interviewees, all interviews were audio-recorded and subsequently transcribed verbatim. The transcription of the audio material required a lot of time and discipline. Depending on the sound quality and the speaker's accent, the transcription of 1 h audio could take up to 8 h of listening and writing. As student resources were not at my disposal, I decided to outsource parts of this tedious task (10 interviews) to a professional transcription services company in India.[5] However, the returned quality varied. Some assigned interviews were perfectly transcribed without any errors, while others needed to go through several iterations resulting in a fair amount of control work. The interviewees expressed to stay anonymous; therefore, the source of each quote given in later sections will be indicated by acronyms.

4.3.3 Data Analysis

In total, the transcription of all semi-structured interviews resulted in 447 pages of text. The data was analyzed using MaxQDA version 11, a professional application for qualitative data analysis. Data analysis followed the standards for qualitative research as reported by Miles and Hubermann (1994). The analysis process is broken down into a series of stages and smaller steps within these. Although the step-by-step-approach by King and Horrocks (2010) was adopted for this study (as illustrated in Fig. 4.1), the analysis was not conducted sequentially. Rather, as is generally the case in qualitative data analysis, it was frequently iterated between stages.

---

[5]For comparison: 1 h of audio transcription in English language cost about 40€ in India and about 150€ in Germany.

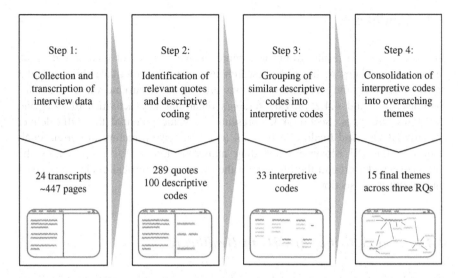

Fig. 4.1 Process of interview data analysis in Chap. 4

At the second step, the goal is to identify those parts of the data (transcripts) that are likely to be helpful in answering the research question. Therefore, while reading through each transcript, relevant material that focuses on participant's views and experiences was highlighted. The next step is to use the highlighted passages in the text to define descriptive codes. Labelling the descriptive codes stays close to the text and with single words or short phrases. Reliability is ensured by coding the data by two independent coders.[6]

At the third step, beyond mere description, a new level of codes is defined which focuses more on the interpretation of the meaning of the descriptive codes. Essentially, it is about grouping together descriptive codes that share some common meaning and creating an interpretative code that captures it.

At the fourth step, overarching themes are identified. This stage builds on grouping interpretative codes, i.e. being on a higher level of abstraction. The overarching themes characterize key concepts in the analysis that are rooted in theoretical ideas or practical concerns. For example, two descriptive codes were "sentiment mining" and "keyword search"; they were grouped under the interpretive code "analyzing group discussions" which eventually wraps up in "sense-making" as the overarching theme. Considering all the codes of the final coding scheme, an intercoder reliability of 93.6% was achieved.

---

[6]I gratefully acknowledge the dedicated support of Mr. Harrison Killefer—at that time MBA student at the Robert H. Smith School of Business, University of Maryland, USA.

4.4   Findings

In this section, the results from the comprehensive analysis of interview data are presented. It relates to the three research questions that motivate this particular study. Therefore, the subsequent sections are organized around these questions. Sections 4.4.1 and 4.4.2 provide findings regarding key activities of OIIs and emerging OII types. Section 4.4.3 presents the value potential that OIIs deliver towards HCOs. And finally, Sects. 4.4.4 and 4.4.5 give a picture of current challenges in the OII ecosystem including numerous mitigations proposed by the interviewees. To ground the findings in the data, rich empirical evidence is given throughout these sections.

4.4.1   Key Activities of OIIs in Healthcare

Research question 2a seeks to identify the unique activities and types of OIIs in healthcare. Analysis of the interview data yielded four distinct key activities of OIIs that are mutually exclusive and collectively exhaustive with respect to this sample. These four key activities are labeled as *facilitation*, *support*, *incubation*, and *sensemaking*. Table 4.4 gives a numeric overview about how these overarching themes derived from the qualitative raw data along the different steps of the analysis process. The essence of these activities will be explained below along with numerous quotes from the interview data for illustration.

Table 4.4 Coding breakdown—OII activities

Theme	Interpretive code	# Interpretive codes	# Descriptive codes	# Coded segments
Facilitation	Linking stakeholders Matching stakeholders	2	10	31
Support	Moderating conversations Guiding conversations Reviewing conversations Admin-technical support	4	13	40
Incubation	Conceiving projects Preparing projects Executing projects Projects w scientific purpose	4	9	35
Sense-making	Interpretation of quant. data Interpretation of qual. data Evaluation	3	12	43
Total 4		13	13 36	149

4.4.1.1 Facilitation

The *facilitation of connections* between complementing stakeholders, e.g. seekers and providers of innovation-related knowledge, is a key activity of OIIs in healthcare. They build bridges between healthcare organizations and healthcare consumers, research institutions and healthcare consumers, but also consumers and consumers by using the reach of the intermediary's network. As noted by the interviewees:

- Our job is to try to bring the two together. (HT, paragraph 38)
- We are a broker bringing together people who otherwise wouldn't get together. (HH, paragraph 45)

The above quotes illustrate the fact that the OII constitutes a crucial link between independent stakeholders. Without that "connecting link", it would be difficult, and perhaps even infeasible, for the stakeholders involved to get into contact. The value is that the OII is able to engage with, e.g., focused patient populations in a way that would be difficult by other means.

Apart from linking stakeholders, the facilitation activity includes an aspect of selecting and matching the right people. In essence, the OII becomes a gatekeeper who filters the reach of his network by a set of criteria determined through the actual project. A positive match is more likely through applying selection criteria. Therefore, the OII may gather detailed information about their users and their professional partners to support the selection procedure. It is exemplified by the following quotes:

- So we collect very detailed profiles of members, so that we can match information from third parties and just show it to the right members. (DU, paragraph 33)
- We are helping to recruit people for clinical trials. (PL, paragraph 83)

4.4.1.2 Support

The second key activity of the OIIs that was evident in the data was one of *active support* during joint innovation projects. In contrast to facilitation, in the support role, the OII engages at an operational level to enable projects through its online platform. The interview data revealed recurring activities that OIIs perform to ensure that projects run successfully, including (i) *moderating conversations*, (ii) *guiding discussion threads*, (iii) *reviewing contributions*, and (iv) *administrative-technical support*. However, there is also variation across OIIs in regard to the different aspects of active support they emphasize.

Depending of the activity levels in a community, *moderating conversations* is important to construct a virtual environment in which users feel engaged and motivated to contribute. Especially for communities of smaller size, a moderator who is part of the OII organization can act as a catalyst for stimulating participation in conversations without being directly involved in the topic-related discussion. This can occur through actions such as writing welcome messages to new users, writing thank you messages for contributions made by users, sending invitations to participate, or writing synopses of what has been discussed so far. All these elements can help to keep the conversation on track. Equally, moderating conversations can help mediate between conflicting users if two or more users do not find common ground on an issue they are discussing. The moderator, as an independent third party, may intervene in these situations. The following quotes from the interview data give evidence for moderating community conversations:

- I think we felt the patients were underserved by many of the existing communities. We felt many of those communities were not properly moderated. So our communities are moderated by life humans. (IN, paragraph 13)
- The groups usually have less than 100 participants. So with such small groups it is necessary to actively moderate in order to keep the conversations going. (CO, paragraph 82)

Enhancing the moderation of conversations, moderators can also actively *determine the topical focus* of community conversations. As such, the users are guided towards specific topics. The moderator then sets the overall themes of discussion and may ask users specific questions. This helps motivate the users to explicate their knowledge and experience regarding a certain topic. Often, if the OII is running a project in collaboration with a healthcare organization, the overall themes of discussion are well aligned with the OII's clients:

- Typically the client is not involved day to day. The client has questions they want to answer and we help answer those questions. (IN, paragraph 65)
- So our clients do not directly engage with the patients... They do that through us. They tell us what questions, what problems they want to solve and we interact with the patients. (IN, paragraph 151)

As it has been extensively documented, in healthcare, the privacy and confidentiality of information is a focal concern among participants in digitally mediated environments (Anderson and Agarwal 2011). With all the contributions in the community, it may become important to *review the quality* of user posts before the information is fully disclosed online. Reviewing includes activities such as sanitizing private or confidential information. It can protect the user of being identified in public or prevent legal actions in case of unjustified criticism. Furthermore, adjusting abusive language can be part of the reviewing role as well. Altogether, it is a mechanism of ensuring quality control:

- People put their stories on and then we moderate them. That means nothing is public until we have read it. We may make a small audit, sometimes we have to remove names or dates because the aims of moderation are to reduce the risk of identifying the patient and to reduce the risk of public criticism of names, health service staff, which could result in legal actions. (PO, paragraph 17)

Another aspect of community management is the *administrative-technical support* for the users. Typically, OII staff is available to answer questions regarding the technical and administrative functioning such as requests concerning setting up and maintaining user accounts, submitting and editing posts, communicating with other online users, and participating in the projects or challenges offered by the OII. The administrative-technical support is vital to keep the community on track as it is a prerequisite to enable users to access the platform and all of the platform's functions to their fullest extent, and to ensure smooth operations from the user's perspective:

- They are mostly supporting patients when... they're a helpdesk. They are helping patients to use the site and supporting them when they have problems. (IN, paragraph 156)

The above support activities are illustrative to the extent of evidence provided by the interview data, while fully recognizing that there may be other support activities that did not surface among the sample of respondents.

4.4.1.3 Incubation

Incubation is a third block of activities that OIIs perform. Some OIIs offer consultancy services to help healthcare organizations to start new co-creation projects. If healthcare organizations do not have much experience in running co-creation projects, OIIs with incubation activities act as enablers. Such OIIs receive wider responsibilities in (i) *conceiving*, (ii) *preparing* and (iii) *executing* co-creation projects. The intensity of the agent's support depends on the earlier work done by the commissioning organization—the findings suggest that it can range from refining existing projects plans to conceiving a new co-creation project from scratch.

For *conceiving new projects*, the HCO approaches the OII with a high-level business challenge for which they think co-creation can be a viable method. Then, the OII proposes a project about how to get the best output from the users within the given context. There are no standard approaches as this is a relatively new field. Often new data needs to be collected and methods of data collection need to be adapted because the goals of the commissioning organizations vary. If the agent's support is required to a lesser degree, then the OII can help with *refining and preparing* co-creation projects suggested by a HCO. To optimize the value of co-creation, it is important to fine-tune a project toward its intended target group. OIIs conceiving new projects are demonstrated by these quotes:

- So our approach is working very much with companies, speaking to them about current standpoints, pain points and challenges what they need to know and why. And then we create the project or the challenge around that. To help meet their needs. It's very much case by case. (PC, paragraph 52)
- So they give us the high level, business pain point or the area that they are trying to tackle. We then go away and have a little brainstorm, think about the best way to work with the crowd/community to get the best output. (PC, paragraph 71)

- A lot of our job is persuading clients to simplify and reduce the complexity and break things down into its component part. (DU, paragraph 36)

In addition to the conceptualization and design, *executing the projects* independently can be part of OII incubation. Executing projects may include building new virtual rooms as a platform for exchange, developing forms of how to canvass the users, e.g. by tailored questionnaires, leading the entire communication with users, and others. A good example here is the development of patient-reported outcome (PRO) measures. It requires the design of a questionnaire, distributing it among the users, and making sure that results are returned on time. The following quotes demonstrate aspects of executing a co-creation project as part of OII incubation:

- Any sponsor or company will literally, once have agreed on whatever we are working on, just sit back and enjoy the ride. And we do all the work for them. So, they can either observe or be proactive in it, it's up to them. (PC, paragraph 106)
- But largely I should be clear: our clients don't want to have direct access to the patient base, they never asked for it because of the regulatory concerns. (IN, paragraph 205)

The interview data also shows that agents set up co-creation projects for *scientific research purposes*. As the OII is best aware of the power of user data available from their network, they may run longitudinal scientific studies that are not always tied to a specific project with one of their partners. The quote below illustrates a setting where OIIs may conduct scientific research as part of their incubation activity:

- The other is now a study where we are collecting data over time. It's an epidemiological cohort study. We're asking the participants and so it's a combined effort between the participants and us. (AW, paragraph 46)

It is noteworthy that agents create an environment for users to support them in advancing their ideas. In this vein, agents are no different from incubators that provide a protective environment for innovative users in which they can develop their ideas under controlled conditions. One of our interview partners made a fine but important distinction:

- Our project approach is not to take ideas from people and run away - but to take ideas and support people to help develop and evolve them. (PC, paragraph 19)

The same interviewee highlighted that they want to create a fertile environment beyond ideation alone. This can be achieved by enabling users to also *"pilot and then scale"* their ideas through the OII's network, namely other users from the community and professional partners.

4.4.1.4 Sense-Making

OIIs collect substantial amounts of qualitative and quantitative data through the OII platform. Hence, *making sense of these data* and extracting insight is one of their key activities. The value of the data collected can be increased by means of data processing, data aggregation, and data interpretation. *Quantitative data* in this context foremost relates to questionnaire data, medical data manually entered by the users, geo-locational data, sensor data from smartphones, and many other forms. At a base level, OIIs can perform the aggregation of quantitative data which enables statistical interpretations as exemplified by the following quotes:

- We are really like the layer like select, analyze, process, interpret these data and then is the mechanism for interventions as you go forward. (GI, paragraph 106)
- We now get into a position that we have collected and validated enough data to run analysis on it. One of the analyses would be "hey where is this blind spot?" For instance in this city there is way too low number of AEDs to create a safe environment. (AD, paragraph 38)

In contrast to quantitative data, *qualitative data* predominantly take the form of forum discussions, wiki-style contributions, submissions from idea contests, and live chats. For example, qualitative data contains experiential knowledge from users about living with a condition, going through prescribed medicines and treatments, and dealing with the challenges imposed. As found in several instances, OIIs can analyze these types of qualitative data by consolidating forum discussions and combining it as a whole. There are several ways in which this is done. For example, by selecting and observing certain communities of interest, or by searching the community discussions for particular key words. The OII then synthesizes the knowledge into a written report that is made available to the stakeholders involved, especially to the healthcare organizations benefitting from this newly gained knowledge. These observations are substantiated by these interview quotes:

- There are a couple of ways to get insights from our community. One is that, I would call that "fly on the wall", where we are just reading, we are just observing non-invasively in the support groups. (IN, paragraph 187)
- We typically write reports, we summarize it and synthesize it in ways that are digestible. We don't just give them raw data. Sometimes statistical work, sometimes sort of natural language processing, sometimes follow-on interviews with patients, you know, it depends on the project. (IN, paragraph 181)

As part of their sense-making activities, some OIIs do *evaluate contributions* from users. Evaluation often happens within the scope of idea contests. Either staff from the OII or an appointed panel of judges, usually manually, evaluate the submissions by users, with a goal of surfacing submissions and their authors that provide the most interesting and innovative content. The following quote illustrates evaluation as one facet of sense-making:

- I mean, it's written submissions when people send in multimedia material, I mean manual evaluation is the only way to do it. We had to go through every single one. (DM, paragraph 98)

The degree to which the OII performs the sense-making activity depends very much on subsequent stakeholders and if they require raw data, pre-processed data, or fully analyzed data.

4.4.2   Emerging OII Types

Although the four activities are each independent and distinctive sets of tasks, the data reveal that the key activities are not exclusively associated with an entity. Rather, each OII can provide one or several of these activities. It was found that the activities typically occur in bundles or configurations, and each exemplifies a distinctive interaction with the ecosystem of stakeholders, i.e. HCCs and HCOs. It was also found that one activity typically dominates and represents the central focus of the OII. The iterative analysis yielded four such types in the sample: the *proactive agent*, the *support provider*, the *community champion*, and the *bridge builder*. Each of these types is described in detail in the following. Figure 4.2 gives a brief overview of the activity bundles that compose the four distinct OII types.

4.4.2.1   Proactive Agent

The first typical bundle of OII activities is the *proactive agent*. It combines three out of four key activities which are: *incubation*, *support*, and *sense-making*. OIIs of this type assume a strong and proactive role in the ecosystem of stakeholders. That is also why HCOs and participating healthcare consumers do not interact directly with each other (see Fig. 4.3). In healthcare, the agent role is critical because some patients may be wary of engaging directly with HCOs (Anderson and Agarwal 2011). The actual process of co-creation happens between the consumers and the OII. As an agent, the OII conceives co-creation projects on behalf of HCOs (incubation) and

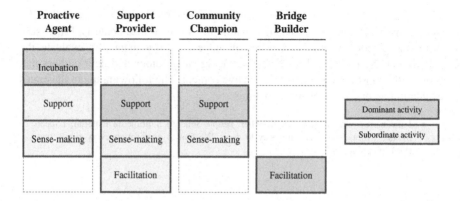

Fig. 4.2 Emerging OII types by activity bundles

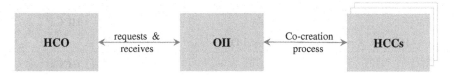

Fig. 4.3 OII type "proactive agent" in context

then manages the entire realization of the projects on a tactical and operative level (support). During and after the project, the OII collects large amounts of data from the users which are being analyzed and reported to the HCOs (sense-making). Typical examples of the agent type are OIIs such as *PatientsCreate*, *Inspire*, or *PatientsLikeMe*.

4.4.2.2 Support Provider

The *support provider* bundles the activities *support*, *sense-making*, and *facilitation*. An OII of this type enables HCOs to interact directly with the consumers by enabling access to the user pool (facilitation). While the interaction takes places through the intermediary's online platform (see Fig. 4.4), the OII supports the co-creation projects in an operational role, e.g. by supervising the day-to-day conversations and ensuring the technological functioning (support). Compared to the proactive agent, the HCO adopts a stronger and more salient role towards the consumers in terms of designing and leading the scope of the project. The OII, in return, can run various analyses on the gathered consumer data to gain insights for the benefit of the involved HCOs (sense-making). Typical examples of the support provider-type are OIIs such as *PatientOpinion*, *HealthUnlocked*, or *HealthTechHatch*.

4.4.2.3 Community Champion

The third type, the *community champion*, integrates *support* and *sense-making* as key activities. This type is somewhat similar to the support provider, with the distinction that the OII does not facilitate between HCOs and consumers on the

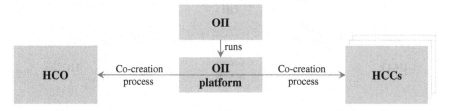

Fig. 4.4 OII type "support provider" in context

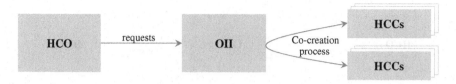

Fig. 4.5 OII type "community champion" in context

basis of specific projects. The reason behind it is the fact that there are HCOs that initiate and sponsor co-creation projects with consumers through OIIs, but they do not expect explicit outcomes for their own innovation capacity on the short-term. Their goal is to empower patients to exchange and develop solutions to their problems with each other (see Fig. 4.5). So the co-creation process itself happens between consumers themselves, while enabled and closely supported by the OII (support). Certainly the HCO sets the overall direction, but it does not get involved in the actual process of co-creation. Any outcome of the process remains with the consumers. The OII, however, can again perform analysis on the process of social interaction or actual outcomes such as specific solutions or improvements on some products or services (sense-making). Typical examples of community champions are OIIs such as the *Patient-Innovation*, *Diabetes Mine Design Challenge*, or *Connecting-Nurses*.

4.4.2.4 Bridge Builder

The final type of OII revealed in the data, the *bridge builder*, provides a single activity of *facilitation*. It is the least complex of OII types. The bridge builder initiates relationships, e.g., by selecting and matching certain criteria, between HCOs and consumers pooled through the OII platform (see Fig. 4.6). Once these connections are made, the HCO and the consumers can interact directly, yet outside of the OII's platform, thereby allowing the co-creation process to continue to run beyond the OII's sphere of activity. Typical examples of the bridge builder-type are OIIs such as *CancerCommons*, *ArmyOfWomen*, or OIIs engaging in clinical trial recruitment, for instance.

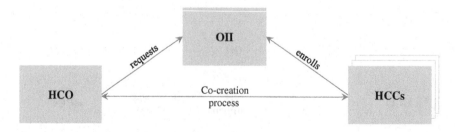

Fig. 4.6 OII type "bridge builder" in context

To summarize, four key activities of OIIs have been identified in reply to research question 2a: facilitation, support, incubation, and sense-making. It was also found that these activities typically occur in bundles. The four OII types are labeled: the proactive agent, the support provider, the community champion, and the bridge builder, to reflect their key.

4.4.3 OII Value Potential for Healthcare Organizations

A question of both theoretical and practical relevance that often arises in the context of intermediaries in general is "what is the value they create for the parties they mediate?" A key objective of this part, as articulated in research question 2b, is to isolate in a more detailed manner the value creating potential of OIIs in healthcare for one set of parties: the HCOs. Analysis of the data reveals that the value-add of OIIs for HCOs can be summarized in four distinct categories: *network reach*, *lay expertise*, *professional expertise*, and *digital literacy*. It is also found that each form of value-add is differentially associated with the archetypical bundles identified for research question 2a. The essence of these categories will be explained in the following along with numerous quotes from the interview data for illustration. Table 4.5 gives a numeric overview about how these overarching categories derived from the qualitative raw data along the different steps of the analysis process.

4.4.3.1 Network Reach

One key area in which OIIs can significantly add value is in *increasing the network reach* of a HCO. It is found that there are ways in which the intermediary organization can do so. First, OIIs give HCOs *access to sources* of information that are

Table 4.5 Coding breakdown—OII value potential for HCOs

Theme	Interpretive code	# Interpretive codes	# Descriptive codes	# Coded segments
Network reach	Access to new/unique sources Acc. to specialized populations	2	15	23
Lay expertise	Value of lay expertise Timeliness of contributions	2	5	14
Prof. expertise	Specialization Experience	2	7	22
Digital literacy	Digital literacy	1	2	4
Total 4		7	7 29	63

new and unique, collectively fueled by the knowledge and experience of the user pools that the OII has gathered over time. Several interviewees highlighted that reporting on patient experiences and interacting with patient pools has traditionally been very difficult for HCOs to do. Through the OII with its bridging function, there is an emerging possibility for HCOs to address these new information sources and patient pools, enabling new conversations between HCOs and users in which they are otherwise not involved. As the availability of these new sources further increases, it became apparent that HCOs increasingly realize the value that lies in these new sources. They look for new possibilities on how to better exploit these new sources of information and how to interact with the healthcare consumers more closely. The following quotes demonstrate that user-based sources of information are novel and unique to healthcare organizations:

- And the value for ConvaTec is that they can learn a lot about all these things I was talking about, they can learn a lot about patient experiences and that's really valuable for them. You know it's very difficult for them to do that otherwise. (IN, paragraph 134)
- It is usually about accessing health information. And you know, being able to act on it. They wanted access to patient information that they couldn't get elsewhere. (HU, paragraph 111)
- Researchers are here about our data and they want to work with it. And so they come back and say, hey, things could be used in this condition and let's try to find a way. (GI, paragraph 55)

Second, OIIs enable *access to highly specialized* patient populations with extremely focused disease patterns. For HCOs it is typically difficult to approach such specialized populations by any other means. The data suggest that these pools often are highly engaged in their health and wellness, far more than the overall population, and are very willing to participate in co-creation efforts. In terms of the patient online behavior, one interviewee highlights the high engagement by the average time of activity on the platform: he noted that users spent over half an hour online every day and over 40% return each single day. While these numbers may be idiosyncratic to this platform and disease condition, they demonstrate the striking positive potential for new knowledge creation. The value for HCOs lies in developing direct relationships with these engaged and focused patient populations which, in return, helps them to increase their network reach, as the following quotes illustrate:

- Our value is that we are able to engage with focused patient populations in a way that's really difficult by other means. If you are a Pharma Company and you want to talk with 100 lung cancer patients or ovarian cancer patients, it's very difficult to find those patients and to find one or two who are engaged and who are willing to be responsive. That's what we do and it's valuable to Pharma Companies. (IN, paragraph 176)
- But these are all high-value chronic patients who are diagnosed, who are costing a system a substantial amount of money. So if you can talk to those five patients and support them and actually reach out to them and then you help; then you can change the cost base dramatically. (GI, paragraph 127)

Network reach is a value-add for HCOs that can be provided by OIIs of all four types (proactive agent, support provider, community champion, or bridge builder).

4.4.3.2 Lay Expertise

A second area of value-add for HCOs is around the *consumers' lay expertise*. OIIs can provide authentic accounts of lay expertise through the user pools that have formed around the OII platform. These user pools range from several hundred users up to, for example, 350,000 users for the OII with the largest user pool in our sample. The lay expertise originates from the lived experience of healthcare consumers (e.g., patients or their caregivers) dealing with a condition, going through procedures and treatments, and using medical products. Some healthcare consumers may also accumulate lay medical knowledge, particularly if they are involved in coping with a condition over several years. Such expertise can surface in different forms such as treatment data recorded in the patient's personal health record, in-depth feedback on products or services, experiential knowledge on coping with a chronic disease over time, or creative ideas to improve the patient's situation. The interview data acknowledges the value of lay expertise that lies in the users' contributions, as the following quotes show:

- So, what the concept accomplished was not only bringing some specific product ideas to life but also just bringing patient needs to light until to what people are looking for, and also kind of simulating this whole conversation and helping to place kind of this next-generation of thinkers into the industry that's creating these devices for people with diabetes. (DM, paragraph 11)
- It is small, practical, incremental improvements typically. It is not a systemic or radical change to processes. (PO, paragraph 56)
- Almost all of the [solution proposals] have a relatable economic benefit, but I think, the platform really speaks to the way that nurses think, which is much more about care and impact of the patient, and the care studying. (CN, paragraph 76)

A crucial advantage here is the *timeliness* of the consumers' contributions. The data are collected temporally proximate to the user's experience and the HCOs can act on it without delay. HCO's are also able, under certain circumstances, to go back to the patients and ask them again if further details or clarifications are needed. This kind of live interaction highly increases the value-add for HCOs, as opposed to other sources of data in which the data may be dated and, thus, less fruitful for the HCOs. The following two examples illustrate this value-add:

- A lot of other people that mine big data say that the data is dead because it happened a year ago or so. You cannot go back and say: 'Ask a patient'. If we are looking at a prescription that has been filled for your drug and maybe you got a very expensive rare drug and it costs quarter a million dollars a year. You could see that the prescription was filled but you don't know if the patient took it. And you don't know if the patient encountered any problems getting it out of the packaging. Or they phoned up the support number and the lady at the other end was rude. You don't know what happened.

- You just see the data that says: one prescription filled in January. The idea is that you have more of a live interaction with patients potentially, if you set this up and if you are willing to listen. (PL, paragraph 34)
- If you are managing a hospital and once a year you get a patient questionnaire that says '90% of my patients are very unhappy', well, that's too late. What we give you is 'I visited my mother yesterday and her bed was disgusting'. So you can do something about it today! So you are speeding up the feedback cycle. It's a different type of information. (PO, paragraph 37)

The data suggests that lay expertise as a value-add for HCOs can be particularly provided by the OII types of proactive agent and support provider.

4.4.3.3 Professional Expertise

Some OIIs have already developed comprehensive professional expertise in their field. Their expertise is of distinct value for HCOs who often have not build up similar in-house capabilities yet. The professional expertise of OIIs arises from two sources: their *specialization* and *experience*. The specialization into a specific area has enabled the OIIs to build a deep understanding their patient pools and how to interact with them, relevant knowledge related to the medical background behind the patients' challenges, and a nuanced understanding of the social and technical requirements to successfully design and run co-creation projects with healthcare consumers in online environments. The OII experience links back to the number of years in service and the number of projects accomplished. A few OIIs have been even able to build a brand-like reputation on the basis of their extensive experience. The quotes below give a brief account of the professional expertise of OIIs:

- So, yeah, we take the business pain point or the identified business pain point and help them to translate that and put that into a challenge. (PC, paragraph 71)
- I think we created value through demonstrating that innovation communities like ours can, indeed, support people in developing compelling ideas. Well, at least this is what the findings of our analysis showed. (ID, paragraph 62)
- We have developed an expertise in developing those measures quickly and more efficiently than traditional methods. (PL, paragraph 29)
- We are going to be focused to give them value of an open and non-structured collaboration. (PI, paragraph 64)

HCOs can obtain this type of professional expertise especially from a proactive agent.

4.4.3.4 Digital Literacy

A final dimension of the OII's value proposition that the data reveal is the notion of *digital literacy*. Many HCOs are challenged in regard to their ability to exploit digital technologies for competitive advantage (Agarwal et al. 2010). While HCOs that are searching to increase their digital literacy acknowledge the positive benefits of online consumers as a source to grow their innovation capacity, they lack confidence and appear to be hesitant in initiating their own co-creation projects. Such HCOs involve with OIIs as a mechanism for building their own capability with digital platforms and interfaces. Taking advantage of the actual consumer contributions on the OII platform seems to be of less priority for the HCO. The data suggests that it is a unique opportunity for them to test and learn from the use of digital tools and technology which, in return, may have indirect implications on future engagements with consumer communities online. As noted by the interviewees:

- What I can see from the meetings that we have, like at the headquarters, they will bring in some of their innovation groups that were working in other things and put those in front of this committee. [] It is this indirect secondary learning that the company is trying to do. It is not directly using these ideas from the platform itself. It is more, everything they are learning from this engagement, that is really the benefit of the company. (CN, paragraph 53)
- That is a new demographic that they have not really working with in the past and they are also able to test and learn from the use of digital platforms and how they can potentially role that back into patients support services, and things that will actually benefit directly their clients. So, working back to support patients for diabetes, the more they understand about digital tools and technology and how to work with it in this space. It is, I think, a company benefit. (CN, paragraph 48)

It was found that the OII type of community champion is particularly instrumental in creating digital literacy value for HCOs. To conclude, the empirical observations show that OIIs create different forms of value-add for HCOs. Figure 4.7 summarizes the value generating potential of each OII type and shows the different associations with each form of value-add.

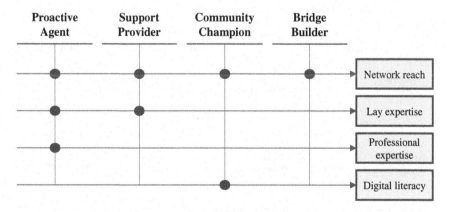

Fig. 4.7 Values added for healthcare organizations per OII type

4.4.4   Reported Challenges

Working with the OII interview data has also shown that there exist a number of critical challenges that may impede co-creation activities in the currently available settings. In reply to research question 2c, this section addresses related findings. Overall, there are seven areas in which major concerns are expressed. The following Fig. 4.8 gives an overview of the challenges identified; they are arranged by stakeholder type as they may dominantly occur at the HCO, OII or HCC side. The arrows between the boxes indicate that one challenge influences another. Some of the challenges show a special relevance in the healthcare context, which is then highlighted with an exclamation mark.

In order to overcome those challenges, solutions are needed. Therefore, possible mitigations are proposed for each challenge identified based on the interviewee accounts. The findings mostly reflect the perspective of the OIIs while some interviewees also speak on behalf of some HCOs addressing particular challenges that HCOs encounter.

The next subsections describe each of the reported challenges in detail, and then Sect. 4.4.5 presents possible mitigations. Rich empirical evidence from the interviews is given throughout. Table 4.6 gives a numeric overview about how these overarching challenges derived from the qualitative raw data along the different steps of the analysis process.

4.4.4.1   Attract User Base

To make the concept of intermediary platforms run, it is essential to attract a user base large enough to provide plentiful inputs. However, *attracting the user base* is one of the key challenges reported. Attraction depends upon three aspects identified

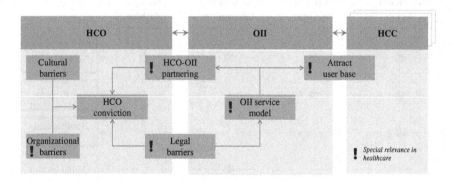

Fig. 4.8   Reported challenges in the OII ecosystem

Table 4.6 Coding breakdown—challenges in the OII ecosystem

Theme	Interpretive code	# Interpretive codes	# Descriptive codes	# Coded segments
Attract user base	Gaining trust Gaining critical mass Provide usability	3	6	17
HCO conviction	Negative attitudes Positive attitudes	2	4	9
Cultural barriers	Cultural barriers	1	2	5
Organizational barriers	Complexity Priorities	2	3	8
Legal barriers	Legal barriers	1	3	8
OII service model	Effective service model Catalyze on ideas Diverging interests	3	10	21
HCO-OII partnering	HCO-OII partnering	1	7	9
Total 7		13	13	35	77

(i) *gaining trust from the users*, (ii) *gaining the critical mass of users*, and (iii) *providing a degree of platform usability* that is rich of features but easy to use at the same time.

First, *gaining trust* is important to attract a user base. The element of trust is important for users in their decision to enroll and participate at the platform. It is about the trust towards the intermediary as the operating organization as well as trust towards the technical implementation of the intermediary platform. Especially in healthcare-related settings, the element of trust may be even more important than elsewhere. If potential users perceive a lack of trust in the intermediary, they are less likely to participate. Hence, it is important for the intermediary organization to have trust-building mechanisms in place. One interviewee finds out that online platforms do not necessarily create a social space. He argues that, on the one hand, online platforms per se may be too detached from the real world and, on the other hand, there is inertia as well which stops people from enrolling. Another aspect that contributes to creating or reducing trust from a technical perspective is the dealing with personal data in online settings. One interviewee reported concerns from users regarding data privacy. The following quotes from the interviews underpin that gaining trust from potential and actual users is a key challenge.

- And I think the big point really is: it's not just a matter of build it [a platform], and they'll come, in terms of people with diseases, the patients. So I think that you really need to have a trust relationship with them. And so how you do that - I think that is important. (AW, paragraph 144)
- The trouble with PatientsLikeMe is, there is nothing about them that would make the average person trust them. They are just giving you a vehicle to get together. They are saying, here is the meeting room you can meet in. And so it will be interesting to see if they can get enough people, that's where I think their challenge is going to be. The advantage we have is, because I have a book and I have a name and all that, you know I have reputation among breast cancer people. So they trust me. But PatientsLikeMe really doesn't, they are just a company. And so how to build that brand and that trust, that will be their challenge. (AW, paragraph 132)
- Online platforms do not necessarily create a social space. One of the things that I found important was to link it to offline communities. It was not just launched to the website and email people about it. It was launched on the website, and then, when we go to conferences and talk to people then we have seen submissions. There is inertia to it as well. So, working with offline communities to create trust and participation in online communities, and focusing on small goals first to get to big goals, I think, was really important for us. (CN, paragraph 70)
- We have also noticed that our target group of users was very cautious with regard to data privacy concerns. That's why we tried to collect as little data as possible, so to say the most indispensable data only. (ID, paragraph 34)
- The ideal situation will be that: we have a core group of like super-creative, empowered patients who use our piece of technology to do what we are doing as the commercial company. You know, crowdsourcing and then crowdfunding, something within their community that they need. But people don't do that off the bath. I think we will need some big wins first. (PC, paragraph 52)

Second, beyond gaining trust, there is the challenge of *gaining the critical mass* of users. To *recruit and retain people* and to finally reach a critical mass of users is important for any intermediary platform. Without a critical mass of users, positive network effects are more difficult to achieve. Several interviewees have reported that retaining users and making them participate again and again has required major efforts. If users do not see what is in there for them, they may be quick in turning away from the platform. Also, many potential users have existing accounts with other social network websites, while being hesitant about the benefits that an additional account at a new platform may hold. According to one interviewee, it is initially doable to make people register, update their profile and start posting occasionally, but then it is quite hard to make them collaborate in a more structured way. Part of this challenge is building up the web traffic through marketing in a variety of online channels and thus making people aware of the platform. Especially in the context of some very special and rare diseases, e.g. neuromuscular diseases, it is per se difficult to reach the relevant population as it is in fact a relatively small and dispersed group. But due to effects of physical paralysis that go along with such diseases, some potential users are physically inapt or highly restricted in using a desktop computer at all. All the above points make it challenging for intermediary organizations to gain a critical mass of users. It is supported by the following quotes.

- People aren't very altruistic as we would like them to be! If there is nothing really in it for them, they turn away. (PC, paragraph 39)
- We were able to move users to register at the site and to post stuff occasionally and to keep their profile up to date. But just not much more than that. They did not develop things in closed rooms together. I have to be straight forward here. After this experience I would not be very optimistic anymore if such concept works at all. (HH, paragraph 45)
- That is a big challenge. Building up the traffic has taken many years and that is a big part of the challenge. Social media has been incredibly helpful in the last three years. Our traffic increased for about 100% in the past year, and that is largely a result of using Twitter and Facebook as ways to increase our profile. But there is no simple solution to that. (PO, paragraph 65)
- Most people never sign up to more than four social networks. And if they do, they don't use more than four on any time. So we are very dubious about trying to create a big social platform and, as well, when we approach a partner that has like 10,000 patients and we ask them to drive traffic to our website, if they fear that somebody is going to take traffic away from their site, we will never be able to work with them again. (PC, paragraph 91)
- And here is the problem: neuromuscular diseases are really rare and special and it goes along with effects of paralysis. This already reduces the potential size of the user community. As I observed during our field work, using a desktop computer is quite hard and tedious for some patients. That reduces the target user group again and it makes the initial challenge even more difficult to build a decent user community. (ID, paragraph 26)

Third, a more technical aspect is the *usability of the intermediary platform* that has influence on the attraction of a user base. Usability is the degree to which the platform is easy to use and a good fit for the people who use it. It takes into account the needs and abilities of users in conjunction with the requirements by the OII. A platform with a high usability will in return create trust and attract users. Several interviewees reported that they had struggled with the technical implementation of features or ongoing technical upgrades. It resulted in unsteady operations of the affected platforms and reduced usability for the users. As a large portion of the Internet is nowadays accessed through mobile devices, high usability needs to be ensured throughout the range of end consumer devices, although this may lead to additional efforts for intermediary organizations to adapt their platforms to the smaller screens of mobile devices. The following quotes refer to usability challenges:

- I think what we learned along the way is that it has to be made very simple, because that are aspirations of universality. And we had actually started over with a more complicated platform that we have narrowed down. (HU, paragraph 14)
- We had a lot of features on the platform, but it could have been implemented much better. We just had technical problems. Some content was not displayed properly; other content which should not be visible was displayed. So I would advocate for not more functionality and features but that the existing functionality is implemented correctly. And in addition to that, it should be easier to use for the users, so the usability should be much better. (GS, paragraph 92)

- Just recently we had a platform upgrade. There were few changes that attracted people in a kind of quite bad way. The system did not work well for a couple of weeks. And you understand the dependency that the people have on the system and how important it is that it is trusted and a good place to be. So you also understand the vulnerability, if you make errors whether through the platform or through the data, there is no place to hide really. And that is why we want everything to be nice and right at the user level. (HU, paragraph 79)
- I think the big challenge now is that such a large proportion of Internet traffic and of website uses is moving into mobile. So, we have to find effective ways to do this on small devices. That is not going to be easy. But we are thinking about how we can address that challenge of making it possible to interact with PO or leave feedback, even when you have small mobile device. (PO, paragraph 78)

4.4.4.2   HCO Conviction

One of the largest challenges is the barely developed conviction by HCOs into the notion of co-creation in general and in the hypothesized benefits of external sources of innovation. The HCO's conviction reflects the beliefs and attitudes towards non-traditional innovation approaches. It is fueled by many aspects, most prominently by own experiences or experiences reported by others. According to the OII's experiences and the companies that they have been working together with, the data reveals that the field is split in two.

One set of HCOs is resistant and shows a *negative attitude* towards new innovation approaches because they simply do not want it, are not used to it, or are not convinced of it. This may then reflect in little demand for the services offered by OIIs. This low degree of conviction links back to different types of barriers found at HCOs that will be discussed later. The following quotes demonstrate the allegedly negative attitude of some HCOs:

- Lots of organizations have been very resistant to PO, and still are. There are lots of organizations that do not want to use it or refused to use it, or think it is a waste of time. And there are organizations that use it, but do not really know what to do with it. I do not think any of it is straight at all, I think, there are lots of barriers there. (PO, paragraph 58)
- We had very little partners who were really convinced about our approach on innovation. Very often we had to explain it through telephone calls, visits or presentations. It dragged on for a long time. And then we were able to get them interested in it - but only in a very few cases. We didn't meet anybody who was really, really keen to go for open innovation. Most of the companies we talked to were not aware of it at all. (HH, paragraph 72)
- The organizational structures were quite hermetic at the companies that we approached. So we weren't really able to enter. And I'm not an industry expert, can't tell why it is like this. But it clearly shows that the companies did not want it. Or maybe it did not yield the same high benefits that were expected. (HH, paragraph 63)
- Yeah, sadly a lot of it is a unidirectional approach from the pharma company towards the users. Just one-way. (DU, paragraph 42)

- Well, there are many ways and methods to structure and integrate the external input. We already do this in other areas. I don't see a problem here. Rather is the question whether there is the determination and motivation to do it at all. And I think, there is still a long way to go. (HH, paragraph 100)

Another set of HCOs has developed a *positive attitude* towards new innovation approaches. At least, they are open to experiment with new practices and are moving, yet slowly, into this direction. Best practices are not yet defined in this field, so many of them are struggling to figure out what the best way of integrating HCC may be and which benefits they might extract from it. They do it for different reasons, e.g., to advance and support their product development function, to increase consumer integration for marketing purposes, or to demonstrate openness for improved agility and reputation. Again, some empirical evidence follows, demonstrating the more positive attitude of some HCOs:

- Pharma is being the slowest one. They know that they need to but it's still a nice-to-have on the hall because they are silo-oriented. (PC, paragraph 96)
- About 20–25% of the organizations we work with are acting on the patients' input. But it is very difficult to say. We have some organizations that really understand this and are making great success. And then there are others that have not, but do not to seem to have a move with that. They apparently have it, but nothing seems to happen very much. We are always surprised that they want to keep going because they do not seem to use it. It is mysterious sometimes. (PO, paragraph 85)
- But my problem with the traditional focus group is that they've already designed this product and gone down the whole path and then they want to see what buttons you push. That's not the same as involving patients from the construction to all the way through prototyping of the product. It is getting better, I admit. I personally have consulted with a number of companies in early stages of product development, not the big, big players but some of the smaller companies. So, I think, everyone is struggling to figure out what the right and best practices are for involving patients. (DM, paragraph 111)
- The company has no interest at all in the content, in the ideas, or in anything of it. But they want to present themselves well in the user community. I find this quite typical, I must say. At the company-side you can often find a more instrumental approach and an approach that is less straight-forward. If you go by the semantics, open innovation and so on, then you probably expect more than what is really going to happen. That is also true in other industries. Look at 3 M for example, or many other innovation platforms that supposedly present ideas from users but then if you look at it in detail, the interest by the users is often differently. (HH, paragraph 99)

One could argue that conviction is a vague construct, i.e. difficult to react on with change. It certainly is a complex construct with many influencing factors. In this analysis, three types of barriers could be observed that influence the HCO's conviction. They can serve to explain the status quo, but also to initiate change. There are cultural barriers, organizational barriers, and legal barriers that are each elucidated in the following sections.

4.4.4.3 Cultural Barriers

There are substantial cultural barriers in HCOs that inhibit change and innovation. Neither such organizations are used to utilizing contributions from HCCs, nor are they used to draw learnings from external sources of innovation. In the pharmaceutical industry for example, a traditional way of thinking prevails that sees clinicians as their customers and not HCCs. This thinking is certainly counterproductive when setting the agenda for co-creation with healthcare consumers. Sometimes innovation is also connected to people's fear of change. This can be linked to fear of new technology, fear of transparency, fear of external contributions and a lack of control over it (referred to as the "not invented here syndrome" in the literature on user innovation, e.g., Antons and Piller 2015). However, there is a trend that the overall cultural environment is changing for the better. According to the interviewee accounts, this is true because, on the one hand, HCOs are more and more interested in the consumer perspective and, on the other hand, peoples' openness to, for instance, social media has increasingly developed in recent years which in turn yields benefits for networks and transparency in healthcare. The following quotes provide corresponding empirical evidence:

- The legacy thinking of pharma was that clinicians were their customers and not patients. So, it's taking a long time to sort of change – move the needle as advanced sort of change that. (DM, paragraph 129)
- There are substantial cultural or organizational barriers. There is no real history of use of feedback, of learning from feedback in the health service. There are plenty of cultural barriers there to using it. (PO, paragraph 58)
- A lot of what inhibits changes is fear, I think. Certainly with this. People are very scared. They are scared of the technology, scared of the transparency, the publicness, and they are scared of the lack of control they have over it. So, there are all kinds of fears that stop people engaging. And to show them that there are other people who are doing it, who had the same fears when they started, but now do not have the fears because they have learned that this is OK. [] We have to show the benefits. It is all very well to say that it should work in theory, but we have to show practical benefits, otherwise people will not want to spend their money on it. That is a big challenge, too. (PO, paragraph 90)
- The biggest challenge for our clients has been that what we're doing is new. So when we started the company in 2005, this was very new. It's getting easier, not because of us, because of the general environment. Corporations are more and more interested in the patient perspective. So I would say that's a challenge that used to exist which is getting easier. (IN, paragraph 237)
- The wider culture has changed a lot in the last five years in terms of peoples' openness to for example social media. That has a big effect on a lot of thinking within health care, and probably in other industries, too, about the benefits of networks and transparency. To some degree, we are supported by the fact that social media has become such a significant cultural force. (PO, paragraph 93)

4.4.4.4 Organizational Barriers

Often the organizational structure and processes at HCOs are not prepared to routinely work with OIIs and external sources of innovation. Many interviewees emphasized the organizational complexity, hierarchical structures, and internal restrictions as barriers that prevent or retard innovation. To achieve change, organizational structures and processes must be adjusted to better work with OIIs and their users and to finally absorb the contributions generated. It is pointed out that successful co-creation requires support from operational and strategic levels of the organization. Mere support from the top management without somebody driving an innovation project at the operational level, or vice versa, will not be sustainably successful as support from across all levels is needed. Another organizational barrier being reported refers to the fact that innovation does not always come on top of the priority queue due to the necessities of daily business and tied up resources. If innovation projects are slowed down for the above reasons, the situation gets more complicated when key contact persons change due to fluctuation and changing responsibilities, as one interviewee has noted. Thus, staff continuity can be a challenging organizational barrier as well. The following quotes provide corresponding empirical evidence:

- But from a pharma perspective, they are still very internally restricted on how they can engage and co-create and innovate with patients. So this is a big milestone, it's a big challenge. (PC, paragraph 115)
- There are no organizational processes or very few for taking feedback in real time and using it to change services. So, this is all very new to these organizations, and it is not something that we can change very fast. For example, the NHS is a massive system, and even the smallest organizations in the NHS will employ thousands of people. There are plenty of organizational barriers there to using it. (PO, paragraph 58)
- It is true that firms are under a big pressure to innovate. But they are far off from developing things over the Internet. It is not set up this way and they are not used to it, at least for this purpose. The employees do milling and filing and many other things, but they don't sit at their computer discussing about it. (HH, paragraph 65)
- The issue is that it is a slower process than you might think. Not because the patients are not willing to tell you, but because… let's say you are working in a drug company and you really believe in this and you are the pioneer, you are one person out of 30,000 people. You have to go and spread that message that we should listen to patients to… you know, you might have 6 levels of manager above you who don't have time for this because they are too busy making advertising campaign or they are getting sued by the FDA/government. They've got other problems. (PL, paragraph 99)
- And sometimes listening to the patients doesn't come to the top of the priority queue. (PL, paragraph 99)
- The issue is: people change jobs a lot at our clients. I have projects that start in January with person A and by December I have gone through person B, C, D, and E. So obviously that continuity can be difficult. Sometimes things take longer than you think. Things get delayed with ethical reviews or you are trying to launch a survey over Thanksgiving or July 4th or Christmas and no one shows up. (PL, paragraph 99)

4.4.4.5 Legal Barriers

HCOs are hesitant to engage with OIIs due to current regulatory and legal standards. For example, in the pharmaceutical industry, every company needs to adhere to what is called pharmacovigilance. The main activity that is most commonly associated with pharmacovigilance is the reporting of adverse events. It is about the collection, monitoring, and prevention of adverse effects with pharmaceutical products. It has to be reported to the regulatory authorities whose jurisdiction is geographically different. In the European Union, for example, the coordination is done by the European Medicines Agency (EMA), in the United States by the Food and Drug Association (FDA), they play a key role in oversight of pharmacovigilance. So far, the FDA has not given updated regulatory guidelines for social media for pharma. So if a HCO wants to work with an OII, then the OII has to adhere to the same regulatory standards as well. This results in extensive effects on the OII side: increased cost levels, processes getting slowed down, legal liability for the OII management, limited technological choices on the platform, to mention a few. So the legal barriers discussed here actually impact both the HCO and the OII side. At the HCO side, it influences the HCO conviction described earlier, and at the OII side it influences the definition of the OII service model that will be discussed as a next challenge. The following quotes provide corresponding empirical evidence:

- Pharma has a huge regulatory fear. The FDA still hasn't really clearly spoken on guidelines for social media for pharma. They can be liable for all kinds of things, so they are really nervous about it. It has gotten better obviously, they've gone ahead and engaged because they had to, even without the clear guidelines from FDA. (DM, paragraph 129)
- So, the funding of the project itself has not been the biggest challenge, it is the continued effort to work through those regulatory issues to make sure that we can participate in creative and innovative online ways. Especially, when you say creative and innovative and new, it usually puts the breaks on for the regulatory and legal side of that company. (CN, paragraph 84)
- As I said because there were restrictions on Pharmacovigilance. Basically if a product is mentioned or if a negative complaint about the company gets put on this website, how do we handle that, what is the outcome. Even though the website itself has nothing to do with the incident. Perhaps an angry customer comes in and it is all these theoretical risk that they like to think about. That ends up in slowing it down. They have a lot of stipulations and they want to know what is going to happen before it happens, what is the plan, who is monitoring the website 24/7. That comes with significant costs, so that is usually the biggest slow down to us. (CN, paragraph 86)
- Why we are in 2013 and there still is not an effective way to communicate health information on the web, it is because it is really complicated. And there is a huge amount of regulation and huge amount of information governance and requirements and consent and all of those things. The role as we evolve is to make a very easy platform for any health organization or institution, of basic use, that they do not have to worry about that. (HU, paragraph 61)
- There is a legal issue. If you start involving with peers, in any way, or how will they structure their ideas, you may be legally liable for whatever comes out of it. And legal

liability means that if anything bad happens, somebody can sue you and you go to jail as a Member of an Executive Board. That's maybe the most pressing issue, a legal issue. What I've learnt from this so far is that: how specific legal frameworks in countries actually limit the technological choices within the platform. (PI, paragraph 29)

4.4.4.6 OII Service Model

The definition of a successful and sustainable service model for the OII remains a major challenge according to the reports collected. The OII service model describes the interplay of the technical platform, the services rendered (cf. Sect. 4.4.1), and the structure and processes enabling it. The service model ultimately defines how an OII creates value between the user population and the innovation-seeking body of the HCOs. There are some more advanced examples which have existed for a few years now, but many platforms are struggling to define their edge that allows for longevity. It still is a new innovation approach with which many have insufficient experiences. Only a few OIIs have been able to establish a business model that ensures continued revenues; the majority of OIIs in the data set operate on seed funds. Surprisingly many interviewees expressed that the value of co-creation projects remains vague for both OIIs and HCOs. What is termed here as a co-creation project does not have to serve the goal of innovation; many different people understand many different things under innovation. Interviewees report that marketing goals such as refreshing the brand or improving the customer experience may supersede the initial innovation goals of such projects. The service model defined at the beginning needs to be iterated and improved along the way. This is how OIIs can sharpen their value proposition. Part of this is experimenting with a more active or a more passive OII role with regard to process interventions between the different stakeholders (cf. emerging OII types in Sect. 4.4.2). The following quotes provide corresponding empirical evidence:

- I think a lot of commercial partners are not quite sure what they are doing. One of the areas around that whole value generation is that, I think, it is not completely clear on these innovation projects where the value lies. Which is why, in some ways, until that should be clearer, we want to move to this more transactional kind of model, whether it is recruiting for clinical trials or advertising good approved content or whatever happens to be. It is only little concrete that in some of the innovation cycle both the potential clients and the providers, I think, they sometimes struggle with. (HU, paragraph 105)
- In part of the start processes, your product what you are building evolves as you're learning more about what the market is interested in. So, when we started a couple of years ago, we were writing on our experiments because that's the only way that you can learn. Right? So you start out, you iterate and that's how you discover your value proposition. (GI, paragraph 86)
- Ideas mean nothing without the business model and the intellectual property around it. (PC, paragraph 19)
- Often these kinds of innovation platforms are in its early stages and it is hard to show direct return early on. So, what are the metrics and the measures for success in the early

stages of projects? Metrics that help to track participation and to track the uptake or the kind of health and the innovation kind of collaboration platform? (CN, paragraph 109)

- Eventually we were lacking enough staff resources. I guess, you could have done more out of it. But also the professional partners could have benefitted from it much more. But at the end, the problem is that you need people who do it. We had supporters from our partners but these were all not very big, non-commercial organizations. Among others Centres for Rares Diseases, centres organizationally attached to hospitals. We had the impression that they also didn't have the resources to support the ideas from the patients. I guess, they didn't know yet how to derive benefit for them. (GS, paragraph 45)

Another important yet challenging aspect is that the service model needs to answer how OIIs can catalyze on the ideas and inputs generated through the users. Once ideas or concepts are created, it is important that OIIs provide an environment in which these inputs can grow and are developed further in a systematic way. For example, OIIs can trigger and actively support the piloting and scaling of such innovation inputs. Acting as a catalyst sets OIIs apart from just the big number of social websites for sharing and exchanging such as online discussion boards or forums. The following quotes provide corresponding empirical evidence:

- So how do we catalyze on these ideas that patients have and actually grow them? Rather than just say 'oh, that's a nice idea, that worked once'? That's a huge challenge. (PL, paragraph 73)
- But at the moment there is nothing to help to (a) pilot and then (b) scale. It's kind of pointless if it's talking for the sake of talking. (PC, paragraph 20)
- If it's a great idea, one of the first things we do is get hold of that member and invite them to prototype days, ask them to develop it with us, with the sponsor. Because you know, a startup in healthcare is probably one of the hardest startups to do. Given the environment, it's unlikely that most people, who come on the platform and have substantial experiences or have ideas, will have the means and the infrastructure to roll something out. (PC, paragraph 23)

Working out an effective service model may be complicated by one more aspect: a few times it is reported about diverging interests of the parties involved, mainly diverging interests between HCCs as users of OII platforms and the HCOs as professional partners of the OII. Diverging interests stand for differences in what the parties involved understand as innovation, change or advancement. Here the OII with its core characteristic of mediation between parties becomes particularly important. Especially in healthcare, this challenge underlines the need for independent third parties such as OIIs. Often patients have a very different perspective on innovation than HCOs and patients' ideas turn out to be a different kind of innovation as referred by examples given in the quotes below. As a specialty defined through the structure of the healthcare system, diverging interests may partly be rooted in the fact that a HCC is usually neither the payer nor the decision maker for the healthcare products or services he actually consumes. This sets restrictions to how innovation can be rewarded as compared to other sectors. The following quotes again provide corresponding empirical evidence:

- The complaint we got from women was, they were being used, as I said, because the researchers in fact didn't want to do what they claimed. In terms of a business and making companies to do this, this is a really important point because what people say they want isn't always what they really want. (AW, paragraph 29)
- What is funny is if I think of the three stories that have been most closely been linked to the development of a new drug... In those cases, patients told clients what was imported. And it turned out to be a different kind of innovation. They said things like 'I would be worried that this cool gizmo means that my drug is gonna cost more. What I probably gonna do is take all my pills out and put them into my packaging that I take around with me every day to remind me of my pills. Don't do the innovative thing! Keep the costs down and give me option B, not option C'. And the company actually did that which was interesting. But you know, you have to listen to what patients say. I think that there is a risk in this innovation game that we get so in love with Google Glass, but we forget that for some people a 99 cent fishing tackle box is actually the best way to handle their pills. And that can be innovation! (PL, paragraph 80)
- If you are hit by a motorbike and you are disabled and you don't have a job anymore, and you are claiming insurance, the idea of spending 20,000€ on a wheelchair that has some more features that are innovative... well, you don't have any money, and you don't have a way of getting more money, you are not there by choice. You probably also don't have transparency about what the price of this thing is. Most likely of what is happening is your insurance company says 'You can have this 5000€ wheelchair, but not the 20,000€ one.' There is a disconnect between you as the consumer versus you as the patient, which means that innovation cannot be rewarded in the same way that it is in the consumer space. (PL, paragraph 75)

4.4.4.7 HCO-OII Partnering

The last challenge in this row is about the partnering between HCO and OII. From the OII perspective it is crucial to get the right HCOs onboard who can process and benefit from the inputs created through the OII platform. Hence, the HCO-OII partnering strategy is of great importance, yet it remains a key challenge as reported from the interviewees. This challenge is tightly related to the definition of the OII service model and the attraction of the user base discussed earlier. To catalyze ideas, it needs HCOs who are motivated and able to technically implement and scale it. Otherwise, it will be hard to materialize the idea into a product or service. However, for some interviewees it seems complicated to find and engage with HCOs who do act in the interest of the OII and its represented user base. Any position and strength that an OII can gain in the interactions through the OII platform must be well-balanced to avoid an HCO dominance that could interfere with peer to peer openness. One interesting aspect of a HCO-OII partnering strategy could be to systematically involve non-profit organizations. This may help to balance interests and to increase trust of all participants.

- It is critical for success to have companies onboard who can potentially implement the idea at stake. And if this company listens in from the very beginning at the platform interactions, then credibility and motivation increases. This was always clear to us, but so to speak, we failed at this point though. (HH, paragraph 55)
- Our partners did not really support us to grow or implement the patients' ideas. It is true we had a jury of experts to assess the ideas and to decide over which idea is to be developed further. So they did their job and then they did not care anymore about the progress of the initiative. (GS, paragraph 36)
- Whether we are going to have our facilitation of the relationships with legal entities, whether they are involved in some kind of commercialization, this is still a subject of careful analysis. Why do we say careful analysis? That's an advantage to have such entities onboard, and also a threat. Because they may take it over and destroy the whole process of peer-to-peer openness, right. And that's something that we are trying to avoid. (PI, paragraph 27)
- I have my doubts that people will just go to a company and give all our data away freely. Rather I think the non-profits probably have a stronger position. So the Michael J. Fox Foundation, they are doing it with Parkinson. Then you've got the myeloma people, you have the diabetes people. So most of the big non-profits in this country are doing it for different diseases. I think the non-profits probably have a more trusted position that would allow them to do it. So maybe what these companies or these smart guys with technology need to do is really care more with the non-profits - so you get the advantage of both, rather than trying to do it themselves. (AW, paragraph 134)

4.4.5   Proposed Mitigations

The previous section has given detailed accounts of current challenges in the OII ecosystem. As consumer co-creation via OIIs is still a subject of current academic research, the above challenges may provide relevant directions for further development and improvement. In addition to these challenges, the interviewees who were quite aware of the given constraints also proposed mitigations to overcome these challenges. This helps to increase the functional understanding of consumer co-creation via OIIs. The following table provides mitigations to each of the seven major challenges as reported by the interviewees (see Table 4.7).

4.5   Discussion

This section discusses the results of the study and is divided into two subsections. The first subsection reflects upon findings about OII activities and types and derives propositions. The second subsection captures important limitations of the study at hand and directly denotes fruitful starting points for further research endeavors.

Table 4.7 Proposed mitigations to current challenges in the OII ecosystem

Challenge	Sub-Challenge	Problem	Proposed Mitigation	Anchor Quote
Attract user base	Gain trust	Creating a trust relationship with users is difficult, yet important, particularly in healthcare settings	Actively manage/ enforce trust-building mechanisms	"And I think the big point really is: it's not just a matter of build it (a platform), and they'll come, in terms of people with diseases, the patients. So I think that you really need to have a trust relationship with them. And so how you do that - I think that is important." (AW, paragraph 144)
↳	↳		Build a brand/company that users can trust in; Reputation of founder, own publications, offline events can help	"The trouble with PatientsLikeMe is, there is nothing about them that would make the average person trust them. They are just giving you a vehicle to get together. [...] The advantage we have is, because I have a book and I have a name and all that, you know I have reputation among breast cancer people. So they trust me. But PatientsLikeMe really doesn't, they are just a company. And so how to build that brand and that trust, that will be their challenge." (AW, paragraph 132)
↳	↳		Link online and offline worlds, e.g., through conferences, HC associations, patient groups	"Online platforms do not necessarily create a social space. One of the things that I found important was to link it to offline communities. It was not just launched on the website and email people about it. It was launched on the website, and then, when we go to conferences and talk to people then we have seen submissions. There is inertia to it as well. So, working with offline communities to create trust and participation in online communities, and focusing on small goals first to get to big goals, I think, was really important for us." (CN, paragraph 70)
↳	↳		Show benefits through successful OII projects; create tailored projects for HCOs; later on automate, using a high usability platform	"The ideal situation will be that: we have a core group of like super-creative, empowered patients who use our piece of technology to do what we are doing as the commercial company. You know, crowdsourcing and then crowdfunding, something within their community that they need. But people don't do that off the bath. I think we will need some big wins first." (PC, paragraph 52)
↳	↳	Users have privacy concerns	Establish a transp. data privacy policy; only ask for necessary inform.	"We have also noticed that our target group of users was very cautious with regard to data privacy concerns. That's why we tried to collect as little data as possible, so to say the most indispensable data only." (ID, paragraph 34)

(continued)

Table 4.7 (continued)

Challenge	Sub-Challenge	Problem	Proposed Mitigation	Anchor Quote
Attract user base	Gain critical mass	Building up the traffic takes long time	Online marketing and social media can help	*"That is a big challenge. Building up the traffic has taken many years and that is a big part of the challenge. Social media has been incredibly helpful in the last three years. Our traffic increased for about 100% in the past year, and that is largely a result of using Twitter and Facebook as ways to increase our profile. But there is no simple solution to that." (PO, paragraph65)*
↳	↳	Community management is difficult due to topical complexity	Strengthen role of moderator as translator to mitigate topical complexity for users; Improve initial project set-up through OII	*"Overall there is the problem that the community management turned out to be quite difficult. In the context of such disease patterns, it is extremly hard to trigger nourishing discussions or to give profound comments. It is quite specific indeed and you only understand it to its full extent if you are affected yourself or if you know somebody who is affected. As a moderator you are ususally not." (ID, paragraph29)*
↳	↳	Users are not altruistic; if there is nothing really in it for them, they turn away	Focus on as pecific topical area, e.g. by condition; Use incentive scheme to make users come back	*"People aren't very altruistic as we would like them to be! If there is nothing really in it for them, they turn away." (PC, paragraph39)*
Attract user base	Ensure Usability	Large proportion of the Internet traffic and of website uses is moving onto mobile devices	Build mobile app or easily scalable website	*"I think the big challenge now is that such a large proportion of Internet traffic and of website uses is moving into mobile. So, we have to find effective ways to do this on small devices. That is not going to be easy. But we are thinking about how we can address that challenge of making it possible to interact with PO or leave feedback, even when you have small mobile device." (PO, paragraph75)*
↳	↳	Platform features are implemented unsatisfactorily	Increase developer ressources	*„Wir hatten echt viele Funktionen, aber man hätte es besser machen können. Wir hatten einfach technische Probleme. Manche Inhalte wurden falsch dargestellt, Inhalte, die man eigentlich hätte nicht sehen dürfen, wurden angezeigt. Also nicht mehr Funktionalität, aber die bestehende Funktionalität besser umsetzen oder auch einfacher für den Nutzer machen, benutzerfreundlicher quasi." (GS, paragraph92)*
↳	↳	Platform is too complicated for users	Rethink usability concept, make it very simple	*"I think what we learned along the way is that, there has to be made very simple, because that are aspirations of universality. And we had actually started over with a more complicated platform that we have narrowed down." (HU, paragraph14)*

(continued)

Table 4.7 (continued)

Challenge	Sub-Challenge	Problem	Proposed Mitigation	Anchor Quote
☞	☞	Upgrade of the platform software creates issues. System does not run properly, detracts users	Improve upgrade releases	"Just recently we had a platform upgrade. There were few changes that attracted people in a kind of quite bad way. The system did not work well for a couple of weeks. And you understand the dependency that the people have on the system and how important it is that it is trusted and a good place to be. So you also understand the vulnerability, if you make errors whether through the platform or through the data, there is no place to hide really. And that is why we want everything to be nice and right at the user level." (HU, paragraph 79)
HCO conviction	–	Best practices are not available	Test and experiment with new practices	"But my problem with the traditional focus group is that they've already designed this product and gone down the whole path and then they want to see what buttons you push. That's not the same as involving patients from the construction to all the way through prototyping of the product. It is getting better, I admit. I personally have consulted with a number of companies in early stages of product development, not the big, big players but some of the smaller companies. So, I think, everyone is struggling to figure out what the right and best practices are for involving patients." (DM, paragraph 111)
☞	☞	Little demand for OII services	Show benefits for HCOs through successful OII projects	"I should have talked about it. The market research services have actually not been used as much as I expected it would do." (DU, paragraph 59)
☞	☞	Responsibles at HCOs are not entirely convinced about the new, non-traditional approach	Show benefits for HCOs through successful OII projects	"We had very little partners who were really convinced about our approach on innovation. Very often we had to explain it through telephone calls, visits or presentations. It dragged on for a long time. And then we were able to get them interested in it - but only in a very few cases. We didn't meet anybody who was really, really keen to go for open innovation. Most of the companies we talked to were not aware of it at all." (HH, paragraph 72)
Cultural barriers	–	Fear of change	Show benefits for HCOs through successful OII projects	"A lot of what inhibits changes is fear, I think. Certainly with this. People are very scared. They are scared of the technology, scared of the transparency, the publicness, and they are scared of the lack of control they have over it. So, there are all kinds of fears that stop people engaging. And to show them that there are other people who are doing it, who had the same fears when they started, but now do not have the fears because they have learned that this is

(continued)

Table 4.7 (continued)

Challenge	Sub-Challenge	Problem	Proposed Mitigation	Anchor Quote
		Resistance to new, non-traditional approach	Set up HCO organizational processes for taking feedback in real time and using it to change health services	OK. [] We have to show the benefits. It is all very well to say that it should work in theory, but we have to show practical benefits, otherwise people will not want to spend their money on it. That is a big challenge, too." (PO, paragraph 90) "Lots of organizations have been very resistant to PO, and still are. There are lots of organizations that do not want to use it or refused to use it, or think it is a waste of time. And there are organizations that use it, but do not really know what to do with it. I do not think any of it is straight at all, I think, there are lots of barriers there. There are substantial, cultural, or organizational barriers. There is no real history of use of feedback, of learning from feedback in the health service. There are no organizational processes or very few for taking feedback in real time and using it to change services. So, this is all very new to these organizations, and it is not something that we can change very fast. The NHS is a massive system, and even the smallest organizations in the NHS will employ thousands of people. There are plenty of org. or cultural barriers to using it." (PO, paragraph 58)
Organizational barriers	-	Insufficient and insular support from HCO to drive OII projects	Install support from both top management and operational level	"Yes, some organizations have subscribed [to our service] but then nothing very much seems to happen. Organizations are very complex and very different things and sometimes, there will be one person in an organization that drives something forward and makes something happen and makes something really interesting happen, and then another kind of organization, there is only some kind of top-level support but there is nobody driving it, so nothing happens." (PO, paragraph 85)
Legal barriers	-	Legal Liability for Involving with Patients	Adjust technological features to the legal liability that you can take	"There is a legal issue. If you start involving with peers, in any way, or how will they structure their ideas, you may be legally liable for whatever comes out of it. And legal liability means that if anything bad happens, somebody can sue you and you go to jail as a Member of an Executive Board. That's maybe the most pressing issue, a legal issue. What I've learnt from this so far is that: how specific legal frameworks in countries actually limit the technological choices within the platform." (PI, paragraph 29)

(continued)

Table 4.7 (continued)

Challenge	Sub-Challenge	Problem	Proposed Mitigation	Anchor Quote
OII service model	OII concept	HCOs are complex and sometimes slow organizations, partially open for change only	Do not overwhelm HCO with change - fit in seamlessly in some parts	"I think, the easiest way to fit into these institutions right now is to actually not change in too many ways. The best thing you can do is actually fit in seamlessly in some parts of their intervention processes."(GI, paragraph118)
⮧		Insufficient OII ressources	Increase OII ressources and HCO ressources; get partners onboard with a genuine interest in the ideas	"Eventually we were lacking enough staff. I guess you could have done more out of it. But also the professional partners could have benefited from it much more. But at the end, the problem is that you need people who do it. We had supporters from our partners but these were all not very big, non-commercial organizations. Among others Centres for Rares Diseases, Centres organizationally attached to hospitals. We had the impression they also didn't have the resources to support the ideas from the patients. I guess, they didn't know yet how to derive benefit for them." (GS, paragraph45)
⮧		OII broker model is difficult in health	Move away from "broker model" to "agency model"	"What we are trying to do is to move away from is kind of locked value-generating model where it takes quite a lot time and effort to set up an individual relationship. You are acting as a broker between the patient population and the kind of commercial body. That is complicated in health. And what we are doing now really is moving to a model where we can get pretty much everyone adopt a community position within our platform. So we are moving towards digital health agencies who use us as a sort of platform that can mediate between patients and commercial companies. And hospitals or pharmaceutical companies can start getting a presence in our platform rather than just being a third party in the platform." (HU, paragraph23)
⮧		OII has no direct returns early on	Define success metrics for early phase to better justify this type of innovation work	"Often these kind of innovation platforms are in its early stages and it is hard to show direct return early on. So, what are the metrics and the measures for success in the early stages of projects? Metrics that help to track participation and to track the uptake or the kind of health and the innovation kind of collaboration platform?" (CN, paragraph109)
⮧		OII's contribution to a project is too little	Link online and offline worlds	"We had a lot of activities, not only interviews, through the platform, but also as offline events, meetings, etc. We didn't fail at the bottom level. What I mean is that we were not able to contribute to a real project and to see its outcome." (HH, paragraph19)

(continued)

Table 4.7 (continued)

Challenge	Sub-Challenge	Problem	Proposed Mitigation	Anchor Quote
↪	↪	Value proposition too vague	Continuously iterate and adjust the current OII service model; in order to discover your value proposition	"In part of the start processes, your product what you are building evolves as you're learning more about what the market is interested in. So, when we started a couple of years ago, we were writing on our experiments because that's the only way that you can learn. So you start out, you iterate and that's how you discover your value proposition." (GI, paragraph 86)
OII service model	Catalyze / scale ideas	Idea adoption and scaling is difficult	Get stakeholders involved early on to adopt the new ideas	"So, coming up with ideas is not the hard part. It is actually getting patient, doctors and everyone to really adopt these things and to scale. And my reaction to that: if you get people involved in the conversation on day one, in designing and developing these products or services, when it comes to finally launching, you already got the audience engaged. So that becomes a much easier job. So, just scale the product." (PC, paragraph 33)
	↪	Idea adoption and scaling is difficult	Link online and offline worlds, for example through on-site prototype days	"If it's a great idea, one of the first things we do is get hold of that member and invite them to prototype days, ask them to develop it with us, with the sponsor. Because you know, a startup in healthcare is probably one of the hardest startups to do. Given the environment, it's unlikely that people who come on the platform have substantial experiences or have ideas, will have the means and the infrastructure to roll something out." (PC, paragraph 23)
OII service model	Diverging interests	Diverging interests between patients and HCOs	Install OII role as a real mediator between diverging interests	"The complaint we got from women was, they were being used, as I said, because the researchers in fact didn't want to do what they claimed. In terms of a business and making companies to do this, this is a really important point because what people say they want isn't always what they really want." (AW, paragraph 29)
HCO-OII partnering	–	For-profit HCOs have limited position of trust	Cooperate with non-profit organizations	"There is a big potential in this field and there is a lot of people engaged-but they are coming at it from the informatics side. But the question is will the public want it? And will they really be able to develop it into a sustainable business? [...] I have my doubts that people will just go to a company and give all our data away freely. Rather I think the non-profits probably have a stronger position, a more trusted position that would allow them to do it. So maybe what these companies or these smart guys with technology need to do is really care more with the non-profits- so you get the advantage of both, rather than trying to do it themselves." (AW, paragraph 134)

(continued)

Table 4.7 (continued)

Challenge	Sub-Challenge	Problem	Proposed Mitigation	Anchor Quote
↩	↩	HCO dominance could destroy peer-to-peer openness	OII to mediate between diverging interests	"Whether we are going to have our facilitation of the relationships with legal entities, whether they are involved in some kind of commercialization, this is still a subject of careful analysis. Why do we say careful analysis? That's an advantage to have such entities onboard, and also a threat. Because they may takeover this and destroy the whole process of peer-to-peer openness, right. And that's something that we are trying to avoid." (PI, paragraph 27)
↩	↩	Limited implementation of ideas at HCOs	Select HCOs who have the skills to eventually implement users' solutions	"It is critical for success to have companies onboard who can potentially implement the idea at stake. And if this company listens in from the very beginning at the platform interactions, then credibility and motivation increases. This was always clear to us, but so to speak, we failed at this point though." (HH, paragraph 55)
↩	↩	No HCO involved who could professionally exploit the patients' solutions	Get HCOs onboard with genuine interest to grow patients' ideas	Our partners did not really support us to grow or implement the patients' ideas. It is true we had a jury of experts to assess the ideas and to decide over which idea is to be developed further. So they did their job and then they did not care anymore about the progress of the initiative. (GS, paragraph 36)

4.5.1 OII Activities and Types

Based on an analysis by Lopez-Vega et al. (2009) who studied the activities of innovation intermediaries in general (see Table 4.1), Hallerstede (2013) had nominated some activities that are particularly served by OIIs in virtual environments (cf. Sect. 4.2.1). The current findings on the identified key activities of OII include some new insight that is discussed in the following.

Overall, the current findings merge into the prior grouping and confirm Hallerstede's assessment. However, the findings do partly overlap but identify new activities of OIIs that have not been described earlier. It thus contributes to the research stream on virtual intermediaries for co-creation that are termed OIIs in this work. This new category of intermediaries fulfills traditional functions of intermediaries, but also deals with the requirements of its specific environment. Moreover, as co-creation describes a dynamic process of creating something, OIIs have to deal with more than just exchanging self-contained artifacts and need to assist the dynamic creation process between the involved parties. This is reflected in the findings. Figure 4.9 compares the newly found activities to prior knowledge and depicts its relations. The relations are explicated next.

First, the *facilitation activity* covers core functions of an intermediary, such as linking and matching stakeholders. This activity thus fits well in the prior *connection group* and is largely covered by the foregoing *gatekeeping and brokering* activity.

Second, the observed *support activity* of OIIs consist of sub-activities like managing online conversations of the OII online users and related administrative-technical support. It enables a productive interaction between users

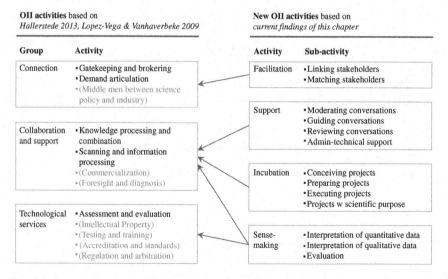

Fig. 4.9 Found OII activities in relation to prior grouping

and the OII and relates well to the prior *collaboration and support group*. This is not just because 'support' is in its name already, but because the new support activities can be subsumed in the prior *information processing* and *knowledge processing* activities. The new support activities, however, present a clear focus on virtual environments which is not explicitly covered by the prior listing. Hence, at this point the new activities not just confirm but enhance the prior listing.

Third, the reported *incubation activity* of OII is not reflected as such in the existing grouping. It seems to be an activity that is special to OIIs in the analyzed context. Hence, it enhances the existing grouping at this point. Incubation activity can certainly be understood as an activity that suits well in the *collaboration and support group*. If an OII offers incubation activity, it certainly strengthens the collaboration between HCO and OII and provides support for the HCO in terms of the setup and execution of co-creation projects. In this case, the OII takes a more active role than just serving as a broker between two parties.

Fourth, the last activity identified is the *sense-making activity*. In the investigated empirical setting, sense-making covers the interpretation of collected information and its evaluation. It is an activity that confirms prior findings. However, the interpretation of collected information can be subsumed under *knowledge combination*, while the evaluation sub-activity rather falls into *assessment and evaluation*.

Based on typical configurations of these key activities, the analysis reveals four types of OIIs. Each OII type suits best to different approaches of HCOs towards co-creation depending on the development of in-house capabilities. In a next step, initial theoretical propositions are developed based on the insights from the data. It suggests the contingencies under which the different OII types would be most useful for HCOs. Among all four types of OIIs, the proactive agent has clearly the most power to shape co-creation projects for HCOs. Due to the OII's incubation, support, and sense-making activities, the proactive agent positions itself as a strong middleman between HCOs and consumers. The proactive agent is ideal for HCOs who have not developed own capabilities to design and implement co-creation projects with HCCs. Accordingly, it can be posited that:

> **Proposition 4.1**: Proactive agents including their designated activities and value potential enable consumer co-creation for HCOs with limited in-house capabilities in this field.

The support provider is the most common OII type in the sample. Support providers have often developed a distinct platform technology which enables them to offer specific tools and methods for co-creation through their platform. Their strength lies in activities on support, sense-making, and facilitation. HCOs with well-developed plans for co-creation projects may find an ideal partner in the support provider. It can be proposed that:

> **Proposition 4.2**: Support providers including their designated activities and value potential enable consumer co-creation for HCOs with advanced in-house capabilities in this field.

The community champion operates co-creation projects for the benefit of the consumer community itself. HCOs assume a more passive role as they do not have an agenda for specific co-creation projects. HCOs partnering with community champions acknowledge the positive potential that lies in co-creation projects with HCCs. It can be posited that:

> **Proposition 4.3**: Community champions including their designated activities and value potential enable consumer co-creation for HCOs with lacking in-house capabilities in this field and a passive innovation approach.

The bridge builder is the least complex of OII types. Its capability lies in matchmaking HCO requests to relevant consumers from the OII user pool. HCOs using bridge builders are aware of their extensive network reach and acknowledge the innovation potential of healthcare consumers for their own co-creation projects that they may conduct detachedly from the intermediary's online platform.

> **Proposition 4.4**: Bridge builders including their designated activities and value potential enable consumer co-creation for HCOs with advanced in-house capabilities in this field.

The proposed OII types go beyond Chesbrough's (2006) and Howells' (2006) seminal description of the role played by innovation intermediaries. Whereas Chesbrough discussed a type of intermediary facilitating the participation of external sources of ideas and Howells mostly referred to industry and technology research associations, the current analysis focuses on pure OIIs that seek to leverage the innovation potential of (healthcare) consumers.

4.5.2   Directions for Further Research

The investigation conducted in this chapter has three limitations, which yield implications for future research. First, as it is commonly the case with qualitative research, the sample size of 24 interviewed platform representatives is not large although the search process for appropriate OIIs was extensive. Because of the exploratory nature of the analysis, it is not possible to statistically generalize the findings to populations or organizations or markets. Further confirmatory empirical research that validates the above findings and propositions could provide more insights on the relative impact of the four OII types on innovation outcomes. The emerging OII types could also be tested in other contexts than healthcare.

Second, the current state of OIIs that the interviewees conveyed is only a "snapshot" at a particular point in time. This field has a highly dynamic pattern of growth and development, so some existing OIIs may fail in the short-term or some new entrants may emerge. Continued research is warranted to investigate the types of OIIs and their value generating potential because it remains an emerging and yet promising lever for healthcare innovation.

Third, when investigating the value generating potential of OIIs and related challenges, the views of the HCOs as the actual beneficiaries should be taken into account; that was out of the scope for the current study. The challenges described above could prompt risk-averse and predictability-seeking HCOs to avoid co-creation. More empirical and analytical studies, particularly including the HCO perspective, are justified on the trade-offs between the value potential and the challenges of consumer co-creation in the short and long run.

Future research should also measure the specific impact of the OII phenomenon on the innovation process, ideally in a quantitative manner. In this respect, it would be important to compare the efficiency and effectiveness of the innovation process at HCOs that use OIIs and at HCOs that do not collaborate with OIIs. In the end, any outcome stimulated through OIIs and co-creation respectively should be measured by its impact on the organization's innovation performance. Dalziel and Parjanen (2012) suggest three ranks of impact levels: *immediate impacts* such as increased resources or capabilities, *intermediate impacts* such as improved performance or revenues, and *ultimate impacts* such as socio-economic benefits. To realize these kinds of impacts, academics and practitioners alike need to identify ways of planning, managing, and implementing complex processes of co-creation on all levels, as noted by Hoyer et al. (2010).

It is the intent of this chapter that the presented findings will inform future theoretical and empirical studies regarding strategies of OIIs and interactions between OIIs and their innovation-seeking clients.

4.6 Conclusion

Using a qualitative research design, this chapter uncovers what online innovation intermediaries (OIIs) in healthcare actually do when they engage in co-creation projects with the ecosystem of stakeholders, i.e. healthcare organizations (HCOs) and healthcare consumers (HCCs). The interview data suggest that there are four key activities that OIIs perform: *facilitation*, *support*, *incubation*, and *sense-making*. These activities can be grouped into archetypical bundles which give rise to four distinct types of OIIs in healthcare. The types are designated as the *proactive agent*, the *support provider*, the *community champion*, and the *bridge builder*. Furthermore, the study discloses different forms of value-add for HCOs that are differentially generated by the OII types. The value generated falls in the areas of *network reach*, *lay expertise*, *professional expertise*, and *digital literacy*. Lastly, the study uncovers seven areas of challenges that impede current co-creation practices in the OII ecosystem. Mitigations for these challenges are proposed as well.

The results make two important contributions to the research literature. First, it enhances the research stream on co-creation and innovation intermediaries. It adds theoretical nuance towards a conceptual understanding of OIIs in healthcare. Based on rich empirical evidence, the activities of OIIs are outlined in greater detail. Compared to an analysis by Lopez-Vega et al. (2009) who studied the activities of innovation intermediaries in general, it is observed that activities of OII in healthcare partly overlap but are much more focused on a few core activities. All four key activities contribute to create social relationships and an atmosphere of trust and confidentiality—aspects that are particularly important in the healthcare set-up where some HCCs are highly affected by their conditions. Moreover, this investigation advocates for the crucial role of OIIs in healthcare, and extends the understanding of Nambisan and Nambisan (2009) by suggesting that the assumption of a direct co-creation process between HCOs and consumers deserves revisiting. In many settings, this relationship is often mediated through OIIs and their platforms respectively. For HCOs, this can be a major advantage as some are restricted by regulatory requirements to step into direct contact with HCCs. Other organizations may just want to start interacting with HCCs on a more independent and neutral platform that is less influenced by a specific company reputation. Further, the empirical data informs the understanding of individuals (here HCCs) as external sources of innovation, responding to the call by West and Bogers (2013) that this domain is under-researched.

Second, this study adds healthcare-specific findings to the research streams on online health communities and innovation intermediaries. Existing studies have examined aspects such as the motivations and concerns of patients to participate, the confidentiality of medical information, or social value creation in online health communities. This study adds a new perspective that is informed by open innovation and co-creation as it suggests that some of these online health platforms can be part of OII organizations who systematically support and run co-creation activities. However, it becomes clear that the healthcare domain entails specific challenges regarding the design and management of platform-based intermediation for co-creation in healthcare. In particular, OIIs have to deal with trust issues of HCCs and persistent organizational and legal barriers of HCOs, to name a few.

The managerial implications of the results suggest that innovation managers at HCOs need to consider OIIs as a valuable mechanism for improving their innovation outcomes. OIIs can help HCOs to adopt appropriate strategies and practices to embrace HCCs as partners in the development and delivery of innovative healthcare products and services. The findings also underscore the need for alignment in choice of OII types: an engagement with an OII should seek congruence with the in-house capabilities available, and the type of OII and its activities provided. Independent of the breadth and maturity of available OIIs today, a majority of the experts interviewed confirm the widely untapped potential of healthcare consumers' knowledge pool and its increasing importance while HCOs seek new ways to enhance the quality and the value of their offerings. As one interviewee compellingly observed: *"There is lots of talk now of feedback and needing to hear from patients in a way that there wasn't ten years ago. So, that is a sort of outcome we are also pleased with"*.

Chapter 5
Empirical Study III: Organizational Adoption of User Innovation Inputs

5.1 Needs and Goals[1]

As the benefits of platform-based open innovation approaches are widely reported (Bullinger et al. 2010; Chesbrough and Brunswicker 2013; Nambisan and Baron 2010; Sawhney et al. 2005), there are many examples of organizations that have initiated the use of self-developed or third party operated online platforms for innovation. The previous two studies of this work investigated OIIs in detail. The focus was to understand their role as middlemen between HCCs and HCOs. However, to complete the conceptual picture, the perspective of HCOs who have retained OII services for consumer co-creation should be added.

According to the theoretical framework presented in Chap. 2, it is the said goal that effective consumer co-creation mediated by OIIs shall contribute to the HCO innovation performance. One important link for this to happen is the *adoption* of consumer-generated input by the innovation-seeking organization. However, it seems that the organizational adoption of user innovation input (UII) generated through OII platforms is not always successful, i.e. neither does it necessarily lead to sustained innovation in the form of novel or improved products and services, nor does it imply commercial advantage for innovating HCOs by default. It appears there is a disconnection between sometimes outstanding innovative ideas from HCCs and its systematic professional development and commercial exploitation by HCOs (Cepiku and Savignon 2015). Therefore, this chapter focuses on the HCO perspective and, in particular, on the organizational adoption of consumer-generated innovation input.

---

[1]An earlier version of this chapter was presented at the 10th Research Seminar on Innovation and Value Creation as Kuenne (2015). For more details concerning the communication of the research, see Annex A.

© Springer International Publishing AG 2018
C.W. Künne, *Online Intermediaries for Co-Creation*, Progress in IS,
DOI 10.1007/978-3-319-51124-5_5

In their comprehensive literature review on "leveraging external sources of innovation", West and Bogers (2013) suggests a four-phase model in which a linear process—(1) obtaining, (2) integrating, and (3) commercializing external innovations—is combined with (4) interaction between the innovation-seeking organization and its collaborators. In the integration phase, abundant research has studied the role of *absorptive capacity* (Cohen and Levinthal 1990) as a complement for integrating external innovation. This concept subsumes the effect that internal R&D capabilities have on the ability to utilize external knowledge for innovation (Cohen and Levinthal 1990). However, it seems that absorptive capacity remains a broad and sometimes vague concept. It does not provide insights on how UII is adopted. Explanations mostly remain on the generic level of 'the more absorptive capacity, the more successful/effective is the UII adoption'. West and Bogers (2013:15) conclude their review by stating:

> This review has shown an extensive body of research on the front end of the process of externally sourcing innovation, but leaves major gaps on how such innovation is integrated and ultimately commercialized. As such, it remains unclear how external innovations travel from the outside to a commercial product through the firm's business model and to what extent it requires distinct innovation strategies.

In a similar vein, Hoyer et al. (2010) ascertain that the connections between an organization's effort for consumer co-creation and its positive impact in the marketplace are insufficiently understood. They argue that these connections have to be disclosed and measured in order to warrant investments in consumer co-creation.

For the above reasons, this third study aims to reduce this gap by addressing the adoption process of UII. To the degree that innovation intermediary platforms will become increasingly significant in a sector where knowledge resources within organizational boundaries are limited, the purpose of this third study is to understand the different stages of the organizational adoption process for user innovation inputs in order to maximize successful innovation outputs. Therefore, the following research question is addressed:

RQ 3: How do HCOs adopt user innovation inputs generated through an OII?

Using a qualitative design, this question will be explored along an in-depth case study from the medical device industry. The selection of the case is based on earlier findings of this research. The OII platform used by the focal organization is classified as type 'proactive agent'. With regard to theory, Rogers' well-established theory on the diffusion of innovations (Rogers 2003) serves as a conceptual starting point. A part of this theory is the description of the adoption process of innovations that is of importance for this study.[2] It provides relevant guidance, however, it is argued that it is lacking nuance especially when organizations adopt user innovation inputs.

The remainder of this chapter is organized as follows. The next section presents a theoretical review on the adoption of innovations and elaborates on Rogers' theory. Section 5.3 explains the qualitative research design and introduces the focal healthcare organization analyzed for the case study. Findings based on interviews with key informants and other data sources are presented in Sect. 5.4, including rich empirical evidence. Then, Sect. 5.5 proposes a refined model of adoption while discussing its contribution and limitation to the aforementioned gap. Section 5.6 concludes this chapter.

5.2 Theoretical Underpinning

Based on the elaboration of Chap. 2, this section adds the necessary theoretical underpinning for the third empirical study. The purpose for which co-creation is run is to positive influence the innovation performance of HCOs through jointly created knowledge with HCCs (cf. the definition of co-creation in Sect. 2.1.1.2). In order to evaluate the effect of co-creation, this study looks at the organizational adoption of co-created knowledge artifacts. In line with the knowledge-based theory of the firm (cf. the theoretical framework in Sect. 2.2), knowledge is considered as the most strategically important resource of an organization. Hence, if a HCO adopts knowledge artifacts from co-creation activities, then it can be considered valuable for the organizational performance. Knowledge artifacts from co-creation activities which are potential candidates for organizational adoption are referred to as user innovation input (UII) in this study.

Theories of the adoption of innovations are to be seen in the wider context of organizational change. Adoption happens if an organization recognizes a performance gap that creates a need for change. Therefore, this chapter is organized as follows. The interrelation of organizational change and innovation is explained in Sect. 5.2.1. Then, common elements of innovation adoption are presented and Rogers' theory is introduced as theory of choice for this study (Sect. 5.2.2). Important distinctions regarding the applicability of this theory to the present context are added in Sect. 5.2.3.

---

[2]For conceptual clarity: *adoption* refers the decision of an individual or an organization to make use of an innovation, while *diffusion* refers to the accumulation of users, who have adopted an innovation, in a market (Rogers 2003). This study deals with the organizational adoption of innovations.

5.2.1   Organizational Change

Before approaching the adoption of innovations, it is useful to give an overview of the total change process relating to organizations. Figure 5.1 displays the paradigm of organizational change and innovation based on the representation by Zaltman et al. (1973). To start, every organization exists within a social milieu or megasystem. It consists of two levels. The first level is the general industry that includes rivaling organizations, consumers, suppliers, unions etc. It is thus the direct external environment of the organization. The second level reflects the indirect external environment of the organization, which is the society in general as well as the feeder network of the particular industry that indirectly influences its prosperity, such as education, science, or governmental activity.

If the structure or the functioning of the social milieu alters, particularly on the first level, then *social change* occurs (Rogers and Svenning 1969). This change may entail *performance gaps*. Performance gaps are differences between what the organization could do and what it actually does with regard to exploiting an opportunity. For example, a performance gap may occur when product requirements by consumers or regulatory agencies change. As soon as the performance gap is recognized, i.e. the organization becomes aware of it, a new *need* can be formulated (Zaltman et al. 1973). The awareness of a gap and the resulting need release resources and conditions for changing the structure and the functioning of the organization. This entails a *search for solutions* to bridge the gap. Either existing solutions are tracked down or new solutions need to be developed by internal R&D resources or external agencies.

In case of alternative solutions, the most appropriate option has to be identified through a *decision-making* process by the relevant group within the organization. Ultimately, after narrowing down the solution options, the most appropriate solution is *adopted* for implementation, or is *rejected* at this point. In the positive case of adoption, the sustained *implementation* will lead to a change in the organization that bridges the initial performance gap. In the negative case of rejection, the process may begin again as the gap and its related solution need is not satisfied.

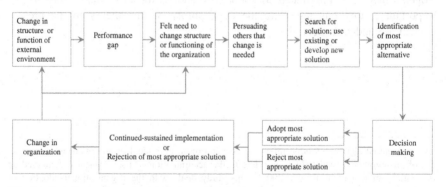

Fig. 5.1 Paradigm of organizational change and innovation (Zaltman et al. 1973)

To conclude, it is important to note that innovations can create social change and social change can create additional innovations in return. The organizational adoption of innovation, which is at the core of this study, takes place against the backdrop of the paradigm of organizational change.

5.2.2 Adoption of Innovations

Innovations come to organizations either through *generation* from internal sources or *adoption* from external sources (Damanpour and Wischnevsky 2006). Proponents of open models of innovation models argue that organizations should strive for a mix of both internal and external sources of innovation (Chesbrough 2003; von Hippel 1988, 2005). The generation of innovations from internal sources is a process that results in an innovation outcome in form of a new product, service, process, structure, program, or technology. If this outcome is for sale and is acquired by an individual or other decision-making unit, then the second entity goes through the process of adopting an innovation from an external source. The adoption process is a sequence of stages that a potential adopter goes through before an innovation is fully assimilated.

From the perspective of the adopting unit, the adoption process of innovations can be subdivided into two major stages *initiation* and *implementation* (Zaltman et al. 1973). At the transition point between the two stages, the idea becomes legitimated by powerholders of the adopting unit and a decision is made to implement it. Subsequently, the stage of implementation deals with the actual procedures of changing the structure and functioning of the adopting unit and its subsystems. Large parts of the literature on organizational change contribute to the latter stage (e.g., Bennis 1966; Hornstein et al. 1971). Figure 5.2 summarizes some of the various process models of organizational adoption. All these models shall not be explained in detail at this point, but, despite their differences, commonalities can be traced with regard to the similarity of stages. This study will lean on the model by Rogers as it found wide dissemination and acceptance over the last decades (first edition 1962, fifth edition 2003).

According to Rogers (2003), the adoption process entails five stages that typically follow each other in a time-ordered manner. First, the *knowledge stage* at which the adopter is exposed to an innovation's existence and gathers information about "what the innovation is and how and why it works" (Rogers 2003:21). Second, at the *persuasion stage* the adopter forms a negative or positive attitude toward the innovation. Rogers clarifies that the mental activity at the persuasion stage is mostly affective, while it is more cognitive at the preceding knowledge stage (Rogers 2003). Third, the *decision stage* at which the potential adopter chooses to adopt or reject the innovation. Rogers (2003:177) defines adoption as "the decision to make full use of an innovation as the best course of action available", while a rejection is a decision not to adopt. At the next fourth stage, the *implementation stage*, the adopted innovation is put into practice. Up to this point,

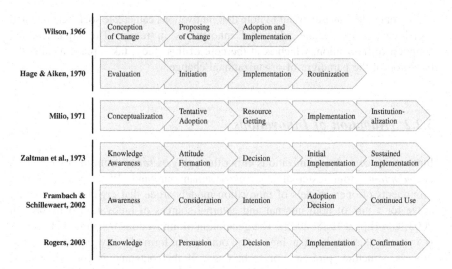

Fig. 5.2 Comparison of organizational oriented models of innovation adoption

the adoption process has been an activity of thinking and deciding only. From this point onwards, the implementation of the innovation is causing structural or behavioral change at the adopting unit. If it becomes necessary to modify an innovation during the course of implementation, then it also happens at this stage (Rogers refers to this as 'reinvention'). And fifth, the *confirmation stage* serves to reassure whether the adoption decision is still right under the additional knowledge gained after implementation. The continued use or the discontinuance of the innovation are the two options here. This process can be considered a success when the adopting unit demonstrates commitment through the sustained use of the adopted element over a period of time (Bhattacherjee 1998).

5.2.3   Distinctions to Present Theory

In this chapter, Rogers' theory is used to analyze the company under study and to unfold the findings later. However, it is important to point out some distinctions. Traditionally, adoption theories, also the one by Rogers, have focused on the adoption of a single innovation (e.g. Apple's iPad) by multiple potential adopters (e.g. customers). However, in the context of this chapter, it is the goal to analyze one single adopter across several innovations. This is a twist to Rogers' original idea. Also, this study strictly focuses on the innovation adoption at the organizational side that may possibly be different than the adoption at the individual's side.

Rogers' theory generally applies to both adopter types but it appears that it is inclined to the individual's side though (Zaltman et al. 1973).

Furthermore, in the existing models of organizational adoption, adoption is often compared to a company buying an innovation, i.e. a novel product, from a supplier. This novel product is a physical product that has been fully developed and marketed by the supplier. Turning over to the context of this study, it deals with the adoption of *user innovation inputs* (as it was termed earlier) and as such they are distinctively different in four ways. First, they are *not fully developed* products but they appear in form of conceptual ideas, knowledge or data from users. Second, they are *intangible* because the UIIs are basically knowledge artifacts. Third, they still require significant *further maturing* from the adopting organization in order to generate an innovation outcome in terms of improved or novel products. And forth, they are generated in *online* settings.

Having clarified the theoretical underpinning for this chapter, the next section is about to present the methodical approach as well as the case company.

5.3 Method and Data

This section details the method and the data of the empirical study at hand. It is the goal of this chapter to add the HCO perspective to the overall understanding of the OII phenomenon. Therefore, the current study examines one HCO in detail using a single-case study design. The first subsection justifies the underlying research approach, followed by a comprehensive introduction to the chosen case company in Sect. 5.3.2. Section 5.3.3 explains the types of data used and how these were gathered and then Sect. 5.3.4 clarifies how this data was analyzed.

5.3.1 Research Approach

To study the emerging phenomenon of organizations adopting UII about which limited understanding exists, a qualitative research design is utilized that supports rich, contextualized insights in nascent domains (Creswell 2009). To answer the research question, a *holistic single-case study* was chosen (Yin 2003). The case study as a research strategy allows the researcher to gain "an understanding [of the] dynamics present within single settings" (Eisenhardt 1989:534). The inherent advantage in case study research is that a multitude of perspectives can be gained through their rich nature of different sources of evidence (Eisenhardt 1991; Yin 2003). The researcher can develop an in-depth understanding about the situation, the relationships, the processes and, thus, the phenomenon under study (Bergenholtz 2011; Dyer and Wilkins 1991).

Yin (2003:47) recognizes several rationales for selecting a single over a multiple case study. Here, the rationale for selecting a single case is the leading character of the chosen case. The case, i.e. the unit of analysis, represents a product development project that was performed by a healthcare organization utilizing an online intermediary platform in order to include healthcare consumers in the development process. It has a leading character because the particular case was the most promising project among many other projects performed. Beyond, the host company has invested heavily in co-creation and user involvement over many years and thus gained extensive experience.

The purpose of this case study is not to test the findings of earlier chapters of this work, but to continue the line of research by further exploring and illustrating how inputs generated in co-creation settings are adopted by HCOs. As such, it is inductive in nature.

5.3.2 Introduction to the Case Company

The unit of analysis of the case study is a specific product development project that started in 2012 at a major international medical device company. In this work, the company will be referred to under the fictitious name *Salpo*. Salpo develops, manufactures and markets medical devices and services related to ostomy, urology, continence, and wound care. About 80% of their activities are in the chronic care business which is mostly continent care and ostomy care. Product development and related product launches are organizationally accommodated in the global research and development (R&D) department which is governed by the board of directors. During the development process, Salpo's global R&D department works closely together with other departments such as commercial, marketing, and production. For example, the commercial team defines the segments that the company wants to be in, the strategic product portfolio, and the user needs that the company wants to address in the future. Then, global R&D works closely with the production side which runs so-called innovation factories that are low-volume production sites in geographically close locations. After a product has been developed, the joint teams ramp up the production for product launches at one of the innovation factories. This includes building up the production equipment and production lines, and stabilizing the production process of the new product. After one, maximum two years and a successful acceptance in the market, the production of the new product is moved to one of Salpo's high volume production sites in Eastern Europe or Far East. Finally, the newly launched product is internally handed over to the product lifecycle management department and it leaves the R&D department.

Apart from traditional internal innovation, Salpo has gained, for more than 20 years, extensive experience with the involvement of external innovation sources (i.e. physicians, nurses, patients) in the product development. It is a fundamental part of the company DNA. The knowledge and experience of the product users is considered a valuable asset for the product development and innovation funnel.

Salpo has established multiple both offline and online approaches to integrate the user's perspective into innovation. One is the *anthropology approach* which serves to observe patients in their homes or in rehabilitation centers in their daily lives handling the products. Often patients cannot express their next great idea. So with these observations, Salpo's teams can identify patients' needs and create some new product ideas and refine existing concepts.

Another approach is *user advisory boards*. These are a worldwide network of healthcare professionals, mainly nurses who deal with the patients on a daily basis either in hospitals, rehabilitation centers or during home visits. It has the advantage of getting an informed perspective from those who are involved in post-operative care and treatment and who can articulate needs which might for the individual patient be difficult or embarrassing to express. They have regular meetings with global product development teams and the member's role is particularly to identify trends, product wishes, product feedback, but also to evaluate concepts and prototypes suggested by Salpo's global R&D. The user advisory boards have also initiated local *focus groups* with selected patients for specific development projects. In terms of numbers, there are about 20–30 specialized nurses in each country in Europe who are part of the user advisory board which in total makes about 500 professional user experts in Europe. In each country, there are usually two to five very clear key opinion leaders that have also gained some reputation internationally. By setting up user advisory boards in different countries, the varying cultural attitudes and concerns could also be built into product design and development.

A third approach, which is important for this chapter, is the introduction of an *online platform based on a community* of about 3500 registered end users. This approach differs from the aforementioned ones in a way that patients as end users are enabled to actively engage in product development-related discussions on a continuous basis. The online platform was branded and marketed in at least twelve countries from Australia to several countries in Europe to ensure a high number of participants. The purpose is to involve end users in the innovation process online and utilize their creativity. The platform centers on *challenges* that are proposed by either Salpo's R&D team, by the platform administrators, or by the users. A challenge aims at triggering a discussion around potential issues with the products in use and discovering unmet needs or possible improvements. Discussion takes place in either *open forums* that are visible to all registered users or in so-called *VIP* ("very innovative person") *rooms* available to selected users if a topic moves towards concept development. The platform has administrators who are users as well, i.e. not staff from Salpo; they ensure to keep momentum on the site, facilitate the community interactions, specify new innovation challenges to be posted on the platform, and do administrative work making sure that users could log-in and could navigate through the platform. Apart from the user administrators, there are three full-time employees from Salpo engaged. Their tasks are mainly to specify the innovation challenges, to do the material for the marketing, to provide the branding material to be used externally, to maintain and develop the system. They would also act as a consultant for each internal development project; so if a project needed some information from some users on a specific topic, then they would help that project to formulate the problem, make awareness of it in the community, and consolidate the feedback. So they were temporarily working on development projects using the co-creation platform as a tool.

Initiated and conceptualized by this online community, Salpo has developed a new product that is a truly co-created product. It is an accessory product for ostomy care patients who have to wear ostomy bags every day. The underlying product development project is analyzed in this paper as it gives insights about the Salpo's adoption process of user innovation inputs.

5.3.3 Data Gathering

Three data sources were used to investigate on the adoption process at Salpo. The triangulation of different sources allows to obtain a richer set of information and to increase the robustness of the results (Anand et al. 2007). As Jick (1979:602) put it:

> Given basic principles of geometry, multiple viewpoints allow for greater accuracy. Similarly, organizational researchers can improve the accuracy of their judgments by collecting different kinds of data bearing on the same phenomenon.

First, the interactions at the online platform were systematically observed during the time early 2012 to late 2013. Particularly, the interventions from the platforms users, the platform administrators, and Salpo R&D project managers were observed with regard to intensity and temporal flow. Second, three expert interviews with Salpo employees from the R&D and commercial departments were conducted after the project had finished. The three interviewees are a Senior Vice President Global R&D with 12 years tenure in the company, a Front-End Innovation Manager Global R&D with 5 years tenure, and a Senior Market Manager with 4 years tenure who have all gathered specific experience on the aforementioned product development project. And third, internal documentation about the Salpo's innovation function was made available. This included detailed information about the intra-organizational structure, the innovation process, and Salpo's approach to innovation.

The interview sessions were planned based on relevant literature on qualitative research (Creswell 2009; King and Horrocks 2010; Robson 2011). Given the exploratory design of the study, the interviews were designed to be open-ended, semi-structured, and in-depth in nature (Yin 2003). The interviews were conducted using a *semi-structured guide*[3] with questions relating to the early idea development in the user community, the evaluation of the idea potential, Salpo's adoption of the idea, and challenges during this development project. With regard to the research objective informing this chapter, namely to explore the organizational adoption process of UII, the critical incident technique was applied within the interview sessions (Flanagan 1954). The interviewees were asked to reflect upon critical incidents influencing the UII adoption in either a positive or a negative way. The interviews were conducted by

---

[3]Refer to Annex E for the complete interview guide including the entire set of questions.

telephone in English language and lasted an average of 73 minutes. With the consent of the interviewees, all interviews were audio-recorded and subsequently transcribed verbatim. Finally, anonymity to the interviewees was assured.

To control potential informant biases, data from different perspectives was collected. On the one hand, employees from different hierarchical levels have been interviewed. On the other hand, the information obtained from the interviews was triangulated with the other sources to reassess its validity (Jick 1979). As each data source has specific strengths and weaknesses, Pettigrew (1990) recommends the use of different types of data such as interviews and observations.

5.3.4 Data Analysis

In total, the transcription of the three semi-structured interviews resulted in 57 pages of text. The data was analyzed using MaxQDA version 11, a professional application for qualitative data analysis. Data analysis followed the standards for qualitative research as reported by Miles and Hubermann (1994). Before any formal coding activity started, a preliminary data analysis was performed to gain a deeper understanding of the case (Yin 1981). Hence, the interview data and other material were studied without assigning specific codes or categories.

Then, the coding procedure of the transcribed interviews began, which was organized by means of template analysis (King and Horrocks 2010). Based on previous research on organizational innovation adoption and with regard to the research questions of this study, an initial coding template was set up containing a priori themes based on the five stages of Rogers' model. With this at hand, a first coding round was done. This helped to segment the material into relevant groups along the organizational adoption process. In a second coding round, new codes were inductively added. Motivated through the critical incident technique, data analysis centered on the question how the case company actively influenced the adoption process of user inputs or if they encountered barriers. Hence, new codes covered various aspects such as sub-phases of the process, decision points, adoption challenges, or process adaptations.

In two rounds of coding, the initial coding template was refined both deductively and inductively. Other data collected beyond the interviews, i.e. platform observations and internal documentations, were used for triangulation and validation; therefore, they were not coded (Yin 2003).

5.4 Findings

This section reports about the emergence and the development of a user-initiated product idea at Salpo's online co-creation platform. The presentation of findings is organized around Rogers' stages, with a special focus on the decision and implementation stages, and enriched by numerous quotes from the interviews.

5.4.1   Knowledge Stage

The topic for the new product idea emerged in one of the open discussion forums at Salpo's co-creation platform. Users had expressed their unmet need in a way that the existing solutions do not cover their problem. It was about the issue of *pancaking* of ostomy bags. It means there is some vacuum in the stoma which sucks the ostomy bag to the stoma preventing faeces from coming out. Then the faeces will creep under the adhesive between the flange and the skin and it will make the bag fall off. It is a problem that a high share of ostomy patients are suffering from.

Then, at some point in time, there was one platform user who was one of the few active users who was also an engineer. He came up with a preliminary idea for a prototype, produced pictures of it, and immediately published it into the online forum. Some other users followed up on the idea and brainstormed on it further. The following anchor quote from the interview data highlights it:

- There was one guy who was one of the few active users who was also an engineer. He came up with a small idea for a prototype. Then he posted some pictures. And then some other users grabbed the idea and brainstormed on it further.

At some point, one of the user administrators of the open forum realized the big potential of the idea and created a separate VIP room. To this virtual room were invited selected users who were committed to bringing the discussions toward the next level of concept development. In a VIP room, there is a slightly higher expectation from the group and the administrators that the selected users participate on a regular basis. The following anchor quote provides empirical:

- At some point, our administrator said, here is something interesting, should we create a VIP room so we can continue the discussion and prototyping.

Staff from Salpo did not intervene at this stage, they just passively observed the interactions und thus learnt to know about the idea's existence. How this proposed idea should work only became clearer to Salpo by the time it was more and more specified by the involved community members in the open forum and the VIP room. Hence during this stage the actual activities were independently managed by the user administrators and the involved users interested in this topic.

5.4.2   Persuasion Stage

At the persuasion stage, Salpo started to take a more active role. There was a front-end innovation manager and somebody from marketing and they became part of the members of the VIP rooms and actively joined the discussions. So from then on there was a dialogue between Salpo employees and users/patients.

Once Salpo gets new ideas or new inputs from any of the user channels (online or offline), it is important to operationalize on it. At Salpo this is handled through a light front-end innovation team. Through a structured process and with the help

Fig. 5.3 Prototype kit including materials, adhesives and other plastic elements (*source*: email newsletter from Salpo received on February 27, 2012)

from the community discussions, they generate a number of so-called *concept directions* that could solve the initial problem. Then they evaluate these concept directions with users and with several other functions such as mechanical construction, industrial designers, production, commercial, and marketing. In order to increase the success rate of the front-end projects, Salpo front-loads with specialists with a big blend of skillsets. Having that early involvement of many stakeholders increases the chance of success instead of numerous alluring ideas that turn out to be not feasible after some time.

- That is part of the front-end innovation. We start out with an unmet need in the market. Through a structured process we generate a number of 'concept directions' as we call them that could meet this need. Then we evaluate these concepts directions with user, with our production guys, with our commercial team, and of course technically, i.e. how feasible they are from a material and mechanical constructing viewpoint.
- We have a big blend of skillsets involved from the very beginning of an idea.
- Because you come up with a lot of ideas. When you then, 6 months later, talk to the production guy, he says it is a nice idea but it is not feasible to produce. So having that early involvement of many stakeholders basically increases the chance of success.
- Before we make the decision, because this is when we really start investing even more money, we have found it very useful to have this cross-functional team to work for six months to make sure what we actually bring into the actual product development phase is actually well qualified.

Salpo created more attention for the ongoing concept development, when they sent out prototype kits to those interested in it (see Fig. 5.3). They received a bit of materials, adhesives and other plastic elements and then people could cut and glue their prototypes and sent pictures of it back and forth between each other. However, it was noted that only a small number of 10-20 users was actively engaged in this activity.

- These prototype kits were sent out to those who wanted it. And actually, then people made prototypes and sent it back and forth between each other. So there was a lot of attention going around it.

The front-end process usually takes six months. During this period, the front-end team proposes concept directions which are evaluated with the community members and the functions just mentioned. Then they come up with a recommendation for a maximum of two but preferably one concept direction that they believe in. So the persuasion stage ends at the finalized state of the front-end process. From the very early start and its initial discussions until the point when Salpo had concluded on the concept directions, it has been going on for about 10 months.

5.4.3 Decision Stage

As introduced in Sect. 5.3.1, Salpo also runs user advisory boards around the world. These boards mainly consist of nurses working in hospitals or rehabilitation centres who are involved in Salpo's product development process as well. They are addressed with all forms of needs and prototype evaluations. At that point of the on-going project, Salpo also addressed these boards with the pancaking issue. It quickly became clear that, also from the perspective of the nurses, a solution is needed in the market. Based on the assessments of online community of users and the user advisory boards, Salpo took the decision to formally adopt the concept into their product development pipeline. As users had already been prototyping, the idea had been driven quite far already, so that now it needed to be matured and finalized in a professional manner. At that decision point, it has also been the senior vice president of global R&D who strongly supported this initiative in coordination with marketing and other functions.

- And we also addressed the COF [the user advisory boards] with this pancaking issue and it was quite clear that a solution is needed in the market. And then we said 'Should we give this a chance?' I was involved at that time. Then it was decided, now let's launch OstomyArch as our first truly co-created product.
- At that decision point, it has probably been out SVP who said 'Ok, let's do it!' Of course, a decision together with marketing. This is something that we want to try.
- When these users had been prototyping, then we said 'Ok, now they have driven it so far, now we need to mature it to finalize it'.

With the decision to adopt this user-initiated concept, the project then became a formal product development project at Salpo. Such projects run through a well-defined stage-gate execution model of internal innovation. However, the project manager in charge of the project came up with a few modifications on how he ran the product development process. He was faced with several challenges as it was new to interact with users through an online platform during a product development project. The responsible manager set up a three step development process with the users. It was important that also the involved users were aligned on timelines and duties. Users should know the plan of how long they should be involved, and what will be the focus during each step. It was important to align the strict Salpo processes with the users who are normally not engaged in such a procedure.

- I planned a 3-stage development process with the users in it. So they also knew that now we start and we will finish in 3–4 months or how long it took. And there were those 3 stages. People knew the plan of how long they should be involved, and what will we focus on during each stage.

However, the decision to adopt this concept for product development turned out to challenge the existing practice. As Salpo intends to be lean in all its processes, the product development pipeline is basically controlled by the innovation roadmap which defines three consecutive years at a time. And the marketing department determines which projects are admitted into that pipeline including all related resources necessary to execute on it. To have products just popping up as extra ones coming from aside, like the ones from an online innovation community, is a managerial challenge difficult to act on as all staff resources are balanced out and flexibly expandable manpower is hardly available.

- To have products just popping up as extra ones because there was something coming from aside, the company is so lean, so all resources were balanced according the projects in this pipeline. So additional small projects coming up, we wouldnt have the manpower.

5.4.4 Implementation and Confirmation Stages

After the adoption decision, the governance of the project shifted from community-driven to Salpo-driven. This is a turning point in fact. The community members were still involved in evaluation decisions if they want to, but the main pace was now determined by the product development team. So at the beginning of the implementation stage, the raw product concept entered *gate 0* of the *stage-gate-execution model* (see Fig. 5.4).

- At the time when it left the community, it was what we define as gate 0. It left the community at the finalized state of the front-end. When we took the OstomyArch in the execution gate process, it was at gate 0.

All remaining work for the implementation stage is meticulously laid out in Salpo's stage-gate model.[4] Such stage-gate models are commonplace in R&D departments for formal product development projects (Cooper 2008). However, this co-creation project was considered a sandbox project that did not formally pass through all the gates. A few status meetings took place, but the usual gate meetings held during large development projects were neglected. In effect, the whole project was executed much faster than normally. This is partly because some of the development and prototyping activities have already been done by the user community in a previous stage, but partly also because Salpo had installed and trusted the user advisory boards as an acting committee.

---

[4]Refer to Annex F for a detailed explanation of Salpo's stage-gate process.

Fig. 5.4 Salpo's   stage-gate   execution   model   of   formal   development   projects (*source*: Salpo internal documents)

- The project didn't go through all these gates as such. There were some small status meetings, but it was ran much faster through than normally.

In order to describe the implementation stage of the UII adoption process in a comprehensive yet concise manner, the granularity of Salpo's execution model is too detailed. Therefore, leaning on present literature, a reasonable subdivision of this stage is inspired by Reichwald and Piller's (2009) idealized innovation process. The three phases *concept maturing, production and test,* and *market launch* will serve as subdivision for the implementation stage. The end of each of these sub-stages raises the question if the implementation is overall on track but offers an option to cancel the process if necessary. So it is suggested to integrate Rogers' separate *confirmation stage* as several decision points at the end of each of the *implementation sub-stages*.

5.4.4.1   Concept Maturing

Looking at the maturity level of the concept at this point, several Salpo managers confirmed that it was at around 40% maturity level compared to a finalized product. The basic ideas were available, but to bring it to full launch it still required significant efforts such as technical drawings, production agreements, a marketing concept, etc. It also includes activities to plan the product positioning as the to-be-product interacts with the current product portfolio of the company. So overall, there were still many areas to address in order to raise the concept to the level of a finalized product.

- Let me think, the maturity level that the idea had once it left the community, I'd say, it was probably not more than 40%. The basic ideas were there, but to get it to work in a construction that allows for a single product it still takes some modifications to get it there. And we are talking about a product that can interact with our current product portfolio because it interacts with our current products.

The maturing part required a lot of time because the responsible project manager did not have enough team resources available in a flexible manner. Due to the staff shortage, the manager in charge was searching for alternative yet effective ways of running the development process. This led to a few modifications of the process such as using the community members as a working resource through the closed online VIP rooms. The community members were thus at all times integrated in evaluations and decisions of this project.

- But the maturing part of it took some time because I didn't have the set-up, I didn't have the manpower.

5.4.4.2 Production and Test

This sub-stage comprises the ramp up of the physical production of the product at a supplier factory, the product test with almost-final product versions, and the market test. Searching for a suitable and cost-effective external supplier to manage the mass production was not an easy venture. This search entailed discussions around intellectual property and product ownership. Once this was accomplished, there was a lot of work to be done for the regulatory documentation that is required for medical device products. Setting up the agreements for mass production took in total about 9 months.

- The initial work with the supplier I had been completely been screwed up with it. Also to initiate the discussion of 'Is it us who owns the product or is it an external partner?', then we needed to find the external partner, and set it up, and help him with all the documentation. Because as a medical device product there is a lot of documentation going into that.
- We also needed to find a cheap enough supplier. So we had a Chinese supplier on top.

The way it was finally set up was that Salpo had an external Chinese partner who got the ownership of the new product. This was due to some regulatory reasons and also to the fact that if the new product would have become a genuine Salpo product then Salpo would need to involve the entire organization in setting it up in all of Salpo's systems from logistics to customer complaints. Salpo's top management, although willing to engage in user-driven innovation, did not want to own the new product initially in an effort to reduce risk if the low-staff and low-budget co-creation project still fails. Salpo wanted to be on the safe side, to test it on a small set-up first, and if it continuously proves to be a commercial success, then, of course, it had been contractually agreed to take it in as one of Salpo's own products. Once the first items of the manufactured product had arrived, Salpo started a pre-launch through its online platform. The pre-launch should ensure to receive final product feedback, to test its acceptance in this highly qualified target group, and if necessary to prompt last modifications before full commercial market launch. During this product and market test, there was the future sales price attached to the product so that patients acknowledged that this new product is really worth something. But eventually the items were given away for free to community members who had requested 'it. Then the item was sent via postal mail to the patients' homes. Figure 5.5 shows the final product that has been invented by the user community and jointly developed with Salpo.

- To be clear, we did not sell it. We were giving it away for free through the platform to people who had requested it. So we had a sales price attached to it, so that people knew that this is actually something that is worth something.

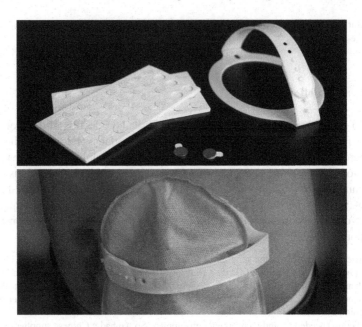

Fig. 5.5 The   co-created   product   that   prevents   pancacking   of   ostomy   bags (*source*: retrieved from www.medicologic.com on August 15, 2015)

- We wanted to see the reaction from the people before. We never went to the stage where we were wanting money for it.

Three months after the pre-launch, Salpo had handed out around 100 pieces of the new product only. Although it solved a critical problem that a large number of ostomy patients are facing, and despite its positive image of a user-developed and community-cocreated product, this result was unexpected and disappointing. Out of the total of 3500 registered users at the platform, Salpo argued that at least 300–400 active users are struggling with the pancaking problem; not counting community members just ordering it for curiosity. So Salpo startled very much with this lack of interest in the new product. Normally, because Salpo is in the disposable business, the company sells their ostomy products by the millions and within catheters it sells over hundreds of millions of items per year. So, naturally, being able to reach out to less than 100 patients during a free pre-launch period is commercially unattractive at all.

From the early discussion of the idea to the start of the pre-launch period, the overall process took approximately 21 months.

5.4.4.3 Market Launch

Finally, Salpo was forced into the discontinuance of the product as it did not predict to be commercially successful despite all previous positive assessments. Thus, the commercial launch was cancelled. If it continued, distinct performance indicators were defined in the company to measure the success of an innovation.

- We basically have 6 KPIs which help to measure a project overall. One is: we have a target for incremental sales value after three years in the market. We have a target for the growth margin that the product is able to be sold at. And we look at the capital expenditure to bring the product to market. Then we look at the development time from the idea until we bring the idea to the market. Then we look at our launch fulfillment which for us means how did we deliver on this pipeline. Were we able to deliver the products on time and to the agreed value?

Linking back to the initial definition of an innovation (see Sect. 2.1.1.3), it is noted that Salpo's endeavor and the original user's idea were innovative indeed. However, the created product cannot be ascribed to be an innovation in the end because it lacked market launch, successful diffusion and positive returns—key elements necessary to turn an initial idea into a successful innovation.

5.5 Discussion

This section is about to interpret the findings and summarizes them into a refined model of UII adoption. Commonalities and distinctions of the proposed model to existing theory are explained, thus deriving the conceptual contribution of this study.

5.5.1 Refined Adoption Model of UII

With the help of Salpo's case, this study demonstrates the organizational adoption of user innovation inputs in one instance. Therefore, Rogers' theory of innovation adoption is leaned on for an initial understanding. After going through the Salpo case, a more detailed understanding is gained suggesting to adapt the idealized adoption process. Figure 5.6 shows the resulting process model of UII adoption summarizing the adoption-related analyses from the perspective of an adopting organization.

5.5.1.1 General Description

The model is composed of two principal phases—*initiation* and *implementation*—which are subdivided into two and three respective stages. At the *knowledge stage*, the potential adopting unit becomes aware of an UII's existence and that there is the opportunity to utilize the UII in the organization. If user innovation input is viewed as any idea or knowledge artifact contributing to the organization's innovation

Fig. 5.6 Process of multi-level organizational adoption of user innovation inputs (*source* own illustration)

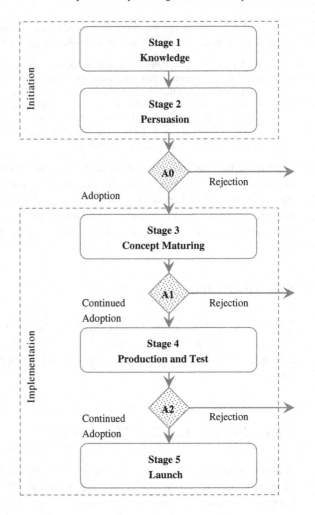

function, then knowledge about the UII is an essential first stage of initiation. In this stage, the organization learns what the UII is about and which value it might have for the organization. It remains open whether the awareness of the UII stimulates the need to adopt it, or vice versa, whether an existing need for a solution increases the search intensity and thus the awareness of appropriate UIIs.

At the *persuasion stage*, the potential adopting unit including its organizational members forms a negative or positive attitude toward the UII. The more organizational members, i.e. key experts or key powerholders, are informed and persuaded, the better are chances for later adoption. Both cognitive and affective elements influence the attitude formation. On the cognitive side, there are the actual potential of the UII to influence innovation and the organizations capability to make use of it. The affective side reflects the general openness towards change that any innovation incurs. This is the point where the concept of the not-invented-here-syndrome (Antons and Piller 2015) comes possibly into play. The not-invented-here syndrome describes a negative attitude-based bias towards knowledge artifacts derived from an external source.

After the persuasion stage, the initiation phase culminates in a crucial *decision point*, named A0. At this point, the organization processes a large amount of information collected during the initiation phase and eventually chooses to adopt or reject the UII. With a decision for adoption, the adopting organization expresses its full intent to implement the UII.

The second major phase begins with the *concept maturing stage*. This stage is key and specifically necessary when adopting UII. As it is noted in the Salpo case, the maturity level of the UII adopted was at 40% only and it still needed significant professional development to grow from a well-conceived idea to a marketable product. The concept maturing stage is thus critical to this transformation and usually not part of classical models of innovation adoption. This stage covers activities such as to mature the concept at a detailed level, to ensure a robust design, to meet cost and quality requirements, to make a matured prototype, to plan manufacturing processes, to assess the regulatory pathway, and to review the patent position. Users are continuously involved for further concept evaluation in this stage, yet to a lesser degree than during the initiation phase.

After this stage, the organization passes to the next adoption-related *decision point*, named A1. If the further maturing of the concept confirms the initial assessment of A0, then the organization continues the adoption. Rejection may occur at this point if the maturing stage has revealed unforeseen and invincible impediments of further implementation.

The decision for a continued adoption leads to the next stage during implementation, the *production and test stage*. From this stage onwards, the implementation of the UII causes structural changes at the adopting unit. Before the production is ramped up, the product is verified from a business, a technical, and a production perspective. Then, the organization contracts production capacity from own or external manufacturing sites and starts the initial production batch. With the first items from the production batch, the product is validated against intended use and user needs. The new product is pre-launched to a selected circle of consumers to test the acceptance.

After the production and test stage, the organization passes to the next adoption-related *decision point*, named A2. If the real-world tests confirm earlier assessments of viability, then the organization continues the adoption. Rejection may occur, as happened at the case company, if the market test provides negative results.

The last stage of the implementation phase is the *launch stage*. The adoption can be defined a success if the adopted UII has been utilized up to this point and cleared its path into a final and marketable product. During the launch stage, the organization establishes the volume production, drives international marketing, and evaluates the business objectives of the novel product.

5.5.1.2 Commonalities with Previous Works

It is the intent of the proposed model to be rooted in earlier works of innovation and adoption scholars. Therefore, it distinctively incorporates several elements from previous works. First, the model reflects the two major phases of initiation and implementation that are common consensus among adoption scholars (e.g., Frambach and Schillewaert 2002; Zaltman et al. 1973). Second, all elements of Rogers' model are accommodated in the modified model. The knowledge and persuasion stages are mirrored as before; the original implementation stage is broken down in three sub-stages; the decision stage has become a decision point; and the original confirmation stage has been continuously intertwined as decision points with the new implementation sub-stages. Third, the new implementation phase embodies three sub-stages that are based on previous works of innovation scholars (e.g., Reichwald and Piller 2009; Verworn and Herstatt 2002). Fourth, inspired by the stage-gate logic (e.g., Cooper 2008), the proposed model uses the semantics of decision points next to stages.

5.5.1.3 Distinctions to Previous Works

The suggested model holds improvements compared to existing models of innovation adoption or innovation generation. These are discussed in the following. First, the present process model basically combines two streams—the innovation *adoption* and the innovation *generation*—which well reflects the nature of co-creation. According to the definition of co-creation, the joint creation of innovations between healthcare consumers and a medical device company in this specific case setting requires their collaboration. Hence, there are process stages during which the healthcare consumers set the direction and other stages during which the adopting organization sets the direction. Both happens according to what each party knows best. Healthcare consumers can provide great ideas, feedback and comments to the *ideation stage* that is at the beginning of each innovation generating process (e.g., Reichwald and Piller 2009). As companies are searching for external sources of innovation, they are listening to external inputs while residing at the *knowledge stage*. It is until they find some interesting innovation input they can scrutinize, so they enter the *persuasion stage*. Then at later stages, organizations are better at providing profound experience and routines to professionally mature the user innovation inputs into a marketable product.

Second, another distinction of the proposed model is that this study refrains from calling the input to the adoption decision already an innovation. Many other papers set in similar contexts (online, co-creation) do so—for comparison see Di Gangi and Wasko (2009). Therefore, this study tries to generalize it to *user innovation inputs* because it does not necessarily have to be ideas or concepts or ready-made products that enter as artifacts into the adoption process. User innovation inputs can also be any kind of knowledge artifacts that bear positive value to the innovation process of the adopting organization.

Third, it is stated in Sect. 2.2 that Rogers' original adoption process is considered a success if the adopted artifact is continually used. The same is true for the model proposed here. If the adopted artifact is continually used (and on this way matured) until the last stage, then the adoption process of user innovation inputs can be considered a success. However, before, the implementation stage could be considered a black box and it was difficult to explain the connection between innovation inputs and innovation outcomes. The proposed model helps to clarify why great innovation inputs from end users may not surface in finalized novel products.

Fourth, at each stage in the implementation phase, it is possible to exit the process. For sure, the same is possible at any of the previous adoption models. Yet, the distinct exit points in the new model increase the awareness of potential failure. They help to understand the perceived disconnect between sometimes outstanding innovative inputs from HCCs and its lacking systematic professional development and commercial exploitation by HCOs. In the Salpo example, it was discovered that the UII adoption process stopped at the decision point A2 (see Sect. 5.4.4.2 again about the why).

Fifth, a last distinction of the proposed model is the semantic differentiation between *decision points* and *activity stages* as opposed to Rogers' original idea that incorporated both in the same semantic manner.

5.5.2 Directions for Further Research

The investigation conducted in this chapter has limitations, which leads to options for further research in this area. First, the main limitation of this study is its basis on a single yet in-depth case study. Therefore, generalizability of the proposed model is limited at this point in time. The proposed model needs to be validated with further organizations adopting UII and, if necessary, the model needs to be amended.

Second, Salpo faced a few challenges when interacting and collaborating with the community members through the online platform. It was reported that mental attitudes between end users contributing in an online innovation platform and R&D employees working in a structured process every day can be quite different. Future research could strive to understand the challenges of different stakeholder types collaborating in virtual settings and suggest mitigations to reconcile both stakeholder types. On the organizational side, this is certainly a question of the absorptive capacity (Cohen and Levinthal 1990) of the UII adopting unit which has not been comprehensively addressed in this study. This may have a positive effect on the rate of successful UII adoptions.

Third, Rogers' theory suggests five perceived characteristics of innovations—relative advantage, compatibility, complexity, trialability, observability—that affect innovation adoption (Rogers 2003:222). These characteristics are difficult to convey in a virtual setting and often require a physical innovation to be present for the adopting unit to test or observe before deciding to adopt (Di Gangi and Wasko 2009). However, through online innovation platforms like the one from the Salpo case, knowledge artifacts contributing to an innovation (aka UII) are exchanged as opposed to a physical innovation that is easily tested or observed. It is not until the UII is adopted by the organization that the development of the physical innovation begins. Future research could investigate if these theoretical constructs remain valid or if others should be added in the specific context of adopting UII via online platforms.

Fourth, to justify investments into consumer co-creation initiatives, it becomes important for organizations to measure the co-creation success and innovation outcomes. If the results from co-creation initiatives have passed the launch stage, then it is easy to find appropriate metrics from classical innovation literature. However, during the early stages of co-creation initiatives, effective metrics remain scarce (e.g., Roser et al. 2009:14) as there are no direct returns early on. Therefore, in accordance with Hoyer et al. (2010), future research needs to develop performance metrics that allow organizations to measure the consumer co-creation efforts quickly and comprehensively. Such metrics are crucial for organizations to manage signs of negative developments proactively while benefitting from the consumer's innovation potential.

Fifth, to end, the successful adoption of UII depends on manifold aspects. This study has distinctively focused on the adoption process and the considerations discussed above. It has to be seen in the overall context though, i.e. other key adoption constructs associated with the adoption process. As mentioned at the outset of Sect. 5.2, the social milieu in which the adopting organizations exists has a socio-political and external influence as well. Apart from that, the organizational characteristics, the characteristics of the UII to be adopted, and the individual characteristics of potential users (staff or clients) are equally important (Wisdom et al. 2014). Further research on the organizational adoption of co-created innovation input could elaborate on the relationships between key adoption constructs and the adoption process in comparison to traditional innovation adoption.

5.6 Conclusion

This chapter aimed at understanding the different stages of the organizational adoption process for user innovation inputs in order to maximize successful innovation outputs. Such user innovation inputs are increasingly generated through OII platforms as HCOs are on a search for external sources of innovation such as HCCs. Although this study is positioned in the context of healthcare, it certainly holds a contribution beyond this domain.

This study has a theoretical and managerial contribution. Based on Rogers' theory on the adoption of innovations, an adapted model of organizational adoption of user innovation inputs is proposed and discussed. This model fills an important gap as adoption models in the context of innovation co-creation with end users are not present in the scholarly literature. The managerial contribution lies in the procedural clarity it provides to R&D departments and innovation managers while HCOs seek new ways to enhance the quality and the value of their offerings.

Chapter 6
Discussion and Conclusion

6.1 Summary

This dissertation investigates online innovation intermediaries (OIIs) in healthcare to help healthcare organizations (HCOs) reap the benefits of consumer co-creation and increase their innovation performance.

The present section summarizes the Chaps. 1–6 of this work. The following section discusses the overall findings across the three empirical studies conducted and clarifies the academic contribution. Section 6.3 derives implications for the management of consumer co-creation at both the OII side and the HCO side. At last, Sect. 6.4 identifies and details directions for further research. The discussions and implications presented in this chapter are based upon the findings gained across the three studies and hence deliver a holistic perspective on the entire research endeavor.

Chapter 1 starts by outlining the complex setup in the healthcare sector that shows structural differences to other sectors. Recent developments in the field of innovation advocate for the approach of open innovation that may help to tackle these challenges. Especially using the innovation potential of healthcare consumers appears to be a critical resource hardly explored. Through the proliferation of health-related online platforms that pool various types of healthcare consumers, the need emerges to better understand the contribution of such platforms for innovation in healthcare. Four examples from practice illustrate available models today and demonstrate its relevance. Apart from its real-world relevance, the academic relevance is derived in Chap. 1 by specifying current research gaps that provide the motivation for this research. Based on that, the research questions for this work are formulated. Chapter 1 then finishes with an overview of the structure of this thesis.

In Chap. 2, a literature review is conducted to elucidate on the key concepts that are important for this work. The goal of that chapter is to establish a theoretical framework that provides the conceptual foundation for this work but also clarifies the chosen perspective of the author. First, the concept of consumer co-creation for innovation is presented. A definition and the main characteristics are given and a

© Springer International Publishing AG 2018
C.W. Künne, *Online Intermediaries for Co-Creation*, Progress in IS,
DOI 10.1007/978-3-319-51124-5_6

clear dividing line is drawn towards related concepts in innovation literature. Second, healthcare consumers are introduced as a construct that serves as input factor for consumer co-creation. Evidence suggests that HCCs are highly innovative and conceive a multitude of valuable solutions to improve their own personal medical situations. Third, the knowledge-based theory of the firm is presented. It provides two important twists to this work: on the on hand, this theory enables to view co-creation activities from a knowledge perspective and, on the other hand, it makes clear that knowledge is the key resource that advances organizations and that leads to competitive advantage. Fourth, the concept of innovation intermediary is introduced. Being of similar importance to this work, it provides the essential perspective that a health-related online platform may serve as an intermediary platform between HCCs and HCOs if it is set up in a certain way by the hosting intermediary organization. Finally, all concepts are consolidated to form the theoretical framework.

In Chaps. 3–5 the three empirical studies are conducted that document the core of this thesis. The content of these three chapters is displayed in a structured manner in the adjacent tables (see Tables 6.1, 6.2 and 6.3). Chapter 3 represents the first empirical study. This study recognizes that a multitude of online health platforms is available and derives the need to identify those platforms that may serve as OII platforms. After deriving dimensions for typology of health 2.0 platforms, a large scale case-study-based approach is chosen. Through desk review, a sample of online health platforms is created (n = 306) from which health 2.0 platforms are filtered (n = 183). For each of the latter, case vignettes are developed. The study

Table 6.1 Summary of Chap. 3 with empirical study I

Chapter 3—Empirical Study I: Identifying Online Innovation Intermediaries in Healthcare	
Builds on	Chapter 2 that elucidates the relevant concepts and derives the theoretical framework
Needs	Multitude of online health platforms is available; need to identify those ones that may serve as OII platform
Research question	How can OIIs be identified within the domain of "health 2.0"?
Theoretical underpinning	Characteristics of health 2.0; Emergence of virtual communities; derivation of dimensions for classification scheme
Method used	Large scale case-study-based approach is chosen; complemented with constant comparison across cases; Case vignettes are developed
Sample	Through desk review a sample of online health platforms is created (n = 306) from which health 2.0 platforms are filtered (n = 183)
Findings	Classification of health 2.0 platforms from an innovation perspective; identification of 30 OII platforms; Examination of descriptive attributes throughout the sample
Implications	State-of-the-art review of health 2.0 platforms; emphasizes the mediating role of designated OII platforms as advocates of innovation
Next step	Detailed analysis of the agency of the identified OIIs and the implications of their emergence as new actors

Table 6.2 Summary of Chap. 4 with empirical study II

Chapter 4—Empirical Study II: Exploring Online Innovation Intermediaries in Healthcare	
Builds on	Chapter 3 that locates relevant online innovation intermediaries serving as basis for deeper investigation
Needs	For this new category of intermediaries, need to understand the OII agency and how they contribute to consumer co-creation; Opposing previous studies, a comprehensive cross-case analysis is needed
Research questions	2a: What are the key activities of OIIs in healthcare, and how do these activities bundle together towards OII types? 2b: What value do OIIs add for the innovation capacity of HCOs? 2c: What are critical challenges during co-creation activities via OIIs, and how can these be mitigated?
Theoretical underpinning	Related works are reviewed with special regard to functions of intermediaries, their value potential and challenges in this field
Method used	Exploratory, multiple case study with cross-case analysis; Based on interviews with key informants
Sample	24 OII organizations from eight countries, mostly US, UK, Germany; Interviews conducted with mainly CEOs and founders
Findings	Four key activities are explored: (i) incubation, (ii), support, (iii) sense-making, (iv) facilitation; Four OII types are derived: (1) proactive agent, (2) support provider, (3) community champion, (4) bridge builder; Their value potential for HCOs classified as: (a) network reach, (b) lay expertise, (c) professional expertise, (d) digital literacy; Seven critical challenges including relevant mitigations identified
Implications	Findings merge into the previous grouping, but provide additional details; Large potential of consumer co-creation in healthcare is confirmed by interviewees; however, it is important to address remaining challenges
Next Step	Explore the HCO perspective on the organizational adoption of innovation inputs generated through OII platforms

Table 6.3 Summary of Chap. 5 with empirical study III

Chapter 5—Empirical Study III: Organizational Adoption of User Innovation Inputs	
Builds on	Chapter 4 that reveals how OIIs work in terms of key activities and types; and Chap. 2 that determines the HCO as receiving unit
Needs	To improve the HCO innovation performance, the integration of external inputs from OIIs lacks understanding; The organizational adoption process of such inputs is an important part of it
Research question	How do HCOs adopt user innovation inputs generated through an OII?
Theoretical underpinning	Organizational Change provides the stage for the adoption of innovations; Rogers' theory on innovation adoption is applied
Method used	In-depth single case study in the medical device industry
Sample	Three interviews, observations and internal documents about one corporate product development project that incorporated the innovation inputs from HCCs through an OII platform
Findings	Adapted process model of the organizational adoption of user innovation inputs; Implementation phase broken down in additional stages; Concept maturing is of particular importance during implementation
Implications	Helps to explain why great innovation inputs from end users do not necessarily surface in finalized product innovations

provides a classification of health 2.0 platforms from an innovation perspective and identifies 30 OII platforms for which further descriptive attributes are found.

Chapter 4 deals with the second empirical study that builds on the findings from the previous chapter. It identifies the need to understand the agency of OIIs in greater detail and how they contribute to consumer co-creation. Also, existing research is lacking a comprehensive cross-case analysis in this field. Therefore, this study aims at developing an understanding about the OII activities, OII types, the OII value potential for HCOs, and critical challenges in the OII ecosystem. Based on an exploratory, multiple case study with a cross-case analysis, 24 interviews with OII organizations from eight countries, mostly US, UK, Germany are conducted. The direct findings state that four key activities are explored: (i) incubation, (ii), support, (iii) sense-making, (iv) facilitation; and four OII types are derived: (1) proactive agent, (2) support provider, (3) community champion, (4) bridge builder. Additionally, their value potential for HCOs is classified as: (a) network reach, (b) lay expertise, (c) professional expertise, (d) digital literacy. Then seven critical challenges including relevant mitigations are presented. The majority of the interviewees confirm the large potential of consumer co-creation in healthcare.

Chapter 5 deals with the third empirical study that switches the perspective of analysis to the beneficiaries of OIIs and co-creation: the HCOs. To improve the HCO innovation performance, the integration of external knowledge artifacts from OIIs lacks understanding. The organizational adoption process of such knowledge artifacts plays an important role here and Rogers' theory on innovation adoption is applied. Through an in-depth single case study in the medical device industry, this study provides a refined process model of the organizational adoption of consumer-generated knowledge artifacts. This model helps to explain why great innovation inputs from end users do not necessarily surface in finalized product innovations.

Chapter 6, the current chapter, concludes by summarizing the findings of the present thesis. Based on this, the results are holistically discussed in the light of the overarching research question and the underlying theoretical framework. To end the thesis, implications for practice and avenues for future research in this compelling field are equally derived.

6.2 Overarching Discussion

This section revisits the entirety of the thesis' findings with regard to the academic contribution it yields. Since the subordinated research questions 1, 2a-2c, and 3 have been answered within each empirical study separately, this chapter will provide an answer to the overarching research question set out in Chap. 1. To refresh, the overarching research question was formulated as:

Research Question: How do online innovation intermediaries (OIIs) enable effective consumer co-creation for innovation between healthcare consumers (HCCs) and healthcare organizations (HCOs)?

This question arose from the need to understand both the large group of HCCs as external sources of knowledge and the emerging multitude of interactive health-related online platforms on the Internet as a unique opportunity to encourage innovation in healthcare. The formulation of the main research question already sets a distinct perspective and abandons others. It relates to co-creation, not open innovation in general; it defines two major stakeholders that should be included instead applying a universal actor-to-actor view; and it establishes the role of a mediating agent that exploits the advantages of virtual environments. Within this framing, the research question clearly addresses an under-researched area according to the research gap identified at the beginning of this work (cf. Sect 1.2). Building upon this research question, the theoretical framework erected in Chap. 2 adds more nuance to how this research is approached. It establishes the understanding that co-creation with HCCs positively contributes to the innovation performance of HCOs. Furthermore, it restricts the research scope to effects that result from the integration of OIIs and their agency.

To give a comprehensive answer to the overarching research question, seven key contributions from this work are discussed in the remainder of this section. To do so, each contribution is elucidated in a structured 4-step format. It covers (i) pointing back to the related research gaps, (ii) explaining what the contribution is all about, (iii) showing its value for existing research, and (iv) showing its value for the overarching research question. These seven contributions are discussed in the remainder of this section. A consolidated view on the contributions is given in Fig. 6.1 that leans on the theoretical framework of Chap. 2.

Contribution #1: A typology to classify health 2.0 platforms from an innovation perspective is proposed and populated with real-world cases, of which 30 qualify as designated OII platforms.

Related research gaps: The characteristic themes of health 2.0—such as increased participation of HCCs, user-generated content, and higher levels of collaboration—appear as suitable prerequisites for an environment in which co-creation can happen. However, the benefits of health 2.0 platforms towards co-creation for innovation is insufficiently addressed in existing research (Boulos and Wheeler 2007; Leimeister et al. 2008; Randeree 2009). A few studies attempt to classify the landscape of health 2.0 platforms (Birnsteel et al. 2008; Goerlitz et al. 2010; Kordzadeh and Warren 2012; Kuehne et al. 2011; Weber-Jahnke et al. 2011), but existing typologies do not explain the potential value of health 2.0 towards

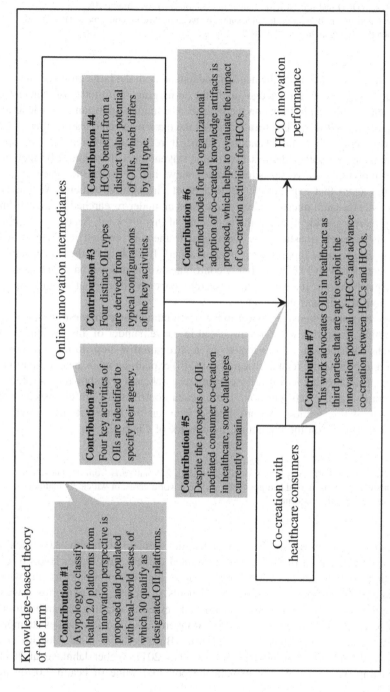

Fig. 6.1 Key contributions of the thesis

co-creation for innovation. Yet, to stimulate innovation in healthcare, several authors pointed out that the innovation potential of HCCs is insufficiently exploited and it should be regarded a beneficial resource (Cepiku and Savignon 2015; Engström and Snyder 2013; Henrike and Schultz 2014; Nambisan and Nambisan 2009). Here, health 2.0 platforms can serve as an instrumental vehicle to approach the group of HCCs.

Details of the contribution: A typology to classify health 2.0 platforms from an innovation perspective is proposed. It distinguishes along two axes: (i) health 2.0 platforms that mediate between innovating companies and external stakeholders, and those who do not; as well as (ii) health 2.0 platforms with a simple or complex coordination level towards the platform users. In addition to that, 183 health 2.0 platforms are identified through an extensive search and are applied to the typology. This leads to the identification of 30 cases that qualify as an OII platform. Hence, the existence of appropriate OIIs in healthcare can be substantiated. A cross-case analysis reveals further characteristic elements of the observed OII platforms, such as OII platforms call for HCCs with profound experience, and OII platforms trigger more intense interaction levels with or between their users than non-OII platforms (cf. Sect. 3.4.2).

Value for existing research: Contribution #1 extends the body of knowledge in two ways. On the one hand, it adds to the debate on prospects of health 2.0 (e.g., Fischer and Soyez 2014) by applying a distinct innovation perspective. On the other hand, it adds to research on innovation intermediaries (Howells 2006; Lopez-Vega and Vanhaverbeke 2009; Verona et al. 2006) as the organizations running the identified OII platforms can be regarded as a new class of intermediaries.

Value for the overarching RQ: Contribution #1 provides an empirical set of relevant OII cases for further investigation and derives first characterizing attributes.

> **Contribution #2**: Four key activities of OIIs are identified to specify their agency.

Related research gaps: Earlier works have provided profound knowledge about the agency of traditional innovation intermediaries that operate in a non-virtual environment (Dalziel 2010; Howells 2006; Lopez-Vega and Vanhaverbeke 2009). However, explanations for online intermediaries in particular remain scarce and their agency is insufficiently explored (e.g., Mele and Russo-Spena 2015; Verona et al. 2006). Further research into OIIs follows Howells' (2006) call for research into the range of intermediaries and a more detailed outline of their functions and activities. For any new category of intermediary, key questions need to be answered, such as what the enabling factors of successful intermediation are, or how innovation intermediaries facilitate the creation and integration of knowledge among various parties (Lopez-Vega and Vanhaverbeke 2009).

Details of the contribution: The analysis uncovered what OIIs in healthcare actually do when they engage in co-creation activities with the ecosystem of stakeholders, i.e. HCOs and HCCs. The interview data suggested that there are four key activities that OIIs perform: *facilitation, support, incubation,* and *sense-making.* To each of these activities, additional sub-activities have been described (cf. Sect. 4.4.1). It thus partly addresses the research gaps described above.

Value for existing research: It contributes to the research stream on online intermediaries for co-creation. This new category of intermediaries fulfills traditional functions of intermediaries, but also deals with the requirements of its specific environment. The findings do partly overlap with prior assessments (Hallerstede 2013; Lopez-Vega and Vanhaverbeke 2009), but also identify new activities of OIIs that have not been described earlier. In particular, the reported *incubation activity* of OII enhances the existing grouping at this point. If an OII performs incubation activities, then the OII takes a more active role than just serving as a broker between two parties.

Value for the overarching RQ: The identified OII activities detail the spectrum of the OII's ability to initiate, control and execute co-creation activities between HCCs and HCOs. It gives a first explanation of their inner workings.

> **Contribution #3**: Four distinct OII types are derived from typical configurations of the key activities.

Related research gaps: As stated by Mele and Russo-Spena (2015), the academic discourse has insufficiently addressed the agency of online innovation intermediaries as a new category of innovation intermediaries. The majority of the discourse is limited by the analysis of single cases of OIIs (cf. Sect. 2.1.4.2), while only a few articles generate overarching findings across several OIIs (e.g., Colombo et al. 2013; Mele and Russo-Spena 2015; Verona et al. 2006). This brings Colombo et al. (2013:2) to the conclusion that "existing research on this topic mainly consists of scattered anecdotal evidence". Moreover, there is a lack of understanding of strategies that different OIIs use, when they interact with their knowledge sources and with their innovation-seeking client organizations (Colombo et al. 2015). On the stream of co-creation research, some authors state that current research lacks a differentiated view on the specific mechanisms enabling consumers co-creation (Greer and Lei 2012; Piller et al. 2012).

Details of the contribution: Based on 24 interviews across different OIIs, four distinct types of OIIs are derived. The types are designated as: the *proactive agent*, the *support provider*, the *community champion*, and the *bridge builder* (cf. Sect. 4.4.2). The OII types crystallize from typical configurations of the OII activities. That means not every type serves every activity. Hence, each type has specific strengths and each type can satisfy their respective client organizations differently. To make the suitability between OIIs and HCOs clear, four theoretical propositions are given (cf. Sect. 4.5.1).

Value for existing research: Contribution #3 directly responds to the related research gaps. It extends the research streams on consumer co-creation with regard to how it can be effectively enabled, and on online innovation intermediaries with special regard to their agency. Previous research has only looked into it by analysis of key activities, which is beneficial without doubt. Yet, it occurs rarely that one OII performs all the activities listed in academic papers. So Contribution #3 gives a twist to it by observing archetypical configurations of OII activities. Hence, it becomes possible to explain the agency of OIIs through OII types, not only through OII activities. An understanding of the OII agency eventually explains how OIIs are able to support consumer co-creation. Each OII type shows a different approach towards the interaction with HCCs and HCOs, which can be interpreted as different strategies that respond to the call from Colombo et al. (2015). Finally, Contribution #3 also follows the earlier call from Colombo et al. (2013) by providing results that are based on the comparison of multiple OII cases.

Value for the overarching RQ: It becomes evident that co-creation activities can be enabled by OIIs that adhere to different types. As each OII type has different strengths, the OII type may influence the co-creation outcome. Hence, a HCO has the choice to engage with different types of OIIs. This choice depends on the in-house capabilities regarding previous co-creation experience and the use of online channels (cf. Sect. 4.5.1). The ideal interaction model hypothesized in Chap 1 (cf. Fig. 1.6) is thus best reflected by the OII type 'proactive agent'.

> **Contribution #4**: HCOs benefit from a distinct value potential of OIIs, which differs by OII type.

Related research gap: This contribution draws on a similar research gap noted earlier. For any new category of intermediary, like the previously discussed OIIs in healthcare, key questions need to be answered, such as what the enabling factors of successful intermediation are, or how their agency facilitates the creation and integration of external knowledge (Lopez-Vega and Vanhaverbeke 2009; Mele and Russo-Spena 2015). This is in line with Howells' (2006) call for research into the range of intermediaries.

Details of the contribution: The prior analysis has disclosed four forms of value-add for HCOs that are generated by the OII types to different degrees. The values added for HCOs lie primarily in benefitting from the *network reach* of the OII, the *lay expertise* that the OII supplies through its attached consumer community, the *professional expertise* based on the OII experience in conducting co-creation projects, and the *digital literacy* to be obtained. Based on these insights, an HCO that reaches out for mediated co-creation with HCCs has the strategic choice to engage with different types of OII embodying different value propositions. To exemplify this point further, an OII of type *proactive agent* can generate benefits for HCOs in the areas of *network reach*, *lay expertise*, and *professional expertise*, while an OII of type *bridge builder* mainly generates benefit in the area of *network reach* (cf. Sect. 4.4.3).

Value for existing research: Contribution #4 adds to the understanding of the agency of OIIs. The value potential of OIIs is another, more indirect way to describe the agency of OIIs. Through the activities that OIIs perform, they create benefits for their client organizations. Thus, it adds to existing research on the benefits that OIIs are able to generate for their client organizations (Hallerstede 2013; Verona et al. 2006). Especially with regard to online intermediaries, the value potential has to be clearly attributed to the advantages of the virtual environment in which they operate. For example, the network reach is known to be a key advantage of OIIs, but, especially in healthcare, this value-add is even more crucial for HCOs as online intermediaries can provide access to specialized populations of certain disease groups that are usually scarcely distributed in the physical environment.

Value for the overarching RQ: Contribution #4 clarifies the distinctive value that OIIs can add to the innovation capacity of HCOs who aim to engage in co-creation activities with HCCs. OIIs allow HCOs to benefit from access to unique sources as well as broad external expertise, which can be understood as positive prerequisites for effective co-creation.

Contribution #5: Despite the prospects of OII-mediated consumer co-creation in healthcare, some challenges currently remain.

Related research gaps: Existing research has provided knowledge about the application of consumer co-creation, often in form of showing the benefits and successful examples (Magnusson 2009; Mahr et al. 2014; Piller et al. 2012). A critical stance towards the existing challenges remains largely unexplored though (Hoyer et al. 2010; Mahr et al. 2014). However, a view on current challenges is indispensable to ensure a successful implementation of consumer co-creation. Especially the context of interacting with HCCs, as opposed to professional counterparts, may impose additional challenges (Hoyer et al. 2010; Spann et al. 2009). At the same time, when approaching co-creation through the agency of OIIs, there is a lack of understanding the challenges that HCOs have to overcome when interacting with the OII, and vice versa (Colombo et al. 2015). This understanding would be very important for those HCOs that wish to extract maximum value from the collaboration with an OII, and for those OIIs that wish to improve their service offering on consumer co-creation.

Details of the contribution: Based on the 24 interviews across multiple OIIs, there are currently seven areas in which major challenges are expressed (cf. Sect. 4.4.4). The discovery of current challenges in the OII ecosystem yields interesting implications. They clearly document some of the specifics of the healthcare-related arena. To tackle these challenges successfully, the management of OIIs and the design of OII platforms have to cater for these specific characteristics. The three most pressing are the following. First, trust is as a component of social relationships that is even more important in healthcare settings than elsewhere. The OIIs reported that attracting a large enough user base appears to be arduous as potential participants are hesitant to engage beyond peer-to-peer interaction despite their high degree of intrinsic motivation. Successful and inspiring co-creation examples from the past may help to convince future participants. Second, the organizational structures at HCOs, especially at large HCOs, are hermetic and reluctant of external change. The buy-in from all hierarchical levels is necessary to conduct and implement co-creation initiatives. Two scenarios seem possible to overcome it. Either by establishing a dedicated innovation hub within the organization that follows a less strict governance and is partly decoupled from classical structures, or by engaging with the proactive agent type that may provide similar dynamic structures as a third party. Third, the regulatory situation is holding some OIIs back from further developments. According to current legislation in the United States and the European Union, OIIs working together with HCOs such as pharmaceuticals or medical device firms have to adhere to their standards. This causes extra costs which puts a burden on OIIs that are rather small entities in size and funding. Overall, these challenges have to be interpreted as an observation at a specific moment in time within a developing field. This work also suggests practical mitigations to each of the challenges, while the mitigations directly derive from the interview data. However, the proposed mitigations cannot provide a complete picture of how the challenges can be solved.

Value for existing research: The results contribute to the research streams on consumer co-creation and online innovation intermediaries. It furthers knowledge on the (sometimes difficult) application of consumer co-creation mediated through OIIs. It makes clear that both research domains are mutually conditional, i.e. knowledge about OIIs enables effective co-creation and knowledge about co-creation contributes to successful intermediation via OIIs. Apart from that, it has to be noted that the challenges are amplified through the distinctive set-up in the healthcare domain. Therefore, the challenges as well as the mitigations discussed in this work provide valid cues for further research in this area.

Value for the overarching RQ: Contribution #5 provides critical aspects that may impede effective co-creation activities. Hence, it adds to a more complete answer of the RQ by illuminating the reverse side. A realistic picture of current challenges in the OII ecosystem is important to understand in order to successfully establish co-creation via OIIs as a new innovation strategy.

> **Contribution #6**: A refined model for the organizational adoption of co-created knowledge artifacts is proposed, which helps to evaluate the impact of co-creation activities for HCOs.

Related research gaps: While the prospects of consumer co-creation have been discussed in prior research, it seems that there is a disconnection between sometimes outstanding innovative ideas from HCCs and its systematic professional development and commercial exploitation by HCOs (Cepiku and Savignon 2015). In a similar vein, Hoyer et al. (2010) ascertain that the connections between an organization's effort for consumer co-creation and its positive impact in the marketplace are insufficiently understood. By creating an understanding of the organizational adoption of co-created knowledge artifacts, these connections might be revealed.

Details of the contribution: Based on Rogers' (2003) model on the adoption of innovations, a refined model for the organizational adoption of co-created knowledge artifacts is proposed. The model is composed of two principal phases—initiation and implementation—which are each subdivided into two and three stages respectively. It includes several distinct decision points that signify that adoption is not a single event. The adoption is considered a success if the adoption process is completed. The model is based on previous knowledge in the domains of innovation adoption as well as innovation generation. The single in-depth case study, which forms the empirical basis for the analysis, demonstrates that the knowledge artifacts to be adopted still require significant professional development to grow into a marketable innovation. Without doubt, this model requires further validation as it is currently based on a single case study. Yet, the case company can be regarded as a pioneer in the field.

Value for existing research: Contribution #6 adds to the scholarly body of knowledge in a twofold way. First, it adds to co-creation research by showing the process that co-created input needs to go through to grow into an explicit innovation. Second, it adds to the literature on innovation adoption that previously was not able to map the adoption of co-created knowledge artifacts. In particular, the proposed model adds nuance in a number of aspects: (i) it explicitly deals with the adoption of co-created knowledge artifacts, not turnkey innovation, (ii) it refines the implementation stage compared to previous models, and (iii) it offers distinct adoption gates.

Value for the overarching RQ: This contribution explains what "effective co-creation between HCCs and HCOs" ultimately means. As the definition of co-creation describes (cf. Sect. 2.1.1.2), co-creation has the objective to form knowledge that is valuable for an organization's innovation process of new products or services. That means that co-created knowledge artifacts can be considered valuable for the organization if they are fully adopted by an HCO. Otherwise, if the adoption is refused, it cannot be considered successful co-creation. Therefore, it can be stated that OIIs enable effective co-creation between HCCs and HCOs if it produces co-created knowledge that is eventually adopted by the HCO. Without the successful organizational adoption of co-created inputs, the pure OII agency would lose its raison d'être.

> **Contribution #7**: This work advocates online innovation intermediaries (OIIs) in healthcare as third parties that are apt to exploit the innovation potential of HCCs and advance co-creation between HCCs and HCOs.

Related research gaps: The innovative potential of HCCs to provide inputs to healthcare innovation has been subject of research in recent years (cf. Sect. 1.2).

Although its potential has been clearly stated, it is exploited only to a marginal extent so far (Cepiku and Savignon 2015; Henrike and Schultz 2014; Nambisan and Nambisan 2009). HCCs should be professionally supported to further their innovation activity (Engström and Snyder 2013; Oliveira et al. 2015). At the same time, research on co-creation for innovation continues to focus mainly on the exchange of professional counterparts (i.e. the B2B context). Hence, research on co-creation lacks studies in the B2C context to which HCCs could provide inputs if enabling mechanisms were available (cf. Sect. 1.2). Interestingly, a similar divide is found in the research on innovation intermediaries that has hardly studied the professional intermediation between organizations and end consumers (cf. Sect. 2.1.4.2).

Details of the contribution: This research argues for establishing distinct third parties (OIIs) for enabling co-creation because of the following four advantages. First, if the co-creation interaction is mediated by an OII, then this may increase independence and reduce a potential commercial image. It may then lead to a more open co-creation environment and increase the users' willingness to participate in co-creation projects. Moreover, due to the independent image of an OII, OII are more likely able to build large communities of online users that are not restricted to the topical focus of single organizations. Second, OIIs have the ability to reconcile the different worlds of healthcare organizations and healthcare consumers. At the co-creation project presented in empirical study 3, the executives mentioned that the collaboration with consumers was difficult due to sometimes opposing mental attitudes. Figure 6.2 describes and summarizes the reported characteristic differences of HCOs and HCCs in co-creation settings. OIIs can create an environment through which these differences can be alleviated through mediation. Third, OIIs may not only act as broker of knowledge artifacts, but an OII could position itself as a professional innovation agency that takes advantage of online platforms and online user communities. It could be seen as a complement for organizations that lack internal capabilities. This could help to increase the maturity level of consumer

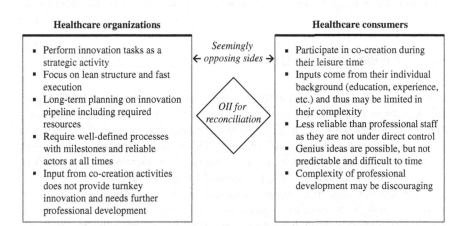

Fig. 6.2 Reported characteristic differences of actors in consumer co-creation

inputs in a systematic manner before it is offered to healthcare organizations for adoption. Fourth, if an OII is engaged for a co-creation project by an HCO, the OII decouples the company brand from the public during the interaction process with the participating healthcare consumers. In any setting of innovation co-creation with consumers and organizations, it is important to think of the implications for the marketing function as well. As co-creation with consumers is a communication with the public, any organization will base its adoption decision of user innovation input on the public image and effects this may cause.

Value for existing research: This contribution responds to the research gaps formulated above and extends research in all the three domains that motivated this work: patient innovation, consumer co-creation, and innovation intermediaries. First, OIIs are apt to access and exploit HCCs through OII platforms. Second, OIIs possess the ability (i.e. through their distinctive agency) to enable co-creation. Third, through engaging in co-creation, OIIs provide further proof of intermediation between organizations and end consumers.

Value for the overarching RQ: Contribution #7 has been an inherent assumption of the formulated RQ. However, the results of this work support its confirmation.

6.3 Managerial Implications

This thesis focuses on online innovation intermediaries (OIIs) in healthcare. It specifically addresses the question how OIIs enable effective consumer co-creation for innovation between healthcare consumers and healthcare organizations. In line with the initial interaction model from Chap. 1 (cf. Fig. 1.6), there are two types of professional actors involved: the HCOs as beneficiaries of co-creation outcomes and the OIIs as mediating agents in co-creation activities. Based on the academic contributions of this research, the present section derives managerial implications for both types of professional actors that are discussed in the following subsections.

6.3.1 Implications for HCOs

The managerial implications for HCOs mostly address managers in R&D departments and other departments that may be charged with innovation-related topics. While HCOs seek ways to enhance the organizational innovation performance with even better and more ideas for new offerings, HCOs might experience a bottleneck of internal knowledge resources because innovation is increasingly the result of novel associations among previously unrelated knowledge domains.

To tackle this challenge, managers should be aware of healthcare consumers who either may be users of the organization's products or services or have gained profound experience through ailments. As stated by current scholarly research, HCCs possess relevant knowledge that can be of critical value for the innovation capacity of an HCO. To connect to the HCCs, the Internet appears to be a valid channel in the today's world. It largely depends on the existing in-house capabilities, if a HCO can reach out and benefit from external inputs to innovation. If the in-house capabilities are insufficient, then there is the option to hire an external agent like an OII who can do the job. Innovation managers at HCOs might draw a number of learnings from this work that are detailed next.

First, this work provides a state of the art review of health 2.0 platforms. These contemporary, interactive online platforms demonstrate the high degree of participation and the profound knowledge pool of HCCs. Some of these health 2.0 platforms are run by organizations who offer intermediary services to connect and collaborate with HCCs through their online platform. HCO managers can find profiles of these online intermediaries in the Annexes B and C of this work. With this overview of identified OIIs, it is possible to sketch a preliminary picture of the market for OIIs in healthcare. It gives managers from HCO environments the necessary orientation when it comes to the decision whether to start their own online innovation platform or to engage with already existing actors in the field.

Second, the results of this work suggest that innovation managers at HCOs should consider OIIs as a valuable mechanism for improving their innovation outcomes. OIIs as third parties can help HCOs to adopt appropriate strategies and practices to embrace HCCs as partners in the development and delivery of innovative healthcare products and services. OIIs provide a distinct value potential for HCOs. In particular, HCOs can benefit from (i) the extended network reach of OIIs giving access to unique and specialized HCC populations, (ii) the authentic accounts of lay expertise of HCCs, (iii) the professional OII expertise acquired through previous co-creation activities, and (iv) the increased digital literacy gained through working in the virtual environment.

Third, when engaging with OIIs, managers can choose from four types of OIIs. The choice largely depends on the in-house capabilities available with regard to consumer co-creation for innovation. Available types of OIIs are (i) the *proactive agent* that offers the most comprehensive set of intermediary activities including consultancy-like activities, (ii) the *support provider* that has operational strength in supporting the conversations and making sense of data, (iii) the *community champion* that allows for a more passive approach towards co-creation, and (iv) the *bridge builder* that is strong at facilitating connections. The in-house capabilities should be well aligned with the chosen OII type. For example, the second and fourth types require advanced in-house capabilities with regard to consumer co-creation, while the first type allows for limited in-house capabilities.

Fourth, in order to enhance internal innovation with knowledge from co-creation activities, the co-created knowledge needs to be adopted from the HCO. This work provides a process model that describes five stages of adoption. Once the adoption process starts, the co-creation process does not end. Managers should keep HCCs continuously involved during the adoption process since HCCs are apt to provide valuable input also during, e.g., the concept maturing and the test stage. The managerial contribution of the adoption model lies in its procedural clarity and the guidance it may provide to innovation managers. However, managers should be aware that an innovation project that integrates HCCs may deviate from the tight processes that are usually applied. Since other actors are involved than in a standard innovation project, coordination costs may rise and adequate staff resources should be reserved. Therefore, it may be recommendable to create an organizationally separated innovation hub that specializes on innovation projects fueled by co-creation with HCCs.

6.3.2 Implications for OIIs

The results of this work also hold implications for the management of OIIs. It is intended for managers at the executive levels of OIIs who should be aware of the following crucial aspects from this work.

First, the market of innovation intermediaries that offer their services through the Internet is still developing. The review from this work delivers a preliminary picture of the OII market in healthcare, which can help managers at OIIs to review competitors and reflect on their position in the market. As the review reveals, some approaches are subsidized with public money and there are only a few cases which have been able to turn into a for-profit business. Managers should validate their current service model with the results from this work. This work provides a classification of OII activities, OII types, and OII value-adds for HCOs. By classifying your own organization into the given scheme, it may help to sharpen the own service offering.

Second, managers should be well aware of the adoption process of co-created knowledge artifacts at HCOs. Hence, the OII service model should be well adjusted to the needs of their client organizations. If OIIs are able to increase the quality of co-creation outcomes, then it is more likely to pass the organizational adoption that will likely induce client satisfaction and follow-on projects.

Third, OIIs offer multiple activities to their client organizations. These activities do exploit the inherent strengths of virtual environments, which is the main asset of OIIs. However, compared to traditional intermediaries, the portfolio of activities is less. Therefore, OIIs could consider to add activities from the traditional range to their offering and thus enhance the competitive advantage. Overall, OIIs should be clear about their original purpose, i.e. to mediate between different parties. With special regard to the reported characteristic differences between HCCs and HCOs (cf. Fig. 6.2), OIIs should take a balancing position that builds bridges between the actors.

Fourth, this work provides a review of current challenges in the OII ecosystem. Towards the HCC side, it seems critical to gain trust from HCCs in order to build up a large enough user base. In addition to that, OIIs often struggle with cultural, organizational, and legal barriers at the front of HCOs. Managers should be well aware of these challenges and should reflect if the current service model needs further realignment. Practical mitigations to each of these challenges are proposed in this work. For example, to grow the user base of HCCs, OIIs should optimize their online platform for high usability, enforce trust-building mechanisms, use an incentive scheme to make users come back. However, one mitigation that was repeatedly mentioned is that OIIs should link the online communities from the platform to offline communities in the real world, i.e. conferences, healthcare associations, patient self-help groups.

With these managerial implications at hand, the following, very last section outlines directions for further research endeavors in this field.

6.4 Directions for Future Research

The goal of this thesis was to acquire fundamental insights into consumer co-creation in healthcare supported by online innovation intermediaries. Although the theoretical framework (Chap. 2) as well as the empirical studies (Chaps. 3–5) help to address the initially formulated gaps in research and to better understand underlying mechanisms from a practice and academic point of view, valuable directions for future research are identified. Since some further research directions have already been discussed in each chapter of the three empirical studies, this section adds overarching research topics and offers pre-formulated research questions.

Grouped along the major stakeholders of the OII ecosystem, Table 6.4 outlines future research directions that are explained in the following. Concerning the HCO side, the first suggestion for future research relates to the power balance between R&D and marketing departments. This work has focused on the effects of

Table 6.4 Directions for future research on mediated co-creation with consumers

#	Topic	Research question
HCO		
1	Power balance R&D and marketing	What are the links between marketing and R&D and its influences on successful co-creation?
2	Knowledge integration	What are effective organizational approaches to enable the organization for integrating external sources of knowledge?
OII		
3	OII business model	What are sustainable business models of OII in healthcare and beyond?
4	Services	Should further services be added to the portfolio of activities of OIIs? How can OIIs best manage the divide between different stakeholder types in B2C contexts?
5	Ethics	What are the ethical implications of OIIs in healthcare? (e.g. with regard to funding models, their objectives, the ways of obtaining patient knowledge)
6	Impact	How to measure the impact of OIIs?
HCC		
7	Locus of consumer innovation in HC	Concerning the knowledge asymmetry in highly technological areas between consumers and organizations, in which areas of healthcare are HCCs best capable to deliver valuable innovation inputs on a broad scale?

co-creation with regard to innovation performance. However, co-creation activities with consumers also present a communication with the public and as such it is of interest for marketing and customer relationship management. Hence, it would be interesting to understand the links between marketing and R&D and its influences on successful co-creation. The second suggestion for future research relates to effective organizational approaches that are needed for integrating external sources of knowledge, such as HCCs. According to the reports from the OIIs interviewed, a significant number of HCOs still faces organizational barriers that prevent them from engaging in co-creation and benefitting from external sources of knowledge.

Concerning the OII side, the third suggestion relates to OII business models. Most of the OIIs from the sample of this work do perform other activities beyond intermediation in order to survive. Hence, the development of sustainable business models that serve mediated co-creation between consumers and organizations would certainly advance this domain. Moreover, future research could investigate if further services should be added to the portfolio of OII activities in order to provide improved agency for co-creation in the B2C context (cf. Fig. 6.2). Further research could also help to determine how OIIs can best manage the characteristic differences between the stakeholder types that are often present in B2C contexts. The fifth topic for future research asks about the possible ethical implications of OIIs in healthcare. This topic becomes particularly relevant with regard to funding models, their objectives, and the ways of obtaining patient knowledge if it includes classified information. The sixth research topic relates to the impact of OIIs and how it can be best measured. This work has used the adoption decision of an organization as an indicator to measure the immediate impact. However, according to Dalziel and Parjanen (2012), there are other levels of impact such as socio-economic benefits that need to be measured.

Concerning the HCC side, the seventh research suggestions refers to the locus of consumer innovation in healthcare. Since the knowledge asymmetry can be considered large between HCCs and HCOs, there may be more or less appropriate areas in healthcare in which HCCs are best capable to deliver valuable innovation inputs on a broad scale. So far, it is not clear whether the locus of consumer innovation lies in, e.g., technology, delivery, treatments, devices, or accessories.

In addition to the research directions above, the scholarly contributions that this thesis has provided (cf. Sect. 6.2) should be approved by confirmatory research. With regard to the identified OII activities, OII types, and the OII value potential, future research could apply and enhance these conceptualizations. Similarly, the presented model for the organizational adoption of user innovation input should be validated with more empirical cases in co-creation settings.

With this very last section, this thesis completes the comprehensive research journey on OIIs in healthcare and provides fruitful starting points for researchers to stimulate further analyses and conversations from both a scholarly and managerial perspective.

Chapter 7
Annexes

7.1 Annex A: Communication of the Research

Parts of this research have earlier been presented to the academic community at international conferences, research colloquia, and related proceedings. This author is sincerely grateful to all peer reviewers who helped to improve this work. The major contribution to each of the below articles remains with the author of this thesis. In chronological order, parts of this research were presented to:

2011

Kuenne, C. W., Rass, M., Adamczyk, S., Bullinger, A. C., & Moeslein, K. M. (2011). Patients as innovators: An open innovation perspective on health 2.0. In *Proceedings of World Conference on Mass Customization, Personalization, and Co-Creation (MCPC)*. San Francisco, CA.
Kuenne, C. W., Adamczyk, S., Rass, M., Bullinger, A. C., & Moeslein, K. M. (2011). IT-Based interaction platforms to foster virtual patient communities. In *Proceedings of GeNeMe 2011* (pp. 153–162). Dresden, Germany.
Kuenne, C. W. (2011). Patients as innovators: Opening up healthcare innovation. In *Proceedings of the 6th Research Seminar on Innovation and Value Creation*. Beilngries, Germany.

2012

Bessant, J., Kuenne, C. W., & Moeslein, K. M. (2012). *Opening up healthcare innovation: Innovation solutions for a 21st century healthcare system*. London: Advanced Institute of Management Research.

The updated online version of this chapter can be found at
http://dx.doi.org/10.1007/978-3-319-51124-5_7

© Springer International Publishing AG 2018

163

C.W. Künne, *Online Intermediaries for Co-Creation*, Progress in IS,
DOI 10.1007/978-3-319-51124-5_7

Kuenne, C. W. (2012a). Towards patients as innovators: Open innovation in healthcare. In *EURAM Doctoral Colloquium 2012*. Rotterdam, Netherlands.

Kuenne, C. W. (2012b). Identifying web-based innovation intermediaries in healthcare. In *Proceedings of the 7th Research Seminar on Innovation and Value Creation*. Chemnitz, Germany

2013

Kuenne, C. W., Moeslein, K. M., & Bessant, J. (2013). Towards patients as innovators: Open innovation in health care. In C. Mukhopadhyay, K. B. Akhilesh, & R. Srinivasan (Eds.), *Driving the economy through innovation and entrepreneurship: Emerging agenda for technology management* (pp. 315–327). Bangalore: Springer India.

Kuenne, C. W., Akenroye, T., & Moeslein, K. M. (2013). Online innovation intermediaries in healthcare. In *Proceedings of the European Conference on Information Systems (ECIS) 2013*. Utrecht, Netherlands.

2014

Kuenne, C. W. (2014). Bridging the knowledge divide: Toward a conceptual understanding of online innovation intermediaries in healthcare. In *Proceedings of the 9th Research Seminar on Innovation and Value Creation*. Nuremberg, Germany.

2015

Kuenne, C. W., & Agarwal, R. (2015). Online innovation intermediaries as a critical bridge between patients and healthcare organizations. In O. Thomas & F. Teuteberg (Eds.), *Smart Enterprise Engineering: 12th International Conference on Wirtschaftsinformatik, WI 2015*. (pp. 1268–1282). Osnabrueck, Germany.

Kuenne, C. W. (2015). Multi-level organizatonal adoption of patient innovations. In *Proceedings of the 10th Research Seminar on Innovation and Value Creation*. Leipzig, Germany.

7.2   Annex B: Repository of Health 2.0 Online Platforms

Platform name	Webpage	Explicit user enquiry	Knowledge exploitation	Innovation intermediary	Level of coordination
2nd MD	www.2nd.md	N	N	N	One-to-one
3G Doctor	www.3gdoctor.com	N	N	N	One-to-one
AED4.eu	www.aed4.eu	Y	Y	Y	One-to-one
AMD Netz NRW	www.amd-netz.de	N	N	N	Many
Apothekenumschau	www.apotheken-umschau.de	N	N	N	Many
Apps for Healthy Kids	www.appsforhealthykids.devpost.com	Y	Y	Y	One-to-one
Army of Women	www.armyofwomen.org	Y	Y	Y	One-to-one
Ärzte Zeitung Online Community	www.aerztezeitung.de/community	N	N	N	Many
Ashoka Changemakers	www.changemakers.com	Y	Y	Y	One-to-one
AskDr.Wiki	www.askdrwiki.com	Y	N	N	Many
Association of Cancer Online Resources	www.acor.org	N	N	N	Many
Autism 360	www.autism360.org	N	N	N	Many
Blabladoctor	www.blabladoctor.com	N	N	N	Many
Bodimojo	www.bodimojo.com	N	N	N	Many
BrainTalk Communities	www.braintalkcommunities.org	N	N	N	Many
CakeHealth	www.cakehealth.com	N	N	N	One-to-one
Cancer Commons	www.cancercommons.org	Y	Y	Y	Many
CancerConnect	www.cancerconnect.com	N	N	N	Many
Cancer Contribution	www.cancercontribution.fr	Y	N	N	Many
Care Pages	www.carepages.com	N	N	N	Many
Careflash	www.careflash.com	N	N	N	Many
Carenity	www.carenity.com	N	N	N	Many
Caring.com	www.caring.com	N	N	N	Many
CaringBridge	www.caringbridge.org	N	N	N	Many
ChickRx	www.chickrx.com/home	N	N	N	Many
Cleveland Clinic	www.my.clevelandclinic.org/online-services	N	N	N	One-to-one
Coliquio	www.coliquio.de	Y	Y	Y	Many
Connecting Nurses Care Challenge	www.connecting-nurses.com	Y	Y	Y	One-to-one
Cosmiq	www.cosmiq.de	N	N	N	Many
Cröhnchen-Klub	www.croehnchen-klub.de	N	N	N	Many
CrowdMed	www.crowdmed.com	Y	Y	Y	One-to-one
Curado	www.curado.de	N	N	N	Many
Cure Together	www.curetogether.com	Y	Y	Y	Many
Daily Strength	www.dailystrength.org	N	N	N	Many
Data Design Diabetes	www.datadesigndiabetes.com	Y	Y	Y	One-to-one
DCCV	www.dccv.de	N	N	N	Many

(continued)

(continued)

Platform name	Webpage	Explicit user enquiry	Knowledge exploitation	Innovation intermediary	Level of coordination
Deutsches Ärzteblatt Online	www.aerzteblatt.de	N	N	N	Many
Deutsches Medizin Forum	www.medizin-forum.de	N	N	N	Many
DGM Ideenschmiede	www.dgmideenschmiede.de	Y	Y	Y	Many
Diabetes Mine Design Challenge	www.diabetesmine.com/designcontest	Y	Y	Y	One-to-one
Diabetic Connect	www.diabeticconnect.com	N	N	N	Many
Disaboom	www.disaboom.com	N	N	N	Many
dLife	www.dlife.com	N	N	N	Many
Doc2doc	www.doc2doc.bmj.com	N	N	N	Many
DocCheck	www.doccheck.com	N	N	N	Many
Doctoralia	www.doctoralia.com	N	N	N	One-to-one
Doctors.net.uk	www.doctors.net.uk	Y	Y	Y	Many
Doktorsitesi (Turkey)	www.doktorsitesi.com	N	N	N	Many
Dooox	www.dooox.de	N	Y	N	Many
Dossia	www.dossia.org	N	Y	N	One-to-one
Doximity	www.doximity.com	N	N	N	Many
DrEd	www.dred.com	N	N	N	One-to-one
Dr-Gumpert	www.dr-gumpert.de	N	N	N	Many
Drimpy	www.drimpy.com	N	N	N	Many
DrThom	www.drthom.com	N	N	N	One-to-one
Edison Nation Medical	www.edisonnationmedical.com	Y	Y	Y	One-to-one
eHealth Opinion	www.ehealthopinion.com	N	N	N	One-to-one
e-med Forum Multiple Sklerose	www.emed-ms.de	N	N	N	Many
e-med Forum Osteologie	www.emed-os.de	N	N	N	Many
EPI-Vista	www.epivista.de	N	N	N	One-to-one
Esanum	www.esanum.de	N	N	N	Many
Eugenol	www.eugenol.com	N	N	N	Many
EverydayHealth	www.everydayhealth.com	N	N	N	Many
FertilityPlanIt	www.fertilityplanit.com	N	N	N	Many
Fibromyalgie Aktuell	www.fibromyalgie-aktuell.de	N	N	N	Many
Follow me	www.followme.com	N	Y	N	One-to-one
FoundHealth	www.foundhealth.com	N	N	N	Many
Function Medicine	www.functionmedicine.com	N	N	N	One-to-one
Gemeinsam für die Seltenen	www.gemeinsamselten.de	Y	Y	Y	Many
Gesundheit Heute	www.gesundheit-heute.de	N	N	N	Many
Gesundheit.de	www.gesundheit.de	N	N	N	Many

(continued)

(continued)

Platform name	Webpage	Explicit user enquiry	Knowledge exploitation	Innovation intermediary	Level of coordination
Gesundheit Kompakt Community	www.community.gesundheitkompakt.de	Y	N	N	Many
Gesundheitsfrage.net	www.gesundheitsfrage.net	N	N	N	Many
Gesundheitswerkstatt	www.gesundheitswerkstatt.de	N	N	N	Many
Ginger.io	www.ginger.io	Y	Y	Y	Many
GiveForward	www.giveforward.com	N	N	N	One-to-one
Hamburg Living Lab	www.hamburglivinglab.de	Y	Y	Y	Many
Health Tech Hatch	www.healthtechhatch.com	Y	Y	Y	One-to-one
Health Unlocked	www.healthunlocked.com	Y	Y	Y	Many
HealthcareMagic	www.healthcaremagic.com/ask-doctor-online	N	N	N	One-to-one
HealthCentral	www.healthcentral.com	N	N	N	Many
HealthCorpus by Nhumi	www.healthcorpus.com	N	N	N	One-to-one
HealthGrades	www.healthgrades.com	Y	N	N	One-to-one
HealthyHeroes	www.healthyheroes.se	N	N	N	One-to-one
HealthyPlace	www.healthyplace.com	N	N	N	Many
HeiaHeia (Finland)	www.heiaheia.com	N	N	N	Many
Hello Health Patients	www.hellohealth.com	N	Y	N	One-to-one
HippokraNet	www.hippokranet.de	N	N	N	Many
Hubbub Health	www.hubbubhealth.com	N	N	N	One-to-one
I Had Cancer	www.ihadcancer.com	N	N	N	Many
iDoc24	www.idoc24.com	N	N	N	One-to-one
Imedo	www.imedo.de	N	N	N	Many
iMobileWellness	www.imobilewellness.com/heart-health	N	N	N	Many
Innovation By You	www.innovationbyyou.com	Y	Y	Y	Many
Inspire	www.inspire.com	Y	Y	Y	Many
iWantGreatCare	www.iwantgreatcare.org	Y	Y	Y	One-to-one
Jameda	www.jameda.de	N	N	N	One-to-one
Jooly's Join (MS Webpals)	www.mswebpals.org	N	N	N	Many
Kamasz Panasz	www.kamaszpanasz.hu	N	N	N	Many
KISP Prostatakrebs	www.prostatakrebse.de	N	N	N	Many
Koozala	www.koozala.com	N	Y	N	One-to-one
Krebsgemeinschaft für Brustkrebs	www.krebsgemeinschaft.de	N	N	N	Many
Lexevita	www.lexevita.de	N	N	N	Many
Lifeline	www.lifeline.de	N	N	N	Many
LifeVest Health	www.lifevesthealth.com	N	N	N	One-to-one
Med1	www.med1.de	N	N	N	Many
Med2Click	www.med2click.de	N	N	N	Many
Medfriend	www.medfriend.de	N	N	N	Many

(continued)

(continued)

Platform name	Webpage	Explicit user enquiry	Knowledge exploitation	Innovation intermediary	Level of coordination
MedHelp	www.medhelp.org	N	N	N	Many
Medical Plexus	www.medicalplexus.com	N	N	N	Many
Medical Valley Innovation	www.medical-valley-innovation.de	Y	Y	Y	One-to-one
Medizin Forum	www.medizinforum.com	N	N	N	Many
Medizinberichte.de	www.medizinberichte.de	N	N	N	Many
Medknowledge.de	www.medknowledge.de	N	N	N	Many
Medpedia	www.medpedia.com	N	N	N	One-to-one
Medperts	www.medperts.de	N	N	N	Many
Medscape by WebMD	www.medscape.com	N	N	N	One-to-one
Medstartr	www.medstartr.com	N	N	N	One-to-one
MedUniverse	www.meduniverse.se	N	N	N	Many
MedWhat	www.medwhat.com	N	N	N	One-to-one
MensHealth.de	www.menshealth.de	N	N	N	Many
MeQuilibrium	www.mequilibrium.com	N	N	N	One-to-one
Merel Club	www.merel-club.de	N	N	N	Many
Microsoft HealthVault	www.healthvault.com	N	Y	N	One-to-one
MiVia	www.mivia.org	N	Y	N	One-to-one
Mood Institute	www.moodinstitute.com	N	N	N	Many
MS-Gateway	www.ms-gateway.de	N	N	N	Many
MumsNet	www.mumsnet.com	N	N	N	Many
My Handicap	www.myhandicap.de	Y	Y	Y	Many
My MediConnect	www.mymediconnect.net	N	N	N	One-to-one
MyBreastCancerTeam (by MyHealthTeams)	www.mybcteam.com	N	N	N	Many
MyPacs	www.mypacs.net	N	N	N	Many
Nature Network	www.network.nature.com	N	N	N	Many
NetDoctor	www.netdoctor.co.uk	N	N	N	Many
NetDoktor	www.netdoktor.de	N	N	N	Many
Neurosurgic	www.neurosurgic.com	N	N	N	Many
NeuroTalk	www.neurotalk.psychcentral.com	N	N	N	Many
NHS HealthSpace	www.healthspace.nhs.uk	N	N	N	One-to-one
NHS Innovation Challenge Prizes	www.england.nhs.uk/ challengeprizes	Y	Y	Y	One-to-one
No more clipboard	www.nomoreclipboard.com	N	Y	N	One-to-one
Novi Medicine	www.novimedicine.com	N	N	N	One-to-one
Onmeda	www.onmeda.de	N	N	N	Many
Orphanet	www.orpha.net	N	N	N	One-to-one
Ozmosis	www.ozmosis.org	N	N	N	Many
Paradisi	www.paradisi.de	N	N	N	Many
Patient Ally	www.patientally.com	N	N	N	One-to-one
Patient Gateway	www.patientgateway.org	N	N	N	One-to-one
Patient Innovation	www.patient-innovation.com	Y	Y	Y	Many

(continued)

(continued)

Platform name	Webpage	Explicit user enquiry	Knowledge exploitation	Innovation intermediary	Level of coordination
Patient.co.uk	www.patient.co.uk	N	N	N	Many
Patienten Wie Ich	www.patientenwieich.de	N	N	N	Many
PatientOpinion	www.patientopinion.org.uk	Y	Y	Y	One-to-one
PatientsCreate	www.patientscreate.com	Y	Y	Y	Many
PatientsLikeMe	www.patientslikeme.com	Y	Y	Y	Many
Pflegeboard.ch	www.pflegeboard.ch	N	N	N	Many
Practice Fusion	www.practicefusion.com	N	N	N	One-to-one
PsychCentral	www.psychcentral.com	N	N	N	Many
Qpid.me	www.qpid.me	N	N	N	One-to-one
QualiMedic	www.qualimedic.de	N	N	N	Many
QualityHealth	www.qualityhealth.com	N	N	N	Many
QuantiaMD	www.quantiamd.com	N	N	N	Many
QuantifiedSelf	www.quantifiedself.com	N	N	N	Many
RareConnect	www.rareconnect.org	N	N	N	Many
RateMDs	www.ratemds.com	Y	N	N	One-to-one
RateMyHospital	www.ratemyhospital.ie	Y	N	N	One-to-one
Rehacafe Gesundheitscommunity	www.rehacafe.de	N	N	N	Many
Renaloo	www.renaloo.com	N	N	N	Many
Research to Reality Community by NCI	researchtoreality.cancer.gov	N	N	N	Many
Rheuma Online	www.rheuma-online.de	N	N	N	Many
Sanego	www.sanego.de	Y	N	N	Many
SD-Krebs	www.sd-krebs.de	N	N	N	Many
Sermo	www.sermo.com	Y	Y	Y	Many
Springer Medizin	www.springermedizin.de	N	N	N	Many
Stupid Cancer	www.stupidcancer.com	N	N	N	Many
SugarStats	www.sugarstats.com	N	N	N	Many
SURVEYOR Health	www.surveyorhealth.com	N	N	N	One-to-one
TicTrac	www.tictrac.com	N	N	N	One-to-one
TuDiabetes	www.tudiabetes.org	N	N	N	Many
Tyze Personal Networks	www.tyze.com	N	N	N	Many
Vidapost	www.vidapost.com	N	N	N	Many
Was hab' ich?	www.washabich.de	N	N	N	One-to-one
WebMD	www.webmd.com	N	N	N	Many
Who is sick	www.whoissick.org	Y	N	N	One-to-one
Wiki Surgery	www.wikisurgery.com	Y	N	N	Many

Note As this is a highly dynamic field of research, it may be that some websites have altered or were shut down during the course of analysis

7.3   Annex C: Case Profiles of the Identified OIIs

Based upon the empirical study I in Chap. 3, the following online platforms have been classified as online innovation intermediaries. Detailed profile sheets for these 30 OII platforms are presented in this annex. Each profile sheet includes a general description, an assessment of the dimensions derived in Chap. 3, and a screenshot. Order of presentation is alphabetical grouped by coordination level, see Table 7.1.

Table 7.1 List of identified OII cases

Coordination level	
One-to-many	One-to-one
1. Cancer Commons	17. AED4.eu
2. Coliquio	18. Apps for Healthy Kids
3. Cure Together	19. Army of Women
4. DGM Ideenschmiede	20. Ashoka Changemakers
5. Doctors.net.uk	21. Connecting Nurses Care
6. Gemeinsam für die Seltenen	Challenge
7. Ginger.io	22. CrowdMed
8. Hamburg Living Labs	23. Data Design Diabetes
9. Health Unlocked	24. Diabetes Mine Design
10. Innovation By You	Challenge
11. Inspire	25. Edison Nation Medical
12. My Handicap	26. Health Tech Hatch
13. Patient Innovation	27. iWantGreatCare
14. PatientsCreate	28. Medical Valley Innovation
15. PatientsLikeMe	29. NHS Innovation Challenge
16. Sermo	Prizes
	30. Patient Opinion

Name: **Cancer Commons**   *Geographical focus:* US
URL: www.cancercommons.org   *Medical focus:* Cancer

General description: Nonprofit, open science initiative linking cancer patients, physicians, and scientists in Rapid Learning Communities. Patients contribute treatment data through the At the moment of analysis, topical focus covers lung cancer, mel anoma, and prostate cancer. The mission is to ensure that patients are treated in accord with the latest knowledge on targeted therapies and immunotherapies and to continually update that knowledge based on each patient's response.

Coordination Level: One-to-many   *Consumer Involvement:* Chronically ill
Community Access: Non-restricted   *Professional Involvement:* Provider, supplier
Level of Interaction: Cooperation
Potential support in innovation process: Fuzzy front end, new product development

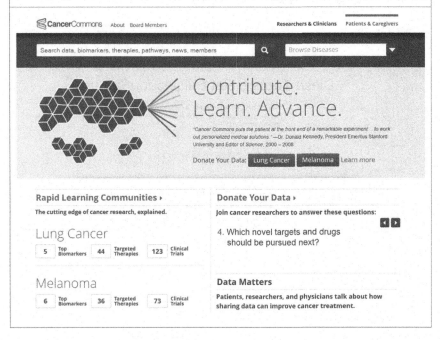

Name: **Coliquio**   *Geographical focus:* Germany
URL: www.coliquio.de   *Medical focus:* Nonspecific

General description: Social networking site exclusive to physicians. Physicians have the possibility to exchange and discuss medical issues of practical cases across disciplines and receive replies from peers within a short period of time. The service is free of charge. One part of the platform activity focuses on open innovation at which physicians and healthcare organizations jointly develop new ideas for innovation and product improvements. The participants submit own ideas and comment the ones of the others.

Coordination Level: One-to-many   *Consumer Involvement:* No
Community Access: Restricted by expertise   *Professional Involvement:* Provider
Level of Interaction: Cooperation
Potential support in innovation process: Fuzzy front end

Name: **CureTogether**   *Geographicalfocus:* Worldwide
URL: www.curetogether.com   *Medical focus:* Nonspecific

General description: Data-driven social networking health site comparing the real-world performance of treatments across 500+ health conditions. It helps healthcare consumers to anonymously track and compare health data, to better understand their bodies, make more informed treatment decisions and contribute data to research. Partnerships with universities exist.

Coordination Level: One-to-many   *Consumer Involvement:* Newly diagnosed, chronically ill
Community Access: Non-restricted   *Professional Involvement:* No
Level of Interaction: Consultation
Potential support in innovation process: Fuzzy front end

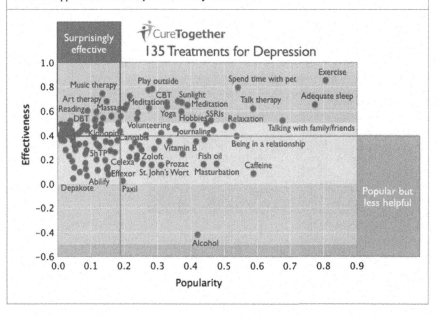

Name: **DGM Ideenschmiede**   *Geographical focus:* Germany
URL: www.dgmideenschmiede.de   *Medical focus:* Myopathy, ALS

General description: To go beyond virtual discussion groups, this platform enables the exchange and new development of ideas for patients affected by ALS (amyotrophic lateral sclerosis). It offers manifold features, such as structured wiki-style interface to edit idea submissions, evaluation of submitted ideas by peers, ranking of most popular ideas, weekly calls for ideas on a given topic.

Coordination Level: One-to-many   *Consumer Involvement:* Chronically ill
Community Access: Non-restricted   *Professional Involvement:* No
Level of Interaction: Collaboration
Potential support in innovation process: Fuzzy front end

Name: **Doctors.net.uk**   *Geographical focus:* UK
URL: www.doctors.net.uk   *Medical focus:* Nonspecific

General description: Social networking site exclusive to UK physicians. As the leading channel for communications and research with physicians, it offers healthcare organizations the ability to reach specific doctor audiences in a measurable way. Organizations in the pharmaceutical and med tech industries, public and private healthcare and recruitment sectors as well as non-health related companies regularly work with this platform. It is a trusted source of medical education, research and communication. The service 'medeConnect' gives clients the opportunity to conduct targeted, fast and affordable research.

Coordination Level: One-to-many   *Consumer Involvement:* None
Community Access: Restricted by expertise   *Professional Involvement:* Provider
Level of Interaction: Cooperation
Potential support in innovation process: Fuzzy front end

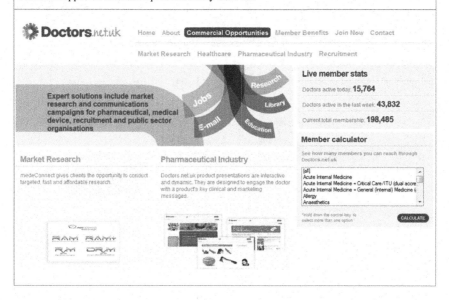

Name: **Gemeinsam für die Seltenen**   *Geographical focus:* Germany
URL: www.gemeinsamselten.de   *Medical focus:* Rare diseases

General description: For patients with rare diseases, the platform (i) organizes a series of idea contest-like challenges to find solutions for improving the quality of life of rare disease patients, (ii) collects patient's problems and needs in a central place, and (iii) creates a community with people from diverse backgrounds to promote knowledge exchange and collaborate on innovative concepts.

Coordination Level: One-to-many   *Consumer Involvement:* Newly diagnosed, chronically ill
Community Access: Non-restricted   *Professional Involvement:* Provider, supplier
Level of Interaction: Collaboration
Potential support in innovation process: Fuzzy front end

Name: **Ginger.io**   *Geographical focus:* US
URL: www.ginger.io   *Medical focus:* Anxiety, depression, mental
health

General description: Behavioral analytics platform that turns data from mobile sensors into health insights. For researchers it is an integrated web platform to collect behavior data and identify novel findings. For providers it is a "check engine light" to improve population management. For patients it provides a mobile application that helps them better understand and manage their health. Ginger.io taps into the continuous sensor data from your mobile phone and other devices to predict individual behavior changes and identify aggregate trends.

Coordination Level: One-to-many   *Consumer Involvement:* Newly diagnosed, chronically ill
Community Access: Restricted   *Professional Involvement:* Provider, researcher
Level of Interaction: Cooperation
Potential support in innovation process: Fuzzy front end, new product development

Name: **Hamburg Living Lab**   *Geographical focus:* Germany
URL: www.hamburglivinglab.de   *Medical focus:* Dentistry, prosthetics, implants

General description: Initiated by TuTech Innovation, this platform that is part of the project Hamburg Living Lab allows companies, researchers, patients and users to jointly work on improvements and new developments of medical products and services in the fields of dentistry, biomechanics and implant technology. Participating companies can thus improve their competitive advantage.

Coordination Level: One-to-many   *Consumer Involvement:* Chronically ill
Community Access: Restricted   *Professional Involvement:* Provider, supplier
Level of Interaction: Collaboration
Potential support in innovation process: Fuzzy Front End, New Product Development

Name: **HealthUnlocked**   *Geographical focus:* UK
URL: www.healthunlocked.com   *Medical focus:* Nonspecific

General description: Patient communities and health tracking for chronic disorders. The difference between HealthUnlocked and other social networks is the level of moderation by trusted patient groups. Apart from that, analyzing the experience of platform users helps to uncover what happens to real people managing their health in the real world. Health institutions (hospitals and charities) and industry (pharmaceuticals or medical devices) collaborate wi th HealthUnlocked to analyze data submitted by consenting users of the platform or to carry out structured studies alongside doctors and patients.

Coordination Level: One-to-many   *Consumer Involvement:* Newly diagnosed, chronically ill
Community Access: Non-restricted   *Professional Involvement:* No
Level of Interaction: Communication
Potential support in innovation process: Fuzzy front end

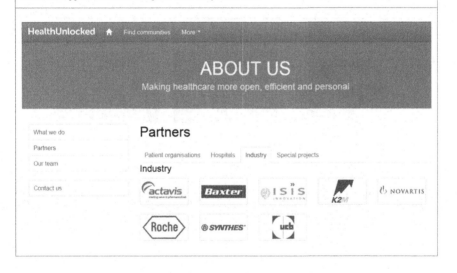

Name: **InnovationByYou**   *Geographical focus:* Worldwide
URL: www.innovationbyyou.com   *Medical focus:* Ostomy, continence

General description: Innovation platform to share ideas and learn from likeminded patients. The goal is to innovate together on products and solutions that can improve the lives of people with ostomy or continence issues. This is also a place for peer support, and tips and tricks. Virtual VIP rooms exist for selected members who have shown a special interest in product development. In these rooms, members work closely together with the sponsor company on a range of confidential innovation projects. The VIP activities include designing prototypes, making 3D models, and distributing toolkits to support creativity.

Coordination Level: One-to-many   *Consumer Involvement:* Chronically ill
Community Access: Non-restricted   *Professional Involvement:* No
Level of Interaction: Collaboration
Potential support in innovation process: Fuzzy front end, new product development

Name: **Inspire**   *Geographical focus:* US
URL: www.inspire.com   *Medical focus:* Nonspecific

General description: Social networking health site that builds communities for patients and caregivers, in partnership with national patient advocacy organizations, and helps healthcare organizations connect with these highly engaged populations. Inspire was created with the belief that patient contributions to medical progress have been historically underappreciated, and great progress in medical research will result from involving patients and fully valuing their contributions.

Coordination Level: One-to-many   *Consumer Involvement:* Newly diagnosed, chronically ill
Community Access: Non-restricted   *Professional Involvement:* No
Level of Interaction: Collaboration
Potential support in innovation process: Fuzzy front end; new product development

Name: **MyHandicap**   *Geographicalfocus:* Germany, Switzerland
URL: www.myhandicap.ch   *Medical focus:* Physical disabilities

General description: Forum and community for disabled people, including large address directory to barrier-free places. It enables patients to exchange among each other and with dedicated professional experts that are partnering with the platform. The forum classifies the contributions into solved and unsolved which conveys a sense of solution orientation. Furthermore, the forum has a special section to submit "ideas for a better world". From time to time, live expert chats are organized that bring companies and patients together to discuss current needs and future developments.

Coordination Level: One-to-many   *Consumer Involvement:* Chronically ill
Community Access: Non-restricted   *Professional Involvement:* Provider, supplier
Level of Interaction: Consultation
Potential support in innovation process: Fuzzy front end

Name: **PatientInnovation**   *Geographical focus:* Worldwide
URL: www.patient-innovation.com   *Medical focus:* Nonspecific

General description: Platform and social network that facilitates the sharing of solutions to improve the quality of life of patients and caregivers of any pathology. Patients and caregivers often develop innovative solutions to cope with the challenges of their conditions. Sharing these solutions may be decisive in improving other people's lives. Idea posts can be improved by adding pictures, links to videos, and symptoms and situation tags.

Coordination Level: One-to-many   *Consumer Involvement:* Newly diagnosed, chronically ill
Community Access: Non-restricted   *Professional Involvement:* No
Level of Interaction: Cooperation
Potential support in innovation process: Fuzzy front end

Name: **PatientsCreate** *Geographical focus:* UK
URL: www.patientscreate.com *Medical focus:* Nonspecific

General description: Patient-centric crowd sourcing platform to empower the patient voice. The goal is to identify the needs of patients and allow bespoke solutions to be produced. Users can create and solve challenges. Other users take up the challenge and offer solutions. The top solutions are showcased on the platform. It also helps companies that are building solutions for patients. Companies are also able to set challenges, often including a financial reward in return for the best solution given.

Coordination Level: One-to-many *Consumer Involvement:* Well, newly diagn., chronic. ill
Community Access: Non-restricted *Professional Involvement:* Supplier
Level of Interaction: Collaboration
Potential support in innovation process: Fuzzy front end, new product development

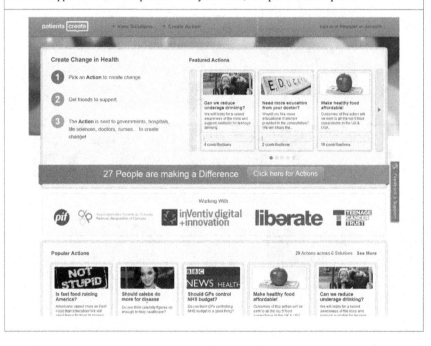

Name: **PatientsLikeMe**   *Geographical focus:* US
URL: www.patientslikeme.com   *Medicalfocus:* Nonspecific

General description: Data-driven social networking health site that enables its members to share condition, treatment, and symptom information in order to monitor their health over time and learn from real-world outcomes. Based on this unique data, PatientsLikeMe has collabora ted with major organizations from industry, academia and the non-profit sector. Through these projects, patients contribute to the advancement of medical research, clinical trials and product development.

Coordination Level: One-to-many   *Consumer Involvement:* Newly diagnosed, chronically ill
Community Access: Non-restricted   *Professional Involvement:* Supplier
Level of Interaction: Collaboration
Potential support in innovation process: Fuzzy front end, new product development

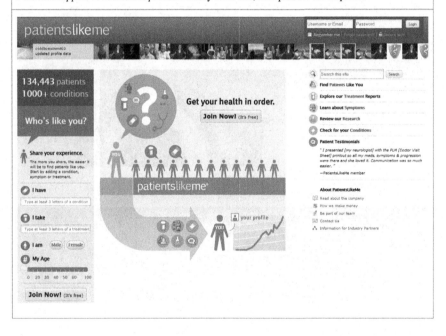

Name: **Sermo**   *Geographical focus:* US
URL: www.sermo.com   *Medical focus:* Nonspecific

General description: Sermo is the largest online physician-only network, where practicing physicians discuss a wide range of topics from clinical cases to advice about drugs, practice management, healthcare reform and more. Besides sharing and solving challenging cases with peers, members can earn honoraria for participating in polls and research studies initiated by healthcare organizations.

Coordination Level: One-to-many   *Consumer Involvement:* No
Community Access: Restricted by expertise   *Professional Involvement:* Provider, supplier
Level of Interaction: Cooperation
Potential support in innovation process: Fuzzy front end

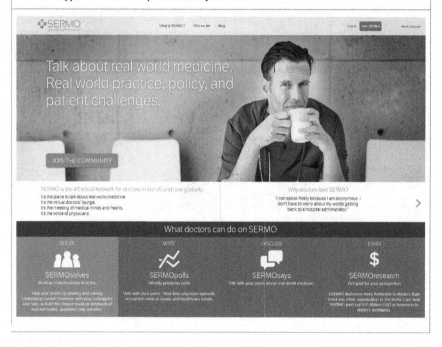

Name: **AED₄.eu**   *Geographical focus:* Netherlands
URL: www.aed₄.eu   *Medical focus:* Stroke

General description: Aed4.eu allows users and public authorities to add GPS locations of automated external defibrillators. This database of locations is then accessible through the application aed4eu on mobile phones. It serves as an example of how authorities and crowdsourc ing can work together to improve healthcare.

Coordination Level: One-to-one   *Consumer Involvement:* Well, newly diagn., chronic. ill
Level of Interaction: Consultation   *Professional Involvement:* Provider, supplier
Potential support in innovation process: Commercialization

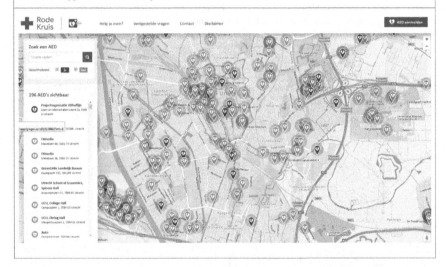

Name: **Apps for Healthy Kids**   *Geographical focus:* US
URL: appsforhealthykids.devpost.com   *Medical focus:* Children's health

General description: Innovation contest to develop fun and engaging software tools and games that contribute to end childhood obesity. Apps for Healthy Kids challenges software developers, game designers, students, and other innovators to develop applications and games that drive children, especial ly ages 9-12, directly or through their parents, to eat better and be more physically active. Financial rewards are set out for winners in different categories.

Coordination Level: One-to-one   *Consumer Involvement:* No
Level of Interaction: Consultation   *Professional Involvement:* Supplier
Potential support in innovation process: Fuzzy front end

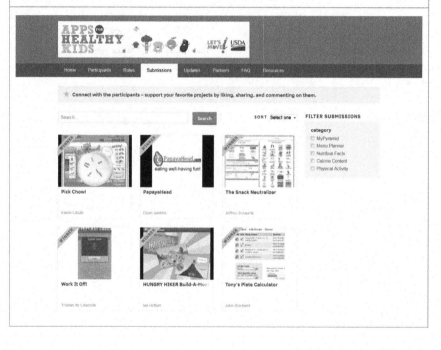

Name: **Army of Women**   *Geographical focus:* US
URL: www.armyofwomen.org   *Medical focus:* Breast cancer

General description: Initiative to recruit woman who may want to participate in breast-cancer-prevention research studies. The goal is twofold: (i) to recruit healthy women of every age and ethnicity, including breast cancer survivors and women at high-risk for the disease, to partner with researchers and directly participate in related studies; (ii) to challenge researchers to expand its current focus to include breast cancer prevention research conducted on healthy women (and not mice only).

Coordination Level: One-to-one   *Consumer Involvement:* Well, newly diagn., chronic. ill
Level of Interaction: Consultation   *Professional Involvement:* Researcher
Potential support in innovation process: Fuzzy front end

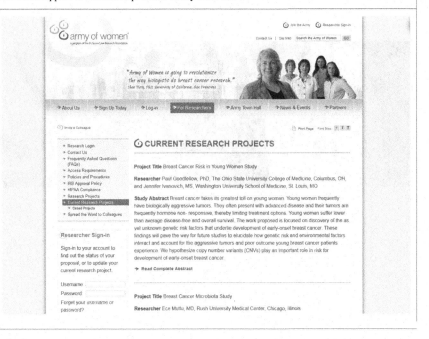

Name: **Ashoka Changemakers**   *Geographical focus:* Worldwide
URL: www.changemakers.com   *Medical focus:* Nonspecified

General description: Innovation marketplace that offers innovation challenges around topics of healthcare and sustainable change. The goal is to connect innovation seekers and solvers through open challenges, coupled with Ashoka's network of social entrepreneurs and impact partners. Users of the platform can either create own challenges or enter a solution on an existing challenge. Together feedback is shared and refined. Ashoka helps to actively spread each project.

Coordination Level: One-to-one   *Consumer Involvement:* Well, newly diagn., chronic. ill
Level of Interaction: Consultation   *Professional Involvement:* Provider, supplier, researcher
Potential support in innovation process: Fuzzy front end

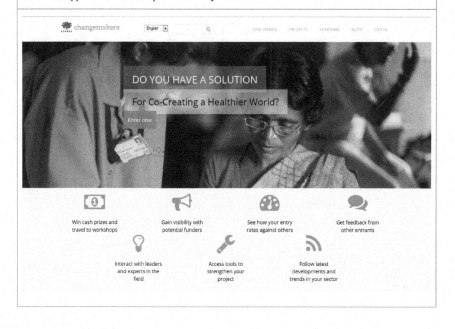

Name: **Connecting Nurses**   *Geographical focus:* Worldwide
URL: www.care-challenge.com   *Medical focus:* Nonspecified

General description: Innovation contest that provides a forum for nurses from around the world to share their ideas, advice and innovations. It is supported by Sanofi in partnership with nurses organizations. The goal is to bring nurses together on-line and in the real world. This network of shared knowledge helps to enhance nursing's role in advancing healthcare. A reviewing committee of nurses evaluates the innovations suggested.

Coordination Level: One-to-one   *Consumer Involvement:* No
Level of Interaction: Consultation   *Professional Involvement:* Provider
Potential support in innovation process: Fuzzy front end

Name: **CrowdMed**   *Geographical focus:* US
URL: www.crowdmed.com   *Medical focus:* Nonspecific

General description: Crowdsourcing platform to identify illnesses that have gone without a diagnosis. The goal is to accelerate and lower the cost of diagnosing rare medical conditions by crowdsourcing and applying prediction market technology to medical data. Patients submit their case against a fee, then so-called medical detectives try to find a solution. Users of the platforms can take both roles, submitting cases or solving cases. Medical detectives, who may earn monetary rewards, are usually medical school students or retired physicians, however, a medical degree is not required.

Coordination Level: One-to-one   *Consumer Involvement:* Newly diagnosed, chronically ill
Level of Interaction: Cooperation   *Professional Involvement:* Provider
Potential support in innovationprocess: Fuzzy front end

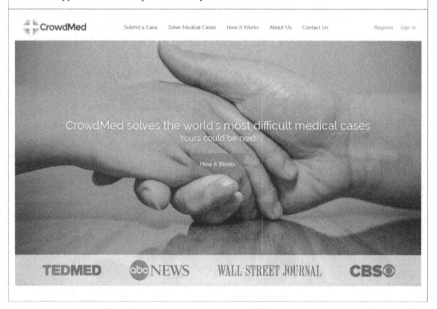

Name: **DataDesignDiabetes** *Geographical focus:* US
URL: www.datadesigndiabetes.com *Medical focus:* Diabetes

General description: Innovation contest to find concepts which help diabetes patients with annually changing topics. The goal is to seek service solutions to improve the experience or outcome of people living with diabetes. It appeals to all innovators regardless of background and current areas of interest. Significant monetary rewards from the commercial sponsors are set for the winners.

Coordination Level: One-to-one *Consumer Involvement:* Well, newly diagn., chronic. ill
Level of Interaction: Consultation *Professional Involvement:* Provider, supplier, researcher
Potential support in innovation process: Fuzzy front end

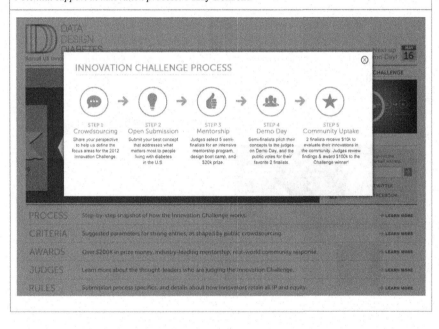

Name: **Diabetes Mine Design Challenge**   *Geographical focus:* US
URL: www.diabetesmine.com/designcontest   *Medical focus:* Diabetes

General description: Idea contest to encourage creative new tools for improving life with diabetes. It welcomes entries from patients, parents, caregivers, entrepreneurs, developers, engineers who are passionate about diabetes and product design. Participants can win monetary rewards and get valuable assistance to realize their design concept. Sponsors are e.g. Sanofi, Animas, LifeScan, Dexcom, and the California Healthcare Foundation.

Coordination Level: One-to-one   *Consumer Involvement:* Chronically ill
Level of Interaction: Consultation   *Professional Involvement:* Supplier
Potential support in innovation process: Fuzzy front end

 Diabetes Mine   A gold mine of straight talk and encouragement

Grand Prize Winner Pancreum: A Small, Modular Artificial Pancreas

Written by Amy Tenderich | Published on June 20, 2011

The Pancreum closed loop (automated insulin + CGM + glucagon) system that won a Grand Prize in the DiabetesMine Design Challenge this year may look like a pipe dream, but designer Gil DePaula assures us it is "visionary but real."

 We are members of
diabetes advocates

 "The glucagon part is definitely a futuristic concept — because there's no predicate device for glucagon delivery with the FDA, so that's a huge question. But the insulin pump and CGM are as real as OmniPod was when I joined Insulet in 2002 (he worked there 5 years). And now that's real and on the market, there are predicate devices out there. So if I want to introduce a new disposable tubeless insulin pump, I can do it. I won't have to climb mountains."

Name: **Edison Nation Medical**   *Geographical focus:* US
URL: www.edisonnationmedical.com   *Medical focus:* Nonspecified

General description: Innovation marketplace for individual innovators and small businesses. It aims at connecting inventors with organizations who are capable of commercializing their ideas. Therefore, Edison National Medical evaluates each submission through an in-depth evaluation process covering technical and clinical feasibility, intellectual property, and commercialization potential. If selected, it will provide active support to commercialize the invention via licensing, sale or company incubation. At the same time, commercial organizations can set innovation searches on the platform addressing a particular topic.

Coordination Level: One-to-one   *Consumer Involvement:* Well, newly diagn., chronic. ill
Level of Interaction: Consultation   *Professional Involvement:* Supplier
Potential support in innovation process: Fuzzy front end, new product development

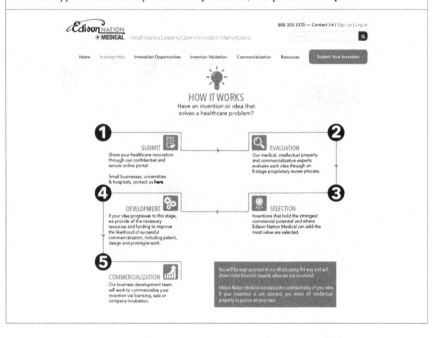

Name: **HealthTechHatch**   *Geographical focus:* US
URL: www.healthtechhatch.com   *Medical focus:* Nonspecified

General description: Platform for launching early-stage innovations in healthcare and putting them into the hands of patients, physicians, wellness professionals and consumers. The platform provides testing, rating, expert advice, and crowdfunding for both non-profit and for-profit entrepreneurs in the health tech field who are holding brilliant ideas ready to hatch. Regular users can participate in the testing part by providing usability feedback on concepts and prototypes. During time of analysis, focus is on apps, which are easy to test through an online setting.

Coordination Level: One-to-one   *Consumer Involvement:* Well, newly diagn, chronic. ill
Level of Interaction: Cooperation   *Professional Involvement:* Provider, supplier
Potential support in innovation process: New product development

Name: **iWantGreatCare**　　　　　*Geographical focus:* UK
URL: www.iwantgreatcare.org　　　*Medical focus:* Nonspecified

General description: At first glance, a feedback platform providing quality ratings and search for UK health services. If healthcare consumers encounter a problem, they can give feedback about doctors, hospitals, GP practices, etc. to ensure the problem gets fixed. The reports are forwarded to the relevant entities. iWant Great Care works with the NHS and independent commissioners to provide detailed, accurate and timely monitoring of patient experience. Quantitative and qualitative feedback for healthcare organizations gives insight that actually allows continuous improvement and is proven to engage front-line clinical teams.

Coordination Level: One-to-one　　　　*Consumer Involvement:* Well, newly diagn., chronic. ill
Level of Interaction: Consultation　　　*Professional Involvement:* No
Potential support in innovation process: Fuzzy front end

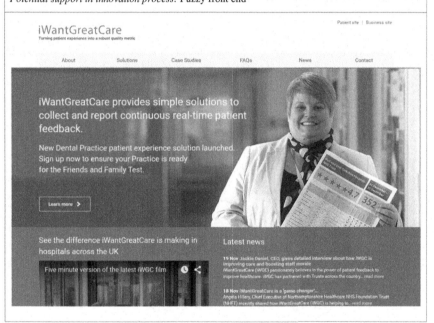

Name: **Medical Valley Innovation**   *Geographical focus:* Germany
URL: www.medical-valley-innovation.de   *Medical focus:* Medical technology

General description: Innovation marketplace for experts in the field of medical technology. The
proposed projects on the site represent innovation challenges from companies of the Medical
Valley network. It is open to companies from that network. Companies that wish to set new
innovation challenges on the platform can contact the platform operator via the site. Solving
these challenges remains open to the general public, i.e. either consumers or professionals,
who can submit the suggested solutions through the site. The platform incorporates typical
elements of innovation contests, e.g. prize money, specified runtime, jury evaluation.

Coordination Level: One-to-one   *Consumer Involvement:* Well, newly diagn., chronic. ill
Level of Interaction: Consultation   *Professional Involvement:* Provider, supplier
Potential support in innovation process: Fuzzy front end, new product development

Name: **NHS Innovation Challenge Prizes**   *Geographical focus:* UK
URL: www.england.nhs.uk/challengeprizes   *Medical focus:* Nonspecified

General description: Innovation contest by the NHS England. This initiative provides an opportunity to reward clinical advances such as new treatments for life-threatening conditions as well as innovations in delivering care and promoting healthy living. It seeks to identify innovations that have the potential for wide scale spread and adoption within NHS delivery. It shall serve the ultimate goal to improve patient outcomes. Contributors come from NHS organizations. The topics and categories for submission are renewed every year. The winning innovations receive prize money and professional mentoring and developmental support from internal and external partners.

Coordination Level: One-to-one   *Consumer Involvement:* No
Level of Interaction: Consultation   *Professional Involvement:* Provider, supplier
Potential support in innovation process: New product development

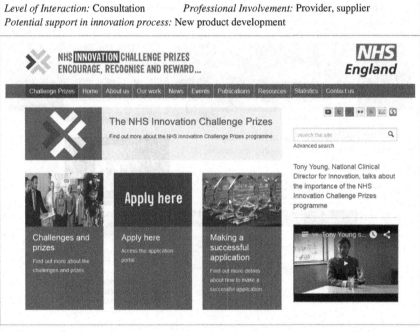

Name: **PatientOpinion**   *Geographical focus:* UK
URL: www.patientopinion.org.uk   *Medicalfocus:* Health service delivery

General description: Non-profit feedback platform for patients or caregivers who recently experienced health services in the UK. It is about both praise and issues to improve. The patient's appraisal is passed on to the respective health organization that can reply to it in return. Each entry has a progress bar next to it that conveys a sense of solution orientation. It indicates in the following order: 'new entry-not read by the healthcare organization', 'read by the organization', 'the organization has given a response', 'change is planned'. Thus, subscribed organizations can effectively improve their services according to the consumers' needs.

Coordination Level: One-to-one   *Consumer Involvement:* Newly diagnosed, chronically ill
Level of Interaction: Consultation   *Professional Involvement:* No
Potential support in innovation process: Fuzzy front end, new product development

7.4 Annex D: Guideline for OII Expert Interviews

Confidentiality Disclaimer: All of your statements are treated confidentially and are anonymously analyzed only. We may agree upon a written consent.

Purpose of this interview: This study deals with so-called online innovation intermediaries, such as your platform. Specifically, we want to explore their role as "bridgers" between healthcare consumers and healthcare organizations (see figure below). At this interface, innovation intermediaries can support the generation, aggregation and transmission of patients' knowledge and ideas towards innovation-seeking firms. Goal of the interview with you is to find out more about the mediating role of your platform [insert name XYZ] as well as the value proposition that this platform makes along the innovation process.

Leading research questions:

> **RQ 2a**: What are the key activities of OIIs in healthcare, and how do these activities bundle together towards OII types?
>
> **RQ 2b**: What value do OIIs add for the innovation capacity of HCOs?
>
> **RQ 2c**: What are critical challenges during co-creation activities via OIIs, and how can these be mitigated?

General information to be obtained:

Interviewee	Company	Online platform
– First and last name – Position, department – Responsibilities – Tenure – Background – Other prof. experience	– Name – #FTE, revenues and profit – Mother company or sponsors – Org chart	– Date of launch – # users/members (+historical +forecast) – % of active users – Page impressions (+historical +forecast) – Major milestones

1. **Please provide a short overview of the goals of your organization! Please also describe your personal responsibility in this setting.**

   - *Which service* do you provide towards partnering HC firms and HC consumers?
   - What is your *core function* of the platform as a service provider?
   - What is the *goal* of the platform today? (Which problem are you trying to solve? Which gap do you serve?)
   - Please tell us your *(strategic) considerations* and objectives related to the implementation and operations of your platform.
   - How would you describe the *business model* behind the platform?
   - Who is the *owner* of the platform's company? Owner = sponsor?
   - What does the parenting company/patron/sponsor *expect* from the platform in return?
   - Do you earn money? If yes, how (pricing)?
   - How would you describe the *market* in which you operate? Who are your *main competitors*?

2. **Who is involved in using or benefiting from the platform?**

   A: Targeted user group: (such as online users/healthcare consumers/patients/ family members)

   - Who is your targeted user group? User segmentation? Actual = target?
   - Do you address individual users, teams, or the community as a whole?
   - Which competencies do you look for?
   - How do you recruit/select users?
   - Why should the users participate? What is in for the user?

B: Targeted partners/organizations/firms:

– Who are your partners today?
– How does the cooperation work? What do your partners expect from you?
– Did you formalize the relationship? How? Why not?
– Which partners could be interested in this aggregated knowledge in the future?

3. What is your role between these stakeholders?

– Describe your (intermediary) role between the users of your platform and your partners (i.e. healthcare organizations).
– How do you create value? What is your value proposition?
– Please describe your service offering towards your partners.
– Do you use/exploit/aggregate the user's data/knowledge? If yes, how?
– Who determines the goal/purpose of the aggregation process?
– Please describe a typical flow from user-generated information via your platform towards the partners/manufacturers.
– Why is the collected data/information from the users useful to you partners?

4. What are your positive/negative experiences while working together with the platform users?

A: Targeted user group:

– What worked well (bad) in the past?
– What do you ask the user to do? What information/knowledge shall/can he contribute?
– How do you engage/incentivize/motivate users?
– To what extent do you control the task solving process? (e.g. regarding task complexity, task formulation, user support, facilitation, proactive motivation, community management).
– Do you receive user feedback? What do they express?
– Did you see motivational issues?
– Are the given technical functionalities for users enough to explicate themselves? Should other, new functionalities be implemented?
– How do you manage data privacy of users while reusing the data for other purposes?

5. **What are your positive/negative experiences while working together with corporate partners?**

  B: Targeted partners/organizations/firms:

  – Please give examples along the following questions.
  – Did you formalize the relationship with your partners, i.e. through contract? If yes, how and why?
  – Can the partner influence the knowledge pack? Can the partner customize the service agreement?
  – Did you experience any barriers and or challenges in cooperation with your innovation partners/manufacturers?
  – Do you know if your partners created innovations based on knowledge received through you/your platform?

Post-interview questions

- Is there anything else that you want to add, that we missed out, that you could not talk about during the interview?

  – What would you like to change in the future?
  – Which changes and trends do you see to come up in the near/mid-term future?
  – How do you see the role of the patient in ten years?

- Are you talking to other researchers?
- To whom else should I speak within your organization?

7.5   Annex E: Guideline for HCO Expert Interviews

INTERVIEW GUIDE
FOR HEALTHCARE ORGANIZATIONS USING OII PLATFORMS

Confidentiality Disclaimer: All of your statements are treated confidentially and are anonymously analyzed only. We may agree upon a written consent.

Leading research question:

> **RQ 3**: How can HCOs adopt user innovation inputs generated through an OII platform?

1. **What are the key activities that IBY and its staff fulfilled as an intermediary between patients and corporate R&D?**

   – Number of staff involved? Who is the "Community Admin Team"? What are their activities?
   – How many total users? How many active users? Who are the users?
   – Through which methods were IBY users engaged?
   – Were there any thematic instructions from corporate to guide IBY?
   – Why would patients leave a great idea to a commercial company? Are they idealistic? Specific incentives? What do they get in return?

2. **To what degree did the patient input created through the IBY platform influence corporate product development? What are real innovation outcomes from IBY? Please give examples**.

   – Which value (benefits) did the IBY platform generate for the Salpo corporate business?
   – Which kinds of projects (topics) are suited for patient involvement?

3. **With regard to the OstomyArch, please describe the process from the early beginnings in the user community until product launch**.

   – When and at which maturity level did the idea enter the formal innovation process?
   – Who was involved—Users versus R&D staff?
   – Which challenges occurred during the development process?
   – How is the process to internalize the patients inputs?
   – Why did the product availability of the OstomyArch end?

4. **Once user innovation input is available, how can healthcare organizations operationalize an innovation strategy that is based on co-creation with patients?**

   – How to match patient inputs with corporate needs/planning/processes?
   – Is corporate open to adapt development agenda to patient ideas?
   – How do internal development processes have to be adjusted in order to allow optimal patient co-creation?
   – In which ways (which areas) is your organization affected by co-creation activities? Change required? E.g. impact on traditional innovation practices and processes?
   – How to measure the success of co-creation activities with patients?

5. **What are critical challenges healthcare organizations face when co-creating innovative insights with patients?**

   – Why did you discontinue IBY? For what reasons couldn't you build a sustainable business case?
   – Future of online innovation platforms: What needs to be improved?
   – Patient-driven   innovation: Which   alternatives   exist   to   a crowdsourced/community platform like IBY? Offline versus online?
   – Do you know of other companies with similar approaches?

Post-interview questions

• Is there anything else that you want to add, that we missed out, that you could not talk about during the interview?

   – What would you like to change in the future?
   – Which changes and trends do you see to come up in the near/mid-term future?
   – How do you see the role of the patient in ten years?

• Are you talking to other researchers?
• To whom else should I speak within your organization?

7.6   Annex F: Stage-Gate Process for Formal Innovation Projects at Salpo

Process flow: Gate 0 → Stage 0 Concept Dev → Gate 1 → Stage 1 Concept Maturing → Gate 2 → Stage 2 Product Verification → Gate 3 → Stage 3 Product Realization → Gate 4 → Stage 4 Global Launch → Gate 5

	Stage 0 Concept Development	Stage 1 Concept Maturing	Stage 2 Product Verification	Stage 3 Product Realization	Stage 4 Global Launch
Objective of Stage	▪ To explore and identify concepts fulfilling the project scope ▪ To recommend concepts with documented principles and functionality for Gate 1	▪ To mature the concept for design verification and prepare for design input freeze at Gate 2	▪ To verify the chosen product concept from a business, a technical and a production point of view (design verification) ▪ To finalize verification of the product and process specifications	▪ To purchase production capacity acc. to launch plan ▪ To start manufacturing products ▪ To perform design validation activities ▪ To obtain regulatory approvals ▪ To carry out design t	▪ To conduct the launch of the new product ▪ To establish volume production ▪ To stabilize production and product quality ▪ To evaluate actual vs. forecasted business

	Gate 0 Project Initiation	Gate 1 Concept Selection	Gate 2 Concept Freeze	Gate 3 Product & Process Freeze	Gate 4 Product Launch	Gate 5 Business Evaluation
Objective of Gate	▪ To initiate an AIM project, signing-off the project direction and scope ▪ To approve the project agreement	▪ To provide a "go" for the selected product concepts to be further matured ▪ To ensure the concept meets the business requirements described in the Innovation Brief	▪ To freeze the prototype and the design specification document ▪ To release pre-investments needed to meet pilot production	▪ To freeze the product ▪ To approve the manufacturing strategy, business case and global launch plan ▪ To release investments needed to meet the capacity	▪ To make final project assessment to give a "go" for launch ▪ To decide on post-launch activities and resources ▪ To decide the date for the	▪ To evaluate the obtained vs. forecasted market position of the product ▪ To close down the project and document learning points from business

Source: Salpo internal documents

Erratum to: Online Intermediaries for Co-Creation

Erratum to:
C.W. Künne, *Online Intermediaries for Co-Creation*,
Progress in IS, DOI 10.1007/978-3-319-51124-5

In the original version of the book, Annexures have to be removed from book back matter and have to be treated as Chapter 7. The erratum book has been updated with the change.

The updated online version of this book can be found at
http://dx.doi.org/10.1007/978-3-319-51124-5

© Springer International Publishing AG 2018   E1
C.W. Künne, *Online Intermediaries for Co-Creation*, Progress in IS,
DOI 10.1007/978-3-319-51124-5_8

References

Adams, S. A. (2010). Revisiting the online health information reliability debate in the wake of "web 2.0": An inter-disciplinary literature and website review. *International Journal of Medical Informatics, 79*(6), 391–400.

Adams, S. A. (2011). Sourcing the crowd for health services improvement: The reflexive patient and "share-your-experience" websites. *Social Science & Medicine (1982), 72*(7), 1069–1076.

Adams-Bigelow, M. (2004). First results from the 2003 Comparative Performance Assessment Study (CPAS). In P. D. M. A. The (Ed.), *Handbook of new product development* (pp. 546–566). Hoboken, NJ, USA: Wiley.

Afuah, A. (2003). Redefining firm boundaries in the face of the Internet: Are firms really shrinking? *Academy of Management Review, 28*(1), 34–53.

Agarwal, R., Gao, G. (Gordon), DesRoches, C., & Jha, A. K. (2010). Research commentary—The digital transformation of healthcare: Current status and the road ahead. *Information Systems Research, 21*(4), 796–809.

Ahuja, G. (2000). Collaboration networks, structural holes, and innovation: A longitudinal study. *Administrative Science Quarterly, 45*(3), 425–455.

Alam, I. (2002). An exploratory investigation of user involvement in new service development. *Academy of Marketing Science Journal, 30*(3), 250.

Alavi, M., & Leidner, D. E. (2001). Review: Knowledge management and knowledge management systems: Conceptual foundations and research issues. *MIS Quarterly, 25*(1), 107.

Alderson, W. (1957). *Marketing behavior and executive action: A functionalist approach to marketing theory.* Homewood, IL: Irwin.

Allen, R. C. (1983). Collective invention. *J Economic Behavior & Organization, 4*(1), 1–24.

Allison, M. (2009). Can web 2.0 reboot clinical trials? *Nature Biotechnology, 27*(10), 895–902.

Anand, N., Gardner, H. K., & Morris, T. (2007). Knowledge-based innovation: Emergence and embedding of new practice areas in management consulting firms. *Academy of Management Journal, 50*(2), 406–428.

Anderson, C., & Agarwal, R. (2011). The digitization of healthcare: Boundary risks, emotion, and consumer willingness to disclose personal health information. *Information Systems Research, 22*(3), 469–490.

Anderson, R., & Funnell, M. (2000). Compliance and adherence are dysfunctional concepts in diabetes care. *The Diabetes Educator, 26*(4), 597–604.

Antons, D., & Piller, F. T. (2015). Opening the black box of "not invented here": Attitudes, decision biases, and behaviorial consequences. *Academy of Management Perspectives, 29*(2), 193–217.

Ardichvili, A., Page, V., & Wentling, T. (2003). Motivation and barriers to participation in virtual knowledge-sharing communities of practice. *Journal of Knowledge Management, 7*(1), 64–77.

Argote, L., Ingram, P., Levine, J. M., & Moreland, R. L. (2000). Knowledge Transfer in organizations: Learning from the experience of others. *Organizational Behavior and Human Decision Processes, 82*(1), 1–8.

© Springer International Publishing AG 2018
C.W. Künne, *Online Intermediaries for Co-Creation*, Progress in IS,
DOI 10.1007/978-3-319-51124-5

Armstrong, A. W., Cheeney, S., Wu, J., Harskamp, C. T., & Schupp, C. W. (2012). Harnessing the power of crowds: Crowdsourcing as a novel research method for evaluation of acne treatments. *American Journal of Clinical Dermatology, 13*(6), 405–416.

Arnstein, S. (1969). A ladder of citizen participation. *Journal of the American Planning Association, 35*(4), 216–224.

Avery, A. (2016). Just do it! Web 2.0 and the breaking of the tacit dimension for knowledge acquisition. In *Proceedings of SAIS 2016*.

Ba, S., & Wang, L. (2013). Digital health communities: The effect of their motivation mechanisms. *Decision Support Systems, 55*(4), 941–947.

Bagozzi, R. P. (1975). Marketing as exchange. *Journal of Marketing, 39*(10), 32–39.

Bansemir, B. (2013). *Organizational innovation communities*. Wiesbaden: Springer Gabler.

Barney, J. B. (2001). Resource-based theories of competitive advantage: A ten-year retrospective on the resource-based view. *Journal of Management, 27*(6), 643–650.

Bartl, M. (2009). *Patients as partners: Co-creation in health care*. www.michaelbartl.com.

Bartl, M., Fueller, J., Mühlbacher, H., & Ernst, H. (2012). A manager's perspective on virtual customer integration for new product development. *Journal of Product Innovation Management, 29*(6), 1031–1046.

Bastian, H. (1994). *The power of sharing knowledge: Consumer participation in the Cochrane collaboration. Cochrane Collaboration*. Oxford: Cochrane Collaboration.

Baum, J., Calabrese, T., & Silverman, B. (2000). Don't go it alone: Alliance network composition and startups' performance in Canadian biotechnology. *Strategic Management Journal, 21*(3), 267–294.

Bendapudi, N., & Leone, R. P. (2003). Psychological implications of customer participation in co-production. *Journal of Marketing*.

Bennis, W. G. (1966). *Changing organizations*. New York: McGraw-Hill.

Berge, S., & Buesching, A. (2008). Strategien von Communities im Web 2.0. In B. H. Hass, G. Walsh, & T. Kilian (Eds.), *Web 2.0: Neue Perspektiven für Marketing und Medien* (pp. 23–37). Berlin, Heidelberg: Springer.

Bergenholtz, C. (2011). Knowledge brokering: Spanning technological and network boundaries. *European Journal of Innovation Management, 14*(1), 74–92.

Berry, L. L., & Bendapudi, N. (2007). Healthcare a fertile field for service research. *Journal of Service Research, 10*(2), 111–122.

Berwick, D. M. (2003). Disseminating innovations in health care. *Journal of the American Medical Association, 289*(15), 1969–1975.

Bessant, J., Kuenne, C. W., & Moeslein, K. M. (2012). *Opening up healthcare innovation: Innovation solutions for a 21st century healthcare system*. London: Advanced Institute of Management Research.

Bessant, J., & Maher, L. (2009). Developing radical service innovations in healthcare—The role of design methods. *International Journal of Innovation Management, 13*(4), 555.

Bessant, J., & Rush, H. (1995). Building bridges for innovation: The Role of consultants in technology transfer. *Research Policy, 24*(1), 97–114.

Bhattacherjee, A. (1998). Managerial influences on intraorganizational information technology use: A principal-agent model. *Decision Sciences, 29*, 139–162.

Bieber, M., Engelbart, D., Furuta, R., Hiltz, S. R., Noll, J., Preece, J., ... Walle, B. Van De. (2002). Toward virtual community knowledge evolution. *Journal of Management Information Systems, 18*(4), 11–35.

Biemans, W. (1991). User and third-party involvement in developing medical equipment innovations. *Technovation, 11*(3), 163–182.

Biemans, W., & Langerak, F. (2015). More research priorities. *Journal of Product Innovation Management, 32*(1), 2–3.

Bill, S., Helleputte, J. Van, Larsson, A., Olsson, A., & Sjölund, F. (2011). Rethinking user involvement in the front end of healthcare innovation. In *18th International Product Development Management Conference*. Delft, Netherlands.

Billington, C., & Davidson, R. (2012). Leveraging open innovation using intermediary networks. *Production and Operations Management*, n/a–n/a.

Birnsteel, L., Hoeksma, J., & Grätzel, P. (2008). *Web 2.0 in the health sector: Industry review with UK Perspective*. London: E-Health Media.

Blazevic, V., & Lievens, A. (2008). Managing innovation through customer coproduced knowledge in electronic services: An exploratory study. *Journal of the Academy of Marketing Science, 36*(1), 138–151.

Bodenheimer, T., Lorig, K., Holman, H., & Grumbach, K. (2002). Patient self-management of chronic disease in primary care. *Journal of the American Medical Association, 288*(19), 2469–2475.

Bogers, M., Afuah, A., & Bastian, B. (2010). Users as innovators: A review, critique, and future research directions. *Journal of Management, 36*(4), 857–875.

Bogers, M., & West, J. (2012). Managing distributed innovation: Strategic utilization of open and user innovation. *Creativity and Innovation Management, 21*(1), 61–75.

Bohnet-Joschko, S., & Jandeck, L. M. (2011). *Erfolg durch Innovation: Das Innovationsmanagement der deutschen Medizintechnikhersteller*. Germany: Witten/Berlin.

Bohnet-Joschko, S., & Kientzler, F. (2010). Medical doctors driving technological innovation: Questions about and innovation management approaches to incentive structures for lead users. *Zeitschrift Für Evidenz, Fortbildung und Qualität im Gesundheitswesen, 104*(10), 721–6.

Boote, J., Telford, R., & Cooper, C. (2002). Consumer involvement in health research: A review and research agenda. *Health Policy, 61*(2), 213–236.

Boudreau, K. J., Lacetera, N., & Lakhani, K. R. (2011). Incentives and problem uncertainty in innovation contests: An empirical analysis. *Management Science*.

Boulos, M. N. K., & Wheeler, S. (2007). The emerging Web 2.0 social software: An enabling suite of sociable technologies in health and health care education. *Health Information and Libraries Journal, 24*(1), 2–23.

Brennan, P. F. (1999). Health informatics and community health: Support for patients as collaborators in care. *Methods of Information in Medicine, 38*(4–5), 274–278.

Brockhoff, K. (2003). Customers' perspectives of involvement in new product development. *International Journal of Technology Management, 26*(5/6), 464.

Brown, J. S., & Duguid, P. (1991). Organizational learning and communities-of-practice: Toward a unified view of working, learning, and innovation. *Organization Science, 2*(1), 40–57.

Bugshan, H. (2015). Co-innovation: The role of online communities. *Journal of Strategic Marketing, 23*(2), 175–186.

Bullinger, A. C., & Moeslein, K. M. (2010). Innovation contests—Where are we? In *Proceedings of the Sixteenth Americas Conference on Information Systems AMCIS Lima* (pp. 1–8).

Bullinger, A. C., Neyer, A.-K., Rass, M., & Moeslein, K. M. (2010). Community-based innovation contests: Where competition meets cooperation. *Creativity and Innovation Management, 19*(3), 290–303.

Bullinger, A. C., Rass, M., Adamczyk, S., Moeslein, K. M., & Sohn, S. (2012). Open innovation in health care: Analysis of an open health platform. *Health Policy (Amsterdam, Netherlands), 105*(2–3), 165–175.

Burt, R. S. (1992). *Structural holes: The social structure of competition*. Cambridge, MA: Harvard University Press.

Cahill, J. (1996). Patient participation: A concept analysis. *Journal of Advanced Nursing, 24*(3), 561–571.

Cain, M. M., Sarasohn-Kahn, J., & Wayne, J. C. (2000). Health e-People: The online consumer experience. *Institute for the Future*.

Carbonell, P., Rodriguez-Escudero, A. I., & Pujari, D. (2009). Customer involvement in new service development: An examination of antecedents and outcomes. *Journal of Product Innovation Management, 26*(5), 536–550.

Cepiku, D., & Giordano, F. (2014). Co-production in developing countries: Insights from the community health workers experience. *Public Management Review, 16*(3), 317–340.

Cepiku, D., & Savignon, A. B. (2015). User innovations in healthcare: Evidence from rare and chronic diseases. In *EURAM Annual Conference 2015, Warsaw*. Warsaw, Poland: Kozminksi University, Warsaw.

Chatterji, A. K., & Fabrizio, K. (2008). *The impact of users on technological development: The role of physician innovation in the medical device industry*. Durham, North Carolina: Fuqua School of Business, Duke University.

Chesbrough, H. W. (2003). *Open innovation: The new imperative for creating and profiting from technology*. Boston, MA: Harvard Business School Press.

Chesbrough, H. W. (2006). *Open business models: How to thrive in the new innovation landscape*. Boston, MA: Harvard Business Review Press.

Chesbrough, H. W., & Brunswicker, S. (2013). *Managing open innovation in large firms— Executive survey on open innovation 2013*. Stuttgart, Germany: Fraunhofer Verlag.

Chesbrough, H. W., Vanhaverbeke, W., & West, J. (2006). *Open innovation: Researching a new paradigm*. Oxford: Oxford University Press.

Chin, W. W., Hamermesh, R. G., Huckman, R. S., McNeil, B. J., & Newhouse, J. P. (2012). *5 imperatives addressing healthcare's innovation challenge*. Boston, MA: Harvard Forum on Healthcare Innovation.

Chreim, S., Williams, B. E., Janz, L., & Dastmalchian, A. (2010). Change agency in a primary health care context. *Health Care Management Review, 35*(2), 187–199.

Cline, R. J. W. (2001). Consumer health information seeking on the Internet: The state of the art. *Health Education Research, 16*(6), 671–692.

Clulow, S. (2013). *Open innovation strategies in the healthcare industry*. Cleveland, Ohio: NineSigma.

Cohen, W. M., & Levinthal, D. A. (1990). Absorptive capacity: A new perspective on learning and innovation. *Administrative Science Quarterly, 35*(1), 128.

Colombo, G., Buganza, T., Klanner, I.-M., & Roiser, S. (2013). Crowdsourcing Intermediaries and problem typologies: An explorative study. *International Journal of Innovation Management, 17*(2), 1–24.

Colombo, G., Dell'Era, C., & Frattini, F. (2015). Exploring the contribution of innovation intermediaries to the new product development (NPD) process: A typology and an empirical study. *R&D Management, 45*(2), 126–146.

Conner, K. R. (1991). A historical comparison of resource-based theory and five schools of thought within industrial organization economics: Do we have a new theory of the firm? *Journal of Management, 17*(1), 121–154.

Cooper, R. G. (2008). Perspective: The stage-gateidea-to-launch process—Update, what's new, and NexGen systems. *Journal of Product Innovation Management, 25*(3), 213–232.

Correia, A. M. R., Paulos, A., & Mesquita, A. (2010). Virtual communities of practice: Investigating motivations and constraints in the processes of knowledge creation and transfer. *Electronic Journal of Knowledge Management, 8*(1), 11–20.

Craincross, F. (1997). *The death of distance: How the communication revolution will change our lives*. Boston, MA: Harvard Business School Press.

Creswell, J. W. (2009). *Research design: Qualitative, quantitative, and mixed methods approaches* (3rd ed.). Los Angeles: Sage Publications.

Dahlander, L., & Gann, D. M. (2010). How open is innovation? *Research Policy, 39*(6), 699–709.

Dalziel, M. (2010). Why do innovation intermediaries exist? In *DRUID Summer Conference 2010* (p. 24).

Dalziel, M., & Parjanen, S. (2012). Measuring the Impact of Innovation Intermediaries: A Case Study of Tekes. In V. Harmaakorpi & H. Melkas (Eds.), *Practice-based innovation: Insights, applications and policy implications* (pp. 117–133). Berlin, Heidelberg: Springer.

Damanpour, F., & Wischnevsky, J. D. (2006). Research on innovation in organizations: Distinguishing innovation-generating from innovation-adopting organizations. *Journal of Engineering and Technology Management, 23*(4), 269–291.

Dannecker, A., & Lechner, U. (2007). Zielgruppenspezifische Dienste für Virtuelle Patientengemeinschaften. In H. K. Oberweis, A. Weinhardt, C. Gimpel & B. A. Pankratius, V. Schmizler (Eds.), *eOrganisation: Service-, Prozess-, Market-Engineering* (Vol. 4, pp. 935–952). Universitätsverlag Karlsruhe.

Davey, S. M., Brennan, M., Meenan, B. J., & McAdam, R. (2010). The health of innovation: Why open business models can benefit the healthcare sector. *Irish Journal of Management, 30*(1), 21–41.

Demonaco, H. J., Ali, A., & von Hippel, E. (2006). The major role of clinicians in the discovery of off-label drug therapies. *Pharmacotherapy, 26*(3), 323–332.

Desouza, K. C., Awazu, Y., Jha, S., Dombrowski, C., Papagari, S., Baloh, P., & Kim, J. (2008). Customer-driven innovation: To be a marketplace leader, let your customers drive. *Research Technology Management, 51*, 35–44.

Desouza, K. C., Dombrowski, C., Awazu, Y., Baloh, P., Papagari, S., Jha, S., & Kim, J. (2009). Crafting organizational innovation processes. *Innovation: Management, Policy and Practice, 11*(1), 6–33.

Di Gangi, P. M., & Wasko, M. (2009). Steal my idea! Organizational adoption of user innovations from a user innovation community: A case study of Dell IdeaStorm. *Decision Support Systems, 48*(1), 303–312.

Diener, K., & Piller, F. T. (2010). *The market for open innovation: Increasing the efficiency and effectiveness of the innovation process*. Aachen: RWTH-TIM Group.

Downes, L., & Mui, C. (1998). *Unleashing the killer app: Digital strategies for market dominance*. Boston, MA: Harvard Business School Press.

Dyer, J., & Singh, H. (1998). The relational view: Cooperative strategy and sources of interorganizational competitive advantage. *Academy of Management Review, 23*(4), 660–679.

Dyer, W., & Wilkins, A. (1991). Better stories, not better constructs, to generate better theory: A rejoinder to Eisenhardt. *Academy of Management Review, 16*(3), 613–619.

Echeverri, P. (2013). *Patient involvement for service innovation: An agenda for research and innovation in healthcare and social service*. Sweden: Karlstad.

Eisenhardt, K. M. (1989). Building theories from case study research. *Academy of Management Review, 14*(4), 532–550.

Eisenhardt, K. M. (1991). Better stories and better constructs: The case for rigor and comparative logic. *Academy of Management Review, 16*(3), 620–627.

Elg, M., Engström, J., Witell, L., & Poksinska, B. (2012). Co-creation and learning in health-care service development. *Journal of Service Management, 23*(3), 328–343.

Engström, J. (2012). *Co-creation in healthcare service development*. Linköping, Sweden: Department of Management and Engineering, Linköping University.

Engström, J., & Snyder, H. (2013). Lead patients—An exploratory investigation of lead users in healthcare. In E. Wästlund, B. Edvardsson, A. Gustafsson, M. J. Bitner, & R. Verma (Eds.), *Proceedings of the QUIS13 Conference* (pp. 309–317). Sweden: Karlstad.

Evans, P., & Wurster, T. (1999). *Blown to bits—How the new economics of information transforms strategy*. Boston, MA: Harvard Business School Press.

Eysenbach, G. (2008). Medicine 2.0: Social networking, collaboration, participation, apomediation, and openness. *Journal of Medical Internet Research, 10*(3), e22.

Eysenbach, G., Powell, J., Englesakis, M., Rizo, C., & Stern, A. (2004). Health related virtual communities and electronic support groups: Systematic review of the effects of online peer to peer interactions. *BMJ British Medical Journal, 328*(7449), 1166.

Ferguson, T. (2007). *E-patient: How they can help us heal healthcare*. San Francisco, CA: www. e-patients.net.

Fichman, R. G., Kohli, R., & Krishnan, R. (2011). The role of information systems in healthcare: Current research and future trends. *Information Systems Research, 22*(3), 419–428.

Field, R. I. (2008). Why is health care regulation so complex? *Pharmacy and Therapeutics, 33* (10), 607.

Fischer, S., & Soyez, K. (2014). Trick or treat: Assessing health 2.0 and its prospects for patients, providers and society. In *Challenges and Opportunities in Health Care Management* (pp. 197–208). Cham: Springer International Publishing.

Flanagan, J. C. (1954). The critical incident method. *Psychological Bulletin, 51*(4), 165–185.

Fleuren, M., Wiefferink, K., & Paulussen, T. (2004). Determinants of innovation within health care organizations. *International Journal for Quality in Health Care, 16*(2), 107–23.

Foss, N. J., Laursen, K., & Pedersen, T. (2011). Linking customer interaction and innovation: The mediating role of new organizational practices. *Organization Science.*

Fox, S., & Duggan, M. (2013). *Health Online 2013*. Washington D.C.

Frambach, R. T., & Schillewaert, N. (2002). Organizational innovation adoption: A multi-level framework of determinants and opportunities for future research. *Journal of Business Research, 55*(2), 163–176.

Franke, N., & Shah, S. (2003). How communities support innovative activities: An exploration of assistance and sharing among end-users. *Research Policy, 32*(1), 157–178.

Freeman, C. (1982). *The economics of industrial innovation* (2nd ed.). Cambridge: MIT Press.

Frey, K., Lüthje, C., & Haag, S. (2011). Whom should firms attract to open innovation platforms? The role of knowledge diversity and motivation. *Long Range Planning, 44*(5–6), 397–420.

Frost, J. H., & Massagli, M. P. (2008). Collaborative uses of personal health information: A study of PatientsLikeMe. In *Information Systems Journal* (pp. 1–4). ACM.

Frost, J. H., Okun, S., Vaughan, T., Heywood, J., & Wicks, P. J. (2011). Patient-reported outcomes as a source of evidence in off-label prescribing: Analysis of data from PatientsLikeMe. *Journal of Medical Internet Research, 13*(1), e6.

Fuchs, C., & Schreier, M. (2011). Customer empowerment in new product development. *Journal of Product Innovation Management, 28*(1), 17–32.

Fueller, J., Bartl, M., Ernst, H., & Muhlbacher, H. (2004). Community based innovation: A method to utilize the innovative potential of online communities. In *Proceedings of the 37th Annual Hawaii International Conference on System Sciences, 2004* (pp. 195–204). IEEE

Garcia, R., & Calantone, R. (2002). A critical look at technological innovation typology and innovativeness terminology: A literature review. *Journal of Product Innovation Management, 19*(2), 110–132.

Gardiner, P., & Rothwell, R. (1985). Tough customers: Good designs. *Design Studies, 6*(1), 7–17.

Gladwell, M. (2000). *The tipping point: How little things can make a big difference*. Boston, MA: Little Brown.

Glaser, B. G., & Strauss, A. L. (1967). *The discovery of grounded theory: Strategies for qualitative research*. Chicago: Aldine.

Goerlitz, R., Seip, B., Rashid, A., & Zacharias, V. (2010). Health 2.0 in practice: A review of German health care web portals. In B. White, P. Isaías, & D. Andone (Eds.), *Proceedings of the IADIS International Conference on WWW/Internet* (pp. 49–56). Timisoara, Romania: IADIS.

Goh, J. M., Gao, G. (Gordon), & Agarwal, R. (2013). *Social value creation in online health communities*. Working paper. College Park, Maryland: Robert H. Smith School of Business, University of Maryland.

Grant, R. M. (1996). Toward a knowledge-based theory of the firm. *Strategic Management Journal, 17*, 109–122.

Greer, C. R., & Lei, D. (2012). Collaborative innovation with customers: A review of the literature and suggestions for future research. *International Journal of Management Reviews, 14*(1), 63–84.

Gregor, S. (2006). The nature of theory in information systems. *MIS Quarterly, 30*(3), 611–642.

Gulati, R., Nohria, N., & Zaheer, A. (2000). Strategic networks. *Strategic Management Journal, 21*(3), 203–215.

Gupta, A. K., & Govindarajan, V. (2000). Knowledge flows within multinational corporations. *Strategic Management Journal, 21*(4), 473–496.

Habicht, H., & Moeslein, K. M. (2015). Open Innovation für Gesundheitsinnovation. In A. C. Bullinger (Ed.), *Mensch 2020—Transdisziplinäre Perspektiven* (pp. 143–155). Chemnitz: Verlag aw&I Wissenschaft und Praxis.

Habicht, H., Oliveira, P., & Shcherbatiuk, V. (2012). User innovators: When patients set out to help themselves and end up helping many. *Die Unternehmung: Swiss Journal of Business Research and Practice, 66*(3), 277–295.

Hage, J., & Aiken, M. (1970). *Social change in complex organizations.* New York: Random House.

Haller, J. B. A. (2012). *Open evaluation.* Wiesbaden: Springer Gabler.

Hallerstede, S. (2013). *Managing the lifecycle of open innovation platforms.* Wiesbaden, Germany: Springer Gabler.

Hanney, S. R., Castle-Clarke, S., Grant, J., Guthrie, S., Henshall, C., Mestre-Ferrandiz, J., ... Wooding, S. (2015). How long does biomedical research take? Studying the time taken between biomedical and health research and its translation into products, policy, and practice. *Health Research Policy and Systems, 13*(1), 1.

Hardyman, W., Daunt, K. L., & Kitchener, M. (2015). Value co-creation through patient engagement in health care: A micro-level approach and research agenda. *Public Management Review, 17*(1), 90–107.

Hargadon, A. (1998). Firms as knowledge brokers: Lessons in pursuing continuous innovation. *California Management Review, 40*(3), 209–227.

Hargadon, A., & Sutton, R. I. (1997). Technology brokering and innovation in a product development firm. *Administrative Science Quarterly, 42*(4), 716–749.

Hartmann, M., Bretschneider, U., & Leimeister, J. M. (2013). Patients as innovators—The development of innovative ideas with the Ideenschmiede. In *Wirtschaftsinformatik Konferenz (WI) 2013.* Leipzig, Germany.

Hartmann, M., Görlitz, R., Prinz, A., Hirde, E., Rashid, A., Weinhardt, C., & Leimeister, J. M. (2011). Ein Literature Review zur Aufarbeitung aktueller Forschungsergebnisse zu Health 2.0 Anwendungen. In *10th International Conference on Wirtschaftsinformatik* (pp. 78–87). Zurich, Switzerland.

Hauschildt, J., & Salomo, S. (2011). *Innovationsmanagement.* Vahlen.

Henrike, H.-W., & Schultz, C. (2014). The impact of health care professionals' service orientation on patients' innovative behavior. *Health Care Management Review, 39*(4), 329–339.

Herek, G. M. (2010). Developing a theoretical framework and rationale for a research proposal. In W. Pequegnat, E. Stover, & C. Anne (Eds.), *How to write a successful research grant application* (pp. 137–145). Boston, MA, USA: Springer.

Hernandez, S. E., Conrad, D. A., Marcus-Smith, M. S., Reed, P., & Watts, C. (2013). Patient-centered innovation in health care organizations. *Health Care Management Review, 38* (2), 166–175.

Hoch, D., & Ferguson, T. (2005). What I've learned from E-patients. *PLoS Medicine, 2*(8), e206.

Hoff, T. (2011). Deskilling and adaptation among primary care physicians using two work innovations. *Health Care Management Review, 36*(4), 338–348.

Hornstein, H., Bunker, B. B., Burke, W. W., Gindes, M., & Lewicki, R. J. (1971). *Social intervention: A behavioral science approach.* New York: Free Press.

Hossain, M. (2012). Performance and potential of open innovation intermediaries. *Procedia—Social and Behavioral Sciences, 58,* 754–764.

Howells, J. (2006). Intermediation and the role of intermediaries in innovation. *Research Policy, 35*(5), 715–728.

Hoyer, W. D., Chandy, R., Dorotic, M., Krafft, M., & Singh, S. S. (2010). Consumer cocreation in new product development. *Journal of Service Research, 13*(3), 283–296.

Hudson, B. (2015). Public and patient engagement in commissioning in the English NHS: An idea whose time has come? *Public Management Review, 17*(1), 1–16.

Huener, A., Stockstrom, C., & Luethje, C. (2011). An empirical analysis of user innovation in the Medical Devices Industry. In *18th International Product Development Management Conference*.

Huff, A. S., Moeslein, K. M., & Reichwald, R. (2013). *Leading open innovation*. Cambridge: MIT Press.

Hughes, B., Joshi, I., & Wareham, J. (2008). Health 2.0 and Medicine 2.0: Tensions and controversies in the field. *Journal of Medical Internet Research, 10*(3), e23.

Huizingh, E. K. R. E. (2011). Open innovation: State of the art and future perspectives. *Technovation, 31*(1), 2–9.

Hunt, S. D. (1976). The nature and scope of marketing. *Journal of Marketing, 40*(3), 17.

Huston, L., & Sakkab, N. (2006). Connect and develop: Inside Procter & Gamble's new model for innovation. *Harvard Business Review, 84*(3), 58–66.

Im, S., & Workman, J. P. (2004). Market orientation, creativity, and new product performance in high-technology firms. *Journal of Marketing, 68*(2), 114–132.

Irani, Z., & Love, P. (2008). *Evaluating information systems: Public and Private sector*. Butterworth-Heinemann.

Jeppesen, L. B., & Lakhani, K. R. (2010). Marginality and problem-solving effectiveness in broadcast search. *Organization Science, 21*(5), 1016–1033.

Jick, T. (1979). Mixing qualitative and quantitative methods: Triangulation in action. *Administrative Science Quarterly, 24*(4), 602–611.

Joshi, A. W., & Sharma, S. (2004). Customer knowledge development: Antecedents and impact on new product performance. *Journal of Marketing, 68*(4), 47–59.

Kane, G. C., & Labianca, G. (Joe). (2011). IS avoidance in health-care groups: A multilevel investigation. *Information Systems Research, 22*(3), 504–522.

Katz, M., & Shapiro, C. (1985). Network externalities, competition, and compatibility. *American Economic Review, 75*(3), 424.

Katz, R., & Allen, T. J. (1982). Investigating the not invented here syndrome: A look at the performance, tenure, and communication patterns of 50 R&D project groups. *R&D Management, 12*(1), 7–19.

Katzy, B. R., Turgut, E., Holzmann, T., & Sailer, K. (2013). Innovation intermediaries: A process view on open innovation coordination. *Technology Analysis & Strategic Management, 25*(3), 295–309.

Kennedy, S., & Berk, B. (2011). Enabling E-Health—A revolution for informatics in health care. *The Boston Consulting Group, Inc.* Retrieved from http://publications.bcg.com/health_care_payers_providers_medical_devices_technology_enabling_ehealth.

Kimberly, J. R., & Evanisko, M. J. (1981). Organizational innovation: The influence of individual, organizational, and contextual factors on hospital adoption of technological and administrative innovations. *Academy of Management Journal, 24*(4), 689–713.

King, N., & Horrocks, C. (2010). *Interviews in qualitative research*. London: SAGE Publications.

Klerkx, L., Hall, A., & Leeuwis, C. (2009). Strengthening agricultural innovation capacity: Are innovation brokers the answer? *International Journal of Agricultural Resources, Governance and Ecology*.

Kodama, F. (1993). Technology fusion and the new R&D. *Long Range Planning, 26*(1), 154.

Kogut, B., & Zander, U. (1992). Knowledge of the firm, combinative capabilities, and the replication of technology. *Organization Science, 3*(3), 383–397.

Kogut, B., & Zander, U. (1993). Knowledge of the firm and the evolutionary theory of the multinational corporation. *Journal of International Business Studies, 24*(4), 625–645.

Kordzadeh, N., & Warren, J. (2012). Toward a typology of health 2.0 collaboration platforms and websites. In *AMCIS 2012 Proceedings*. Seattle, WA.

Kraemer, K., Roth, A., & Moeslein, K. M. (2014). Exploring the diffusion of co-creation expertise in organizations. In *Proceedings of the 21st International Product Development Management Conference*. Limerick, Ireland.

Kristensson, P., Gustafsson, A., & Archer, T. (2004). Harnessing the creative potential among users. *Journal of Product Innovation Management, 21*(1), 4–14.

Kristensson, P., Magnusson, P. R., & Matthing, J. (2002). Users as a hidden resource for creativity: Findings from an experimental study on user involvement. *Creativity and Innovation Management, 11*(1), 55–61.

Kruse, P. (2012). Managing external knowledge in open innovation processes—A systematic review of research. In *Proceedings of the 13th European Conference on Knowledge Management ECKM 2012*.

Kuehne, M., Blinn, N., Rosenkranz, C., & Nuettgens, M. (2011). Diffusion of web 2.0 in healthcare: A complete inventory count in the German health insurance. In *Proceedings of the European Conference on Information Systems 2011*. Helsinki.

Kuenne, C. W. (2015). Multi-level organizational adoption of patient innovations. In *Proceedings of the 10th Research Seminar on Innovation and Value Creation*. Leipzig, Germany.

Kuenne, C. W., & Agarwal, R. (2015). Online innovation intermediaries as a critical bridge between patients and healthcare organizations. In O. Thomas & F. Teuteberg (Eds.), *Smart Enterprise Engineering: 12th International Conference on Wirtschaftsinformatik, WI 2015* (pp. 1268–1282). Germany: Osnabrueck.

Kuenne, C. W., Akenroye, T., & Moeslein, K. M. (2013). Online innovation intermediaries in healthcare. In *Proceedings of the European Conference on Information Systems (ECIS) 2013*. Utrecht, NL.

Kuenne, C. W., Moeslein, K. M., & Bessant, J. (2013). Towards patients as innovators: Open innovation in health care. In C. Mukhopadhyay, K. B. Akhilesh, & R. Srinivasan (Eds.), *Driving the economy through innovation and entrepreneurship: Emerging agenda for technology management* (pp. 315–327). Bangalore: Springer India.

Lakhani, K. R., Lohse, P. A., Panetta, J. A., & Jeppesen, L. B. (2007). The value of openness in scientific problem solving. *Biotech Business, 18S*(Spec No 2), 5533–464.

Lau, A. K. W., Tang, E., & Yam, R. C. M. (2010). Effects of supplier and customer integration on product innovation and performance: Empirical evidence in Hong Kong manufacturers. *Journal of Product Innovation Management, 27*(5), 761–777.

Lee, S. M., Olson, D. L., & Trimi, S. (2012). Co-innovation: Convergenomics, collaboration, and co-creation for organizational values. *Management Decision, 50*(5), 817–831.

Lehner, F. (2014). *Wissensmanagement: Grundlagen, Methoden und technische Unterstützung* (4th ed.). Munich: Carl Hanser.

Lei, D., & Slocum, J. W. (2002). Organization designs to renew competitive advantage. *Organizational Dynamics, 31*(1), 1–18.

Leimeister, J. M., & Krcmar, H. (2005). Evaluation of a systematic design for a virtual patient community. *Journal of Computer-Mediated Communication, 10*(4).

Leimeister, J. M., Schweizer, K., Leimeister, S., & Krcmar, H. (2008). Do virtual communities matter for the social support of patients?: Antecedents and effects of virtual relationships in online communities. *Information Technology People, 21*(4), 350–374.

Leonard-Barton, D. (1995). *Wellsprings of knowledge: Building and sustaining the sources of innovation*. Boston, MA, USA: Harvard Business School Press.

Lettl, C., Herstatt, C., & Gemuenden, H. G. (2006). Users' contributions to radical innovation: Evidence from four cases in the field of medical equipment technology. *R&D Management Journal, 36*(3), 251–272.

Lettl, C., Hienerth, C., & Gemuenden, H. G. (2008). Exploring how lead users develop radical innovation: Opportunity recognition and exploitation in the field of medical equipment technology. *IEEE Transactions on Engineering Management, 55*, 219–233.

Levina, N., & Vaast, E. (2005). The emergence of boundary spanning competence in practice: Implications for implementation and use of information systems. *MIS Quarterly, 29*, 335–363.

Lichtenthaler, U. (2013). The collaboration of innovation intermediaries and manufacturing firms in the markets for technology. *Journal of Product Innovation Management, 30*, 142–158.

Lichtenthaler, U., & Ernst, H. (2008). Innovation intermediaries: Why internet marketplaces for technology have not yet met the expectations. *Creativity and Innovation Management, 17*(1), 14–25.

Lilien, G. L., Morrison, P. D., Searls, K., Sonnack, M., & von Hippel, E. (2002). Performance assessment of the lead user idea-generation process for new product development. *Management Science, 48*(8), 1042–1059.

Littler, D., Leverick, F., & Bruce, M. (1995). Factors affecting the process of collaborative product development: A study of UK manufacturers of information and communications technology products. *The Journal of Product Innovation Management, 12*(1), 16.

Longtin, Y., Sax, H., Leape, L. L., Sheridan, S. E., Donaldson, L., & Pittet, D. (2010). Patient participation: Current knowledge and applicability to patient safety. *Mayo Clinic Proceedings. Mayo Clinic, 85*(1), 53–62.

Lopez-Vega, H., & Vanhaverbeke, W. (2009). Connecting open and closed innovation markets: A typology of intermediaries. *MPRA Munich Personal RePEc Archive*, (27017).

Lorenzo-Romero, C., Constantinides, E., & Brünink, L. A. (2014). Co-creation: Customer integration in social media based product and service development. *Procedia—Social and Behavioral Sciences, 148*, 383–396.

Luethje, C. (2003). Customers as co-inventors: An empirical analysis of the antecedents of customer-driven innovation in the field of medical equipment. In *Proceedings from the 32th EMAC Conference*.

Luethje, C., & Herstatt, C. (2004). The lead user method: An outline of empirical findings and issues for future research. *R&D Management, 34*(5), 553–568.

Lüthje, C. (2004). Characteristics of innovating users in a consumer goods field: An empirical study of sport-related product consumers. *Technovation*.

Lynn, L. H., Reddy, N. M., & Aram, J. D. (1996). Linking technology and institutions: The innovation community framework. *Research Policy, 25*(1), 91–106.

Madhavan, R., & Grover, R. (1998). From embedded knowledge to embodied knowledge: New product development as knowledge management. *Journal of Marketing, 62*(4), 1–12.

Magnusson, P. R. (2009). Exploring the contributions of involving ordinary users in ideation of technology-based services. *Journal of Product Innovation Management, 26*(5), 578–593.

Magnusson, P. R., Matthing, J., & Kristensson, P. (2003). Managing user involvement in service innovation: Experiments with innovating end users. *Journal of Service Research, 6*(2), 111–124.

Mahr, D., Lievens, A., & Blazevic, V. (2014). The value of customer cocreated knowledge during the innovation process. *Journal of Product Innovation Management, 31*(3), 599–615.

Maimbo, H., & Pervan, G. (2005). Designing a case study protocol for application in is research. In P. Y. K. Chau (Ed.), *Proceedings of the 9th Pacific Asia Conference on Information Systems* (pp. 1281–1292). Hong Kong: University of Hong Kong.

Mantel, S. J., & Rosegger, G. (1987). The role of third-parties in the diffusion of innovations: A survey. In R. Rothwell & J. Bessant (Eds.), *Innovation: Adaptation and growth* (pp. 123–134). Amsterdam: Elsevier.

March, J. G. (1991). Exploration and exploitation in organizational learning. *Organization Science, 2*(1), 71–87.

Mayring, P. (2000). Qualitative content analysis. *Forum Qualitative Sozialforschung Forum Qualitative Social Research, 1*(2), 1–12.

McColl-Kennedy, J. R., Vargo, S. L., Dagger, T. S., Sweeney, J. C., & Kasteren, Y. V. (2012). Health care customer value cocreation practice styles. *Journal of Service Research, 15*(4), 370–389.

McEvily, B., & Zaheer, A. (1999). Bridging ties: A source of firm heterogeneity in competitive capabilities. *Strategic Management Journal, 20*(12), 1133–1156.

Mele, C., & Russo-Spena, T. (2015). Innomediary agency and practices in shaping market innovation. *Industrial Marketing Management, 44*, 42–53.

Miles, M. B., & Huberman, A. M. (1994). *Qualitative data analysis: An expanded sourcebook* (2nd ed.). London: Sage Publications, Inc.

Milio, N. (1971). Health care organizations and innovation. *Journal of Health and Social Behavior, 12*(2), 163.

Miller, R. K., & Washington, K. (2012). Consumer use of online health information. In R. K. Miller & K. Washington (Eds.), *The 2012 healthcare business market research handbook* (pp. 569–572). Loganville: Richard K. Miller & Associates.

Moeslein, K. M. (2013). Open innovation: Actors, tools and tensions. In A. S. Huff, K. M. Moeslein, & R. Reichwald (Eds.), *Leading open innovation* (pp. 69–86). Cambridge: MIT Press.

Moorman, C., & Miner, A. S. (1998). The convergence of planning and execution: Improvisation in new product development. *Journal of Marketing, 62*(3), 1–20.

Morris, Z. S., Wooding, S., & Grant, J. (2011). The answer is 17 years, what is the question: understanding time lags in translational research. *Journal of the Royal Society of Medicine, 104* (12), 510–520.

Müller-Prothmann, T., & Dörr, N. (2009). *Innovationsmanagement: Strategien, Methoden und Werkzeuge für systematische Innovationsprozesse*. Munich: Hanser.

Nahapiet, J., & Ghoshal, S. (1998). Social capital, intellectual capital, and the organizational advantage. *Academy of Management Review, 23*(2), 242–266.

Nakamura, C., Bromberg, M., Bhargava, S., Wicks, P., & Zeng-Treitler, Q. (2012). Mining online social network data for biomedical research: a comparison of clinicians' and patients' perceptions about amyotrophic lateral sclerosis treatments. *Journal of Medical Internet Research, 14*(3), e90.

Nambisan, P., & Nambisan, S. (2009). Models of consumer value cocreation in health care. *Health Care Management Review, 34*(4), 344–54.

Nambisan, S. (2002). Designing virtual customer environments for new product development: toward a theory. *The Academy of Management Review, 27*(3), 392.

Nambisan, S. (2009). Virtual customer environments: IT-enabled customer co-innovation and value co-creation. In S. Nambisan (Ed.), *Information Technology and Product Development* (Vol. 5, pp. 109–127). Berlin: Springer.

Nambisan, S., & Baron, R. A. (2010). Different roles, different strokes: Organizing virtual customer environments to promote two types of customer contributions. *Organization Science, 21*(2), 554–572.

Nambisan, S., & Nambisan, P. (2008). How to profit from a better "virtual customer environment". *MIT Sloan Management Review, 49*(3), 53–61.

Nambisan, S., & Sawhney, M. (2007). A buyer's guide to the innovation bazaar. *Harvard Business Review, 85*(6), 109–116, 118, 142.

Neale, M. R., & Corkindale, D. R. (1998). Co-developing products: Involving customers earlier and more deeply. *Long Range Planning, 31*(3), 418–425.

Nelson, R. R., & Winter, S. G. (1982). *An evolutionary theory of economic change*. Cambridge MA: Belknap Press.

Nembhard, I. M., Alexander, J. A., Hoff, T. J., & Ramanujam, R. (2009). Why does the quality of health care continue to lag? Insights from management research. *Academy of Management Perspectives, 23*(1), 24–42.

Nonaka, I. (1994). A dynamic theory of organizational knowledge creation. *Organization Science, 5*(1), 14–37.

Nonaka, I., & Takeuchi, H. (1996). The knowledge-creating company: How Japanese companies create the dynamics of innovation. *Long Range Planning, 29*(4), 592.

Nordgren, L. (2009). Value creation in health care services—Developing service productivity. *The International Journal of Public Sector Management, 22*(2), 114–127.

Normann, R., & Ramírez, R. (1993). From value chain to value constellation: Designing interactive strategy. *Harvard Business Review, 71*(4), 65–77.

O'Reilly, T. (2005). What Is Web 2.0: Design patterns and business models for the next generation of software. *Social Science Research Network Working Paper Series*. SSRN.

O'Hern, M. S., & Rindfleisch, A. (2010). Customer co-creation: A typology and research agenda. In N. K. Malholtra (Ed.), *Review of Marketing Research Vol. 6* (pp. 84–106). Emerald Group Publishing Limited.

OECD. (2014). *Health at a glance: Europe 2014*. Paris: OECD Publishing.

Oh, S. (2012). The characteristics and motivations of health answerers for sharing information, knowledge, and experiences in online environments. *Journal of the American Society for Information Science & Technology, 63*(3), 543–557.

Ojanen, V., & Hallikas, J. (2009). Inter-organisational routines and transformation of customer relationships in collaborative innovation. *International Journal of Technology Management, 45* (3/4), 306.

Oliveira, P., Zejnilovic, L., Canhão, H., & von Hippel, E. (2015). Innovation by patients with rare diseases and chronic needs. *Orphanet Journal of Rare Diseases, 10*(1), 41.

Ophof, S. (2013). Motives for customers to engage in co-creation. In *2nd IBA Bachelor Thesis Conference*. Enschede, The Netherlands: University of Twente, Faculty of Management and Governance.

Ozer, M. (2009). The roles of product lead-users and product experts in new product evaluation. *Research Policy, 38*(8), 1340–1349.

Paterson, C. (2004). "Take small steps to go a long way" consumer involvement in research into complementary and alternative therapies. *Complementary Therapies in Nursing Midwifery, 10* (3), 150–161.

Pavitt, K. (1984). Sectoral patterns of technical change: Towards a taxonomy and a theory. *Research Policy, 13*(6), 343–373.

Penrose, E. T. (1959). *The theory of the growth of the firm*. New York: Wiley.

Perkmann, M. (2009). Trading off revealing and appropriating in drug discovery: The role of trusted intermediaries. *Academy of Management Annual Meeting Proceedings, 8*(1), 1–6.

Pettigrew, A. (1990). Longitudinal field research on change: Theory and practice. *Organization Science, 1*(3), 267–292.

Pharma Relations. (2010). Gesund per Klick? Vom Portal zur Community—Gesundheitswebsites im Wandel. *Pharma Relations*, (12/2010), 30–33.

Piller, F. T., & Ihl, C. (2009). Open innovation with customers: Foundations, competences and international trends. *Expert Study Commissioned by the European Union, The German Federal Ministry of Research, and Europäischer Sozialfond ESF. Published as Part of the Project "International Monitoring,"* (RWTH ZLW-IMA 2009).

Piller, F. T., Ihl, C., & Vossen, A. (2010). A typology of customer co-creation in the innovation process. *Social Science Research Network, 4*, 1–26.

Piller, F. T., Vossen, A., & Ihl, C. (2012). From social media to social product development: The impact of social media on co-creation of innovation. *Die Unternehmung, 65*(1).

Piller, F. T., & Walcher, D. (2006). Toolkits for idea competitions: a novel method to integrate users in new product development. *R&D Management, 36*(3), 307–318.

Piller, F. T., & Wielens, R. (2011). Open innovation in the machinery industry: How a German consortium of SMEs in the drivetrain industry benefited from crowdsourcing of technical problems. *BILAT-USA Symposium on Transatlantic EU-US Cooperation on Innovation and Technology Transfer. Vienna, 22 March 2011*.

Powell, W. W., Koput, K. W., & Smith-Doerr, L. (1996). Interorganizational collaboration and the locus of innovation: Networks of learning in biotechnology. *Administrative Science Quarterly, 41*(1), 116–145.

Prahalad, C. K., & Ramaswamy, V. (2004). Co-creating unique value with customers. *Strategy & Leadership, 32*(3), 4–9.

Prahalad, C. K., & Ramaswamy, V. (2004). Co-creation experiences: The next practice in value creation. *Journal of Interactive Marketing, 18*(3), 5–14.

Prandelli, E., Verona, G., & Raccagni, D. (2006). Diffusion of web-based product innovation. *California Management Review, 48*(4), 109–136.

Probst, G., Raub, S., & Romhardt, K. (2013). *Wissen managen: Wie Unternehmen ihre wertvollste Ressource optimal nutzen* (7th ed.). Wiesbaden: Gabler.

Randeree, E. (2009). Exploring technology impacts of Healthcare 2.0 initiatives. *Telemedicine Journal and E-Health, 15*(3), 255–60.

Reichwald, R., & Piller, F. T. (2009). *Interaktive Wertschöpfung* (2nd ed.). Wiesbaden: Gabler.

Reinhardt, R., Bullinger, A. C., & Gurtner, S. (2014). Open innovation in health care. In *Challenges and Opportunities in Health Care Management* (pp. 237–246). Cham: Springer.

Richter, V. E. (2008). *Der Einbezug von Kunden in den Innovationsprozess: Eine Untersuchung am Beispiel der Branche Medizintechnik unter Berücksichtigung der Informationsökonomie.* Hamburg, Germany: Verlag Dr. Kovac.

Ritter, T., & Walter, A. (2003). Relationship-specific antecedents of customer involvement in new product development. *International Journal of Technology Management, 26*(5/6).

Roberts, E. B. (1988). What we've learned: Managing invention and innovation. *Research Technology Management, 31*(1), 11–29.

Robinson, J. H., Callister, L. C., Berry, J. A., & Dearing, K. A. (2008). Patient-centered care and adherence: Definitions and applications to improve outcomes. *Journal of the American Academy of Nurse Practitioners, 20*(12), 600–607.

Robson, C. (2011). *Real world research* (3rd ed.). Hoboken: Wiley.

Rogers, E. M. (2003). *Diffusion of innovations* (5th ed.). New York: Free Press.

Rogers, E. M., & Svenning, L. (1969). *Modernization among peasants: The impact of communication.* New York: Holt, Rinehart and Winston.

Romero, D., & Molina, A. (2011). Collaborative networked organisations and customer communities: Value co-creation and co-innovation in the networking era. *Production Planning & Control, 22*(5–6), 447–472.

Romm, C., Pliskin, N., & Clarke, R. (1997). Virtual communities and society: Toward an integrative three phase model. *International Journal of Information Management, 17*(4), 261–270.

Rosenberg, N. (1982). *Inside the black box: Technology and economics.* Cambridge: Cambridge University Press.

Roser, T., Samson, A., Cruz-Valdivieso, E., & Humphreys, P. (2009). Co-creation: New pathways to value an overview. *Promise,* 22.

Rotnes, R., & Staalesen, P. D. (2009). *New methods for user driven innovation in the health care sector.* Norway: Oslo.

Rozenblum, R., & Bates, D. W. (2013). Patient-centred healthcare, social media and the internet: The perfect storm? *BMJ Quality & Safety, 22*(3), 183–186.

Russo-Spena, T., & Mele, C. (2012). "Five Co-s" in innovating: A practice-based view. *Journal of Service Management, 23*(4), 527–553.

Salge, T. O., & Vera, A. (2009). Hospital innovativeness and organizational performance: Evidence from English public acute care. *Health Care Management Review, 34*(1), 54–67.

Salmon, P., & Hall, G. M. (2004). Patient empowerment or the emperor's new clothes. *Journal of the Royal Society of Medicine, 97*(2), 53–56.

Sawhney, M., Prandelli, E., & Verona, G. (2003). The power of innomediation. *MIT Sloan Management Review, 44*(2), 77–82.

Sawhney, M., Verona, G., & Prandelli, E. (2005). Collaborating to create: The internet as a platform for customer engagement in product innovation. *Journal of Interactive Marketing, 19* (4), 4–34.

Schreier, M., & Prügl, R. (2008). Extending lead-user theory: Antecedents and consequences of consumers' lead userness. *Journal of Product Innovation Management, 25*(4), 331–346.

Schultz, C., Zippel-Schultz, B., & Salomo, S. (2012). Hospital innovation portfolios: Key determinants of size and innovativeness. *Health Care Management Review, 37*(2), 132–143.

Schultze, U., Prandelli, E., Salonen, P. I., & Alstyne, M. Van. (2007). Internet-enabledco-production: Partnering or competing with customers? *Communications of the Association for Information Systems, 19*(1), 294–324.

Schumpeter, J. A. (1934). *The theory of economic development: an inquiry into profits, capital, credit, interest, and the business cycle.* Cambridge, MA: Harvard University Press.

Seeman, N. (2008). Web 2.0 and chronic illness: New horizons, new opportunities. *Electronic Healthcare, 11*(1), 104–110.

Shapiro, C., & Varian, H. R. (1998). *Information rules: A strategic guide to the network economy.* Boston, MA: Harvard Business School Press.

Shaw, B. (1985). The role of the interaction between the user and the manufacturer in medical equipment innovation. *R&D Management, 15*(4), 283–292.

Sieg, J. H., Wallin, M. W., & von Krogh, G. (2010). Managerial challenges in open innovation: A study of innovation intermediation in the chemical industry. *R&D Management,* 281–291.

Siguaw, J. A., Gassenheimer, J. B., & Hunter, G. L. (2014). Consumer co-creation and the impact on intermediaries. *International Journal of Physical Distribution & Logistics Management, 44* (1/2), 6–22.

Simmel, G. (1902). The number of members as determining the sociological form of the group. II. *American Journal of Sociology, 8*(2), 158–196.

Smith, T. (2003). Can patient choice shape organisational behaviour to provide patients with what they want? *Quality and Safety in Health Care, 12*(6), 473–476.

Spann, M., Ernst, H., Skiera, B., & Soll, J. H. (2009). Identification of lead users for consumer products via virtual stock markets. *Journal of Product Innovation Management, 26*(3), 322–335.

Spender, J. C. (1994). Organizational knowledge, collective practice and Penrose rents. *International Business Review, 3*(4), 353–367.

Spender, J. C. (1996). Organizational knowledge, learning and memory: Three concepts in search of a theory. *Journal of Organizational Change Management, 9*(1), 63–78.

Stevens, G. A., & Burley, J. (2003). Piloting the rocket of radical innovation. *Research Technology Management, 46*(2), 16–25.

Stigler, H., & Felbinger, G. (2005). Der Interviewleitfaden im qualitativen Interview. In H. Stigler & H. Reicher (Eds.), *Praxisbuch Empirische Sozialforschung in den Erziehungs- und Bildungswissenschaften* (pp. 129–134). Innsbruck: Studienverlag.

Stoller-Schai, D. (2003). *E-Collaboration: Die Gestaltung internetgestützter kollaborativer Handlungsfelder.* Bamberg: Difo-Druck.

Swan, M. (2009). Emerging patient-driven health care models: An examination of health social networks, consumer personalized medicine and quantified self-tracking. *International Journal of Environmental Research and Public Health, 6*(2), 492–525.

Szulanski, G. (1996). Exploring internal stickiness: Impediments to the transfer of best practice within the firm. *Strategic Management Journal, 17*(Winter Special Issue), 27–43.

Terwiesch, C., & Xu, Y. (2008). Innovation contests, open innovation, and multiagent problem solving. *Management Science, 54*(9), 1529–1543.

Thallmaier, S. (2014). *Customer co-design: A study in the mass customization industry.* Wiesbaden: Springer Gabler.

Tsoukas, H. (1996). The firm as a distributed knowledge system: A constructionist approach. *Strategic Management Journal, 17,* 11–25.

Van De Belt, T. H., Engelen, L. J., Berben, S. A., & Schoonhoven, L. (2010). Definition of Health 2.0 and Medicine 2.0: A systematic review. *Journal of Medical Internet Research, 12*(2), e18.

Vargo, S. L., & Lusch, R. F. (2004). Evolving to a new dominant logic for marketing. *Journal of Marketing, 68*(1), 1–17.

Vargo, S. L., & Lusch, R. F. (2008). From goods to service(s): Divergences and convergences of logics. *Industrial Marketing Management, 37*(3), 254–259.

Vernette, E., & Hamdi-Kidar, L. (2013). Co-creation with consumers: Who has the competence and wants to cooperate? *International Journal of Market Research, 55*(4), 2–20.

Verona, G., Prandelli, E., & Sawhney, M. (2006). Innovation and virtual environments: Towards virtual knowledge brokers. *Organization Studies, 27*(6), 765–788.

Verworn, B., & Herstatt, C. (2002). *The innovation process: An introduction to process models. Innovation.* Department for Technology and Innovation Management, Technical University of Hamburg, Hamburg, Germany.

von Hippel, E. (1976). The dominant role of users in the scientific instrument innovation process. *Research Policy, 5*(3), 212–239.

von Hippel, E. (1978). Successful Industrial Products from Customer Ideas. *Journal of Marketing, 42*(1), 39–49.

von Hippel, E. (1986). Lead users: A Source of Novel Product Concepts. *Management Science, 32* (7), 791–805.

von Hippel, E. (1988). *The sources of innovation.* New York: Oxford University Press.

von Hippel, E. (2005). *Democratizing innovation.* Boston, MA: MIT Press.

von Hippel, E., & Demonaco, H. J. (2013). Market failure in the diffusion of user innovations: The case of "off-label" innovations by medical clinicians. *SSRN Electronic Journal.*

von Hippel, E., Ogawa, S., & De Jong, J. P. J. (2011). The age of the consumer-innovator. *MIT Sloan Management Review, 53*(105), 27–35.

Voorberg, W. H., Bekkers, V. J. J. M., & Tummers, L. G. (2014). A systematic review of co-creation and co-production: Embarking on the social innovation journey. *Public Management Review*, (July 2014), 1–25.

Wanless, D. (2002). *Securing our future: Taking a long-term view.* London: HM Treasury.

Watkins, D., & Horley, G. (1986). Transferring technology from large to small firms: The role of intermediaries. In *Small business research* (pp. 215–251).

Weber, M. (2011). *Customer co-creation in innovations: A protocol for innovating with end users.*

Weber-Jahnke, J. H., Agah, A., & Williams, J. (2011). *Consumer health informatics services—A taxonomy.* Victoria, Canada: Department of Computer Science, University of Victoria.

Wenger, E. (1998). *Communities of practice: Learning, meaning and identity.* Cambridge: Cambridge University Press.

Werbach, K. (2000). Syndication—The emerging model for business in the Internet era. *Harvard Business Review, 78*(3), 85–93.

Wernerfelt, B. (1984). A resource-based view of the firm. *Strategic Management Journal, 5*(2), 171–180.

West, J., & Bogers, M. (2013). Leveraging external sources of innovation: A review of research on open innovation. *Journal of Product Innovation Management, 31*(4), 814–831.

West, M., & Wallace, M. (1991). Innovation in health care teams. *European Journal of Social Psychology, 21*(4), 303–315.

Wiley, J. (1998). Expertise as mental set: The effects of domain knowledge in creative problem solving. *Memory & Cognition, 26*(4), 716–730.

Wills, C. E., & Holmes-Rovner, M. (2003). Patient comprehension of information for shared treatment decision making: State of the art and future directions. In *Patient Education and Counseling* (Vol. 50, pp. 285–290).

Wilson, J. Q. (1966). Innovation in organizations: Notes toward a theory. In J. D. Thompson (Ed.), *Approaches to organizational design* (pp. 193–218). Pittsburgh: University of Pittsburgh Press.

Winch, G. M., & Courtney, R. (2007). The organization of innovation brokers: An international review. *Technology Analysis & Strategic Management, 19*(6), 747–763.

Wind, J., & Mahajan, V. (1997). Issues and opportunities in new product development: An introduction to the special issue. *Journal of Marketing Research, 34*(1), 1.

Winter, S. G. (1987). Knowledge and competence as strategic assets. In D. J. Teece (Ed.), *The competitive challenge—Strategies for industrial innovation and renewal* (pp. 159–184). Cambridge, MA: Ballinger.

Wisdom, J. P., Chor, K. H. B., Hoagwood, K. E., & Horwitz, S. M. (2014). Innovation adoption: A review of theories and constructs. *Administration and Policy in Mental Health and Mental Health Services Research, 41*(4), 480–502.

Yin, R. K. (1981). The case study crisis: Some answers. *Administrative Science Quarterly, 26*(1), 58–65.

Yin, R. K. (2003). *Case study research: Design and methods* (3rd ed.). London: Sage Publications.

Yin, R. K. (2014). *Case study research: Design and methods* (5th ed.). London: Sage Publications.

Zaltman, G., Duncan, R., & Holbek, J. (1973). *Innovations and organizations.* New York: Wiley.

Zwass, V. (2010). Co-creation: Toward a taxonomy and an integrated research perspective. *International Journal of Electronic Commerce, 15*(1), 11–48.

Printed in the United States
By Bookmasters

Printed in the United States
By Bookmasters